Developmental Policy and the State

STUDIES IN PUBLIC POLICY

Series Editor: Paul J. Rich, Policy Studies Organization

Government in the new millennium demands creative new approaches to managing change. Faced with the impact of globalization, technological revolution, and political reform, what can be done to encourage economic growth, develop more effective public administration at home, and forge strong and lasting relationships abroad?

Lexington Books and the Policy Studies Organization's **Studies in Public Policy** series brings together the very best in new and original scholarship, spanning the range of global policy questions. Its multi-disciplinary texts combine penetrating analysis of policy formulation at the macro level with innovative and practical solutions for policy implementation. It provides the political and social scientist with the latest academic research and the policy maker with effective tools to tackle the most pressing issues faced by government today.

Titles in the Series

Public Policies for Distressed Communities Revisited
Edited by F. Stevens Redburn and Terry F. Buss

Analyzing National and International Policy: Theory, Method, and Case Studies by Laure Paquette

Policymaking and Democracy: A Multinational Anthology
Edited by Stuart Nagel

Policymaking and Prosperity: A Multinational Anthology
Edited by Stuart Nagel

Policymaking and Peace: A Multinational Anthology
Edited by Stuart Nagel

Developmental Policy and the State

The European Union, East Asia, and the Caribbean

Nikolaos Karagiannis

LEXINGTON BOOKS
Lanham • Boulder • New York • Oxford

LEXINGTON BOOKS

Published in the United States of America by Lexington Books
A Member of the Rowman & Littlefield Publishing Group
4720 Boston Way, Lanham, Maryland 20706
www.rowmanlittlefield.com

P.O. Box 317, Oxford OX2 9RU, United Kingdom

British Library Cataloguing in Publication Information Available

Library of Congress Cataloging-in-Publication Data

Karagiannis, Nikolaos, 1964-
    Developmental policy and the state: the European union, East Asia, and the
Caribbean / Nikolaos Karagiannis.
        p.   cm. — (Studies in public policy)
    Includes bibliographical references and index.
    ISBN 0-7391-0396-2 (cl. : alk. paper)
    1. Economic policy. 2. Economic development. I. Title. II. Series.

HD87 .K37 2002
338.9 21
                                                                    2002034907

Printed in the United States of America

♾™ The paper used in this publication meets the minimum requirements of American
National Standard for Information Sciences—Permanence of Paper for Printed Library
Materials, ANSI/NISO Z39.48-1992.

To my newborn son, Vasileios Theophilos, and my family.

Contents

Tables

Preface

An outstanding feature of the real world is the existence and continuation of a variety of economic and social problems, inequalities and disparities. Markets are usually seen to perpetuate inequalities and disparities, and modern capitalist economies do not conform to perfect competition. Neither do market forces generate full capacity utilization and full employment if left to themselves.

Two and a half decades after Keynesian demand management policies were downgraded by most orthodox economists, the market-oriented system of capitalism has regressed to economic performance levels that have not been prevalent since Keynes' revolution. Over 38 million people are unemployed in the Organization for Economic Cooperation and Development (OECD) area. High unemployment rates persist throughout the European Union. The income distribution within most nations as well as globally has become more unequal. Substantial numbers of people around the world have actually experienced declining living standards.

For the past few decades, the theory of development and growth has been building up an empirical record against which many different approaches and models can be tested, and this policy-oriented book draws heavily on many of these empirical studies. Some put great faith in the ability of unfettered markets to set prices and allocate resources, while others argue that development is only possible with substantial state intervention.

However, theories of growth and development in the past decade have met increasingly heavy criticism. In particular, the different views, both "old" and "new," mainly within the mainstream analysis (Solow 1956; Romer 1986; Lucas 1985 and 1988; Krugman 1986 and 1991; Stiglitz 1997, 1998, and 1999, among others) are all different expressions of "development failure," and have come to be considered as intellectually inadequate for explaining the increased diversity and unevenness of development. The result has been described as a "theoretical impasse."

Evidently, no single factor is responsible for development, or a lack of it, and no single policy or strategy can trigger off the complex process of economic development. A wide variety of explanations and solutions to problems of development and growth, or to other economic and social problems, make sense when considered in their proper contexts, but may make no sense at all outside those given sets of circumstances (Cardoso and Faletto 1978: 10-11).

Much of the discussion within this book relates to government involvement in supporting endogenous development. In the past two decades, however, governments have assumed a more conscious economic role in societies and the primary goal of this participation has been in maintaining the economy along a low fiscal deficit/low inflation growth path. Although there has also been a lot of debate about the effectiveness or ineffectiveness of state actions (as a stabilizing force), one thing is evident, namely that the government's role is to "keep the economy from swinging wildly" (Hadjimatheou 1994: 323).

The approach of the beginning of a new century and indeed a new millennium leads inevitably to crystal-ball gazing into the future and to a consideration of the past century; this will no doubt apply as much to economic matters as to others. Therefore, the task today is to meet the challenges of the new millennium without forgetting the valuable lessons of the past; lessons that may include: (1) capitalism comes in many varieties; (2) institutions established through public policy play an important role in determining the performance of capitalism; and (3) "laissez-faire" is a prescription for economic disaster (Minsky and Whalen 1997: 161).

When discussing the development experience of Japan and Newly Industrialized Countries (NICs), there has been a tendency among economists to minimize the role of the state in these economies over the past two decades or so. This trend seems to be closely connected to the general revival of support for the belief of free market forces with its consequence of rolling back the growth of government.

Recent attempts to show that the East Asian experience illustrates why interventionist policies are not necessary for rapid economic growth have tended to focus the debate fairly narrowly on industrial policy. However, the whole array of state management activities needs to be considered. In this vein, the Developmental States of East Asian economies should be seen as both active planners and investors, and more cooperative relations between government and private business have marked their recent history. In fact, these countries managed to promote more orderly adjustments than the market would produce if left to itself.

The book is composed of nine chapters, which provide an integrated discussion between development theory and policy-making. Chapter 1 presents the different approaches, theoretical issues, and models that are related to development and growth, with respect to the role of the government. Chapter 2 provides a general theoretical framework, with special mention to important notions and features of the Developmental State model. Chapter 3 identifies two roles for the state in a market economy: a regulatory one and a developmental one. The fourth chapter focuses on a "new" role for the government and deals with important elements of "modern" interventionism. The fifth chapter provides a survey of regional and industrial policies of European Community (EC) countries in comparison with the Developmental State approach. Chapters 6, 7, and 8 provide an alternative development policy framework for the EC/EU, the Caribbean, and Jamaica respectively, based on the Developmental State analysis. The last chapter summarizes the major conclusions and policy recommendations discussed in previous chapters, as future requirements arise from the present economic and social problems.

My task would have been incomplete if I had not acknowledged those who aided me in completing this book. I would like to thank Neville Duncan and Stuart Nagel for their useful comments and suggestions, Martin Hayward and Karstin Painter for their kind assistance and continuous cooperation, and Floyd Williams, Richard Leach, and Colville Rickards for their valuable technical assistance. I would also like to thank the editors of the *Journal of Eastern Caribbean Studies* for kindly permitting the publication of a shorter version of the article "Alternative Development Policy for the Caribbean: The Challenge of the Developmental State Approach" (originally published in Vol. 27:1, March 2002), which appears as chapter 7 in this book. Last, but not the least, I would like to thank my wife Anthea for her continuous encouragement and support. I owe her more than I can recount.

Chapter 1

Growth Theory and Government

INTRODUCTION

Achieving sustained economic growth has become one of the principal objectives of the economic policies of most countries. A growth in per capita income is supposed to contribute to a general rise in the standard of living of the population in general and the pursuit of such growth has characterized the manifestos of political parties and the writings of economic scientists, for most of the period since the Second World War:

- Policymakers and politicians have often been concerned with the international comparison of rates of economic growth.
- Growth has been seen as a solution to a variety of other economic problems. For example, it is frequently argued that economic growth, rather than the redistribution of income and wealth, provides the main hope of alleviating or eliminating poverty.
- In recent years, many writers have emphasized the costs of economic growth in terms of its effects upon the quality of life (Gillis et al. 1992). Others, following the classical economists of the early nineteenth century, have argued that continued world economic growth is simply not feasible because of the finite quantities of certain essential resources (Gillis et al. 1992).

The systematic application of Keynesian aggregate demand management policies appeared to have resolved the interwar problem of attaining full employment and it is not surprising that attention turned from the problems of aggregate demand for output to the problems associated with increasing the capacity to produce output. In general, the purposes of theories and models of economic growth are the following:

(1) an aid to thinking;
(2) a guide to policy making;
(3) a framework for estimation and prediction; and,
(4) isolating unsuspected possibilities.

However, economic and social development is a highly complex process involving not only economic but also social, political, cultural, and technological changes. It can be defined as the process of adding to resources, increasing the utilization and improving the productivity of available resources—a process which stimulates the growth of national product (and income) and results in an increase in the economic welfare of the community.

The comparatively affluent living standards in industrialized societies provide a clear example of what may be possible for less developed economies. Quality of life is to be regarded as an important index of development but many contend that such quality is not adequately reflected in the index of per capita income growth. Several factors are involved in the measurement of such quality and some of them can be measured in terms of non-monetary rather than monetary indicators.

However, although the level and rate of per capita real income growth is an imperfect index, it is difficult to believe that significant development could take place without a rise in per capita real income. The point should also be made that industrialization is what most countries (especially those in the Third World) aspire to, although a lot of doctrine, and controversy, has been concerned with certain problems of economic coordination that arise in the course of industrialization (e.g., modernization).

Chapter 1 presents the different approaches, theoretical issues, and models which are related to growth and development along with the role of the state and/or government involvement and the available empirical evidence.

BALANCED VERSUS UNBALANCED GROWTH

During the 1950s and 1960s, a lively debate developed between balanced and unbalanced growth as strategies for economic development. These two strategies appear to call for different roles for the state and the market in the process of economic growth and development.

The original exponents of the "balanced growth" doctrine considered the scale of investment that was necessary to overcome indivisibilities on both the supply and demand side of the development process (in the productive process on both sides of the economy). The doctrine has since been extended to refer to the path of economic development and the pattern of investment necessary for the smooth functioning of the economy. The argument for a "big push" is bound up with the assumed existence of external economies of scale.

Enterprises which are not, or do not appear to be, profitable in isolation become profitable when considered as part of a comprehensive plan for industrial expansion including several activities. The balanced growth doctrine stresses the necessity of balance between sectors of the economy in order to prevent bottlenecks developing in some sectors, which may be an obstacle to development, and excess capacity in others, which would be wasteful (Bell 1987: 820-21).

It has also been argued that the transfer of knowledge and techniques from pioneers to latecomers is an inescapable feature of economic growth in latecomers. Latecomers should draw on an existing stock of knowledge and techniques. Little has been said, however, about the nature of the growth process itself or the forms of economic organization which would make the associated investments in plants and equipment. In particular, the role of the government has gone virtually unmentioned.

The balanced growth doctrine was first set out by Rosenstein-Rodan (1943) and subsequently developed and elaborated by Nurkse (1953). The protagonists saw the central problem as one of initiating growth by inducing investment in industry (Bell 1987: 820). Nurkse (1953: 11-17, 20-31) spoke about the case for balanced growth mainly on grounds of demand creation since it is assumed that the less developed countries would not be able to raise their exports substantially (he found problems/difficulties related to capital formation in less developed countries and the prospects or benefits from international trade).

The Rosenstein-Rodan's arguments rest mainly on the desirability of overcoming the indivisibilities in both demand and supply (Rosenstein-Rodan 1943: 203-10). The bottlenecks on the demand side which are imposed by the narrow size of the markets could be removed if a number of industries were set up simultaneously, each catering for the other. A big push (or massive investments in many projects) will enable the economy to "remove the difference between social and private marginal product, and the industries themselves, once set up, would be viable as they would experience neither supply nor demand constraints" (Rosenstein-Rodan 1943: 203-10).

Thus, the Rosenstein-Rodan's view deals with the potentially beneficial effects of the expansion of one firm on the profits of others. According to this view, it is very uneconomical to build roads, railways, and power stations just to meet current demand.

The notion of balanced growth takes on a wider meaning in the work of Kalecki (1976: chs. 2, 4 and 5). He stresses the need for rises and changes in the pattern of demand to be matched by the expansion of output. The case for a big push for supply reasons seems to be quite weak in the absence of resources to attempt such a strategy (Kalecki 1976: 23-24). For Kalecki, the notion of a big push takes on a more complex meaning that also includes institutional change.[1]

Another resource for which industries compete is capital goods. In a closed economy, the capacity of the machine-building sector can impose a limit on how much investment can be undertaken in other industries even if there is a willingness to save more. Indeed, this point is central to the models of Feldman-Domar (1957) and Mahalanobis (1953). In a similar vein, Robinson (1969) argues that:

> In a highly developed industrial economy the physical rate of output of capital equipment is limited by the capacity of certain specialised capital-good industries. . . . Some of the industries producing capital equipment, such as shipyards, cater for a narrow range of types of product, but others, such as iron and steel, engineering and building, cover the provision of equipment for a wide range of industries. Their capacity, at any moment, is limited partly by the amount of plant and partly by the availability of labour with the special skills required. . . . The limit set by capacity upon the rate of output of capital goods may operate through prolonging delivery dates, so that investment plans have to queue up and await completion, or by high prices of new equipment, which . . . causes some investment plans to be cancelled or postponed. (51-52)

The bottlenecks developing in some sectors and/or areas generate less profitable opportunities for firms in these sectors/areas, i.e., the movement of capital into sectors and areas of potentially high profits. Consequently, a case for strong government intervention in order to coordinate individual investments began to emerge from the balanced growth argument (Bell 1987: 821).

A major criticism of the balanced growth doctrine is that it fails to come to grips with one of the fundamental obstacles to development (especially in developing countries), namely, a shortage of resources of all kinds. Critics of balanced growth do not deny the importance of a large-scale investment program as well as the expansion of complementary activities.

However, their argument is that in the absence of sufficient resources, especially capital, entrepreneurs and decision-makers, the attempt for balanced growth may not provide sufficient stimulus to the mobilization of resources and/or the inducement to invest, and will certainly not economize on decision-taking if planning is required. Hence, the case for unbalanced growth rests primarily on the necessity to economize on the use of resources.

The "unbalanced growth" view (as opposed to the "balanced growth" doctrine) formed the basis for Hirschman's thesis (1958). He argued that the real scarcity in developing countries is not only the resources themselves, that is, low income→low demand→low investment→lack of capital, but also the means and ability to bring them into play (Hirschman 1958: 50-54, 63-70 and 73-83). Preference should be given to that stream of projects which maximize induced decision making.

Hirschman (1958: 83-86) explained his argument by considering the relation between social capital (SoC) and directly productive activities (DPA). He called the case in which SoC precedes DPA "development via excess capacity," and the case in which DPA precedes SoC "development via shortages" (Hirschman 1958: 86-89). Both sequences create inducements and pressures which are beneficial to development. He argued that development via excess capacity is essentially permissive, and that to try for balance is equally dangerous because there is no incentive to induced investment expenditure (or induced decision making). On the other hand, development via shortages enforces further investment, and hence the most efficient sequence, as far as induced decision making is concerned, is likely to be that where DPA precedes SoC (Hirschman 1958: 93-97).

Therefore, growth should take place "through shortages and excesses and it is assumed that every challenge would generate its own response" (Thirlwall 1990: 192-93). When growth is unbalanced, capacity in some sectors will outrun others in such a way as to create an imbalance between supply and demand. In an unbalanced growth strategy, such disturbances may be positively welcomed since they offer the opportunity to shake up the system (Bell 1987: 822).

As strategic doctrines, balanced and unbalanced growth appear to call for very different roles for the government as an agent in promoting industrialization. Balanced growth expresses "the desirability of exploiting complementarities through central coordination" when the price mechanism cannot do the job efficiently (Bell 1987: 821). Although neoclassical economists support the view that market growth (i.e., growth through the market mechanism) is or tends to be balanced growth, the concept of planning is often associated with the doctrine of balanced growth.

The association of balanced growth with planning has tended to polarize opinion on the two strategies. On the other hand, unbalanced growth does not preclude planning. With unplanned unbalanced growth there is no guarantee or safeguard against unemployment, inflation, and an unequal distribution of income and resources.

Unbalanced growth is seen to be the outcome of the operation of a free market system. A state pursuing an unbalanced growth strategy will not leave matters entirely to the market but it will try to promote growth in special sectors and/or regions. The promotion could take a number of forms, from taxation to investment by the government itself.

Consequently, unbalanced growth certainly needs the active role of the government, though its rationale favors intervention in a decentralized form (in this connection, Hirschman's argument is against balanced growth or, rather, the centralized mechanism balanced growth demands). In the long run, whether to intervene or not, and if so, in what form, depends on circumstances as different countries have their own economic, social, political, and cultural characteristics.

THEORIES OF GROWTH

Growth theory is mainly composed of three different schools of thought: neoclassical, Keynesian, and Marxist. These three main views on growth are briefly discussed below.

Neoclassical Growth Theory

Neoclassical growth theory is not a theory of development but is one of the equilibrium of a competitive economy through time, and it maintains that market equilibrium exists (Hahn 1987: 625-26). Since a market usually has equilibrating tendencies, excess supplies and demands will tend to sort themselves out sooner or later through a mixture of price and quantity adjustments, as well as wealth and real balance effects. In this sense, the concept of the market is also applicable in the neoclassical growth theory and at this basic level "the markets for macroeconomic aggregates [which usually appear only as market balance–equations] are comparable to the markets for apples and oranges" (Beenstock 1980).

Neoclassical growth theory (starting from Solow 1956) sees economic growth as essentially determined by the growth of supply (to which the growth of demand adjusts). In particular, attention is paid to the accumulation of capital goods, the growth in population and technical progress. Neoclassical growth theory relies on variations in the capital-output ratio through the substitution of labor and capital for the achievement of equilibrium growth with the full employment of labor and capital.

Economic growth is essentially determined by the growth of the total factor productivity of capital and labor, and by (exogenously given) technical progress: the more competitive the product, labor and capital markets in an economy, the more efficient the utilization of resources and, consequently, the faster its economic growth. The state's role in economic growth and development in this approach is regarded as being important but best limited to providing a basic social, legal, and economic infrastructure (for example, public goods) and to creating an appropriate climate for private firms and enterprises (Hahn 1987: 625-26).

Therefore, the total production in the state of general equilibrium[2] is clearly determined by exogenous factors: it is determined by the amount and different types of available resources, by the prevailing knowledge of technology, and by the efficiency with which the available resources, in combination with these techniques, are employed by the entrepreneurs.[3]

Keynesian Growth Theory

Early contributors to the development of post-Keynesian economics emphasised the fact that Keynesian analysis, with its focus on underemployment conditions, ignored the problems of long-run growth and the role of capital accumulation in the process. Harrod (1939, 1948, and 1959) and Domar (1957) attempted to fill this gap by placing and extending Keynes' model into a dynamic setting and argued that to move from the Keynesian static model of analysis to a dynamic situation, income should grow (which implies that planned investment and savings would also grow to match it).

The analysis by Harrod and Domar suggested that a "warranted" growth path may exist, but there may be no mechanism to ensure equality between the warranted growth rate and the growth of labour supply (i.e., the "natural" rate of growth). Secondly, the analysis indicated that the warranted growth path could be unstable, that is, an unsteady growth path or what Harrod referred to as the "knife edge" (Arestis 1992: 206).

In this model, investment, $I_o = c(dY/dt)$, is defined as the total money expenditure that must be made on new investment projects to create an additional unit of output (Harrod 1959: 451-64). For Domar and Harrod, investment creates additional income and increases/improves the productive capacity. In other words, the prime mover of the economy is investment spending which has a dual role to play: it creates demand, but it also creates capacity.

An increase in investment spending stimulates an increase in aggregate demand. Consequently, there is a rise in output, which may generate expectations of further rises in output (Sawyer 1989: 383). The public's decisions to spend and save, expressed as $S = sY_o$, then determines the actual increase in income via the multiplier principle $(dI/dt)/s = dY/dt$.

Entrepreneurs' expectations can only be confirmed if, and only if, $S = I$ or, $c(dY/dt) = sY_o$, which when rearranged produces Harrod's famous growth equation $g_w = (dY/dt)/Y_o = s/c$, with $S/Y_o = I/Y_o$ (Harrod 1948: 46-9). The rate of expansion of national income is thus "warranted" (which is a particular notion of equilibrium growth) and, as entrepreneurs' expectations have been confirmed, they are presumed to expect income to continue to expand at that rate (Kregel 1987: 600).

If the economy happens to grow at the warranted rate, there is no obvious incentive for entrepreneurs to try to increase or decrease the overall rate of growth of output. Just as in Keynes' theory, there is no reason for the warranted rate to be associated with full employment, nor is there any reason for a disturbance of the system from a dynamic equilibrium to lead to a full employment rate (Domar 1957: 22-24, 68-69).

It is clear that the warranted growth rate bears no necessary relation to the natural growth rate, which would ensure full employment ($g_f \neq g_w \neq g_n$ in general). In other words, there is no automatic tendency towards a full-employment equilibrium growth path in a free-market capitalist economy. Consequently, an economy will only be able to achieve continuous full employment if its rate of growth is equal to both g_w and g_n.

It is conceivable, however, to incorporate into Domar-Harrod's model a government sector whose spending and taxes can be manipulated to adjust s in such a way as to keep g_w equal to g_n permanently; the government can also operate on s and c so as to potentially attain full employment and maximum growth, as allowed by the productive potential of the economy (Arestis 1992: 208).

Thus, the role of fiscal policy in promoting economic growth is very important. The relationship between fiscal policy and economic growth can best be analyzed within a Keynesian framework rather than a neoclassical or "New Right" framework. Using the Harrod-Domar equation for growth ($g = s/v$), it is noticeable that fiscal policy, by raising s, raises growth. But no such role can be played by fiscal policy within a neoclassical theory as the population growth rate n determines the growth rate.

A change in taxation or government expenditure can change saving, but this may also change the capital-output ratio v (Sato 1963, 1967). Thus, the Harrod-

Domar model is not only the basis of many macroeconomic growth models but also of macroeconomic management and planning.

Marxist Growth Theory

Marx's discovery of the basic long-term "laws of motion" (development trends) of the "capitalist mode of production" undoubtedly constitutes his most impressive scientific achievement. The Marxist model of economic growth depends on these dynamic "laws," some of which are listed below (Mandel 1987: 378-80):

- the capitalist's compulsion to accumulate;
- the tendency towards constant technological revolutions;
- the capitalists' unquenchable thirst for surplus-value extraction;
- the tendency towards growing concentration and centralization of capital;
- the tendency for the "organic composition of capital" to increase;
- the tendency for the rate of profit to decline;
- the tendency towards growing socialization of labor;
- the inevitability of economic crises under capitalism;
- the inevitability of class struggle under capitalism; and,
- the tendency towards growing social polarization.

No amount of capitalists' self-regulation or state intervention has been able to suppress this "cyclical movement of capitalist production" that is strongly linked to production for profit and private property (competition), which implies too little or too much investment and output, precisely because each firm's attempt at maximizing profit unavoidably leads to a lower rate of profit for the system as a whole (Mandel 1987: 380-81).

Moreover, capitalist growth is always growth with

> Increasing disequilibrium, between different departments of output, between different branches and between production and final consumption. Average capital accumulation leads to over-accumulation which, in turn, leads to under-investment during a depression when output is consistently inferior to current demand. The ups and downs of the rate of profit during a business cycle do not only reflect the variations of the output-disposable income relation, or the organic composition of capital, but they also express the varying correlation of forces between the major classes of society. (Mandel 1987: 381)

Therefore, a major question in growth theory has been whether the level of economic activity (as well as the level of employment) is mainly determined on the supply side or the demand side. Neoclassical tradition views the rate of economic growth as determined by supply-side factors, and the growth of demand (which is not usually explicitly mentioned) is assumed to adjust to support the growth of supply.

On the other hand, the Keynesian perspective stresses demand factors rather than supply factors in the determination of the rate of economic growth. The growth of demand provides the opportunities for growth of supply, but the growth of supply may not be forthcoming (Sawyer 1989: 399).

Finally, according to a Marxist analysis, the ups and downs of the rate of growth and profit in a capitalist economy do not only reflect the variations of the output-disposable income relation, or the organic composition of capital, but they also express the varying correlation of forces between capitalists and workers.

POST-KEYNESIAN AND RADICAL CONTRIBUTIONS

Post-Keynesian, neo-Marxist, Dependency, and other radical views (a rather diverse group outside the mainstream analysis) offer different views which are very important both on theoretical and policy-making grounds, with regard to state involvement. The post-Keynesian school is concerned with problems of growth and income distribution while the Marxist/neo-Marxist/Dependency and other radical approaches analyze development/under-development and economic growth in terms of the "historical process of capitalism."

Post-Keynesian analysis is concerned with an economic system that is expanding over time in the context of history. Central to post-Keynesian growth theory is distributional effects and capital accumulation. Growth dynamics in the post-Keynesian theory is based on Domar-Harrod's model of the growth rate of national income as modified to incorporate the possibility of varying propensities to save out of different kinds of income.

One may thus consider some of the implications of savings propensities out of wages and out of profits (s_1 and s_2 respectively) by writing the following equations (Sawyer 1989: 438-39):

$$S = s_2 P + s_1 W \quad \text{and} \quad S + T + M = I + G + X$$

The above two equations can be combined to give:

$$s_2 P + s_1 W + T + M = I + G + X$$

where T is total taxation, M imports, G total government expenditure and X exports. Rearrangement with national income $Y = W + P$ yields:

$$P = [I + (G-T) + (X-M) - s_1 Y]/(s_2 - s_1)$$

The strong implication of this equation is that investments, government budget deficit and export surplus have the same impact on profits, whereas profits are diminished by workers' savings (Sawyer 1989: 438).

It has also been argued by radical political economists (Luxembourg 1913, 1963; Kalecki 1945; Baran and Sweezy 1966) that there is a tendency for the level of investment spending to be insufficient to support the maximum level of output and employment, so that output and profits are less than they could be.

Their arguments can be simply represented by saying that a surplus of exports over imports, or of government expenditure over taxation, help the realization of profits. While Baran and Sweezy (1966) concentrated on the methods of raising government expenditures, which appear to be acceptable to capitalists (i.e., military spending), Luxembourg and others stressed the need to search for overseas markets in order to stimulate exports and profits (Sawyer 1989: 439).

Kalecki (1971) and other post-Keynesians have emphasized the need for investment and growth to be analyzed together with employment and income distribution (Arestis 1992: 131). For Kalecki, Steindl, Baran, and Sweezy, a higher level of output ensuing from a higher degree of capacity utilization is the source of the higher level of savings required to match a higher level of investment, and vice versa in the case of a lower level of investment. If the level of investment is higher, then the rate of capacity utilization is higher (which implies that the level of output is higher).

Therefore, growth in an economy arises from investment adding to the capital stock, and the prospect of growth generates the demand for net investment. Net investment is closely linked with growth and the expansion of capital stock (Sawyer 1989: 381-84).

Kalecki (1970) wrote the following equation for the rate of growth:

$$r = \Delta Y/Y = (1/m).(I/Y)-a+u \qquad (1)$$

where r is the rate of growth of output, m is the incremental capital-output ratio or the productive effect of gross investment, I is gross investment, a is loss of production due to depreciation and u an increase in output due to the better utilization of equipment or the change in utilization of productive capacity. The above equation is the basic Kaleckian equation for the rate of growth of output and is (with suitable definitions of m, a, and u) an identity.

Kalecki began his analysis by considering a closed economy. The real national income in a given year is denoted by Y, productive investments by I, the increase in inventories by IN, and consumption by C, so that $Y = C + I + IN$. The increase in inventories is taken as proportional to changes in income (i.e., $IN = \mu Y$). Taking into account that $i = (I+IN)/Y$, $k = m+\mu$, and $C/Y=1-i$, the above equation (1) can be written as follows:

$$r = (i/k) - m(a - u)/k \qquad (2)$$

This simple equation is the basis of much of Kalecki's discussion on economic growth, with various extensions to include foreign trade, the employment situation, etc. It is clear from equation 2 that an increase in the rate of growth, r, requires a rise in the investment share, i, and, hence, a decrease in the consumption share. Furthermore, it can be seen that the impact of a higher investment share on the rate of growth will depend on how the other parameters respond to a change in i (Sawyer 1985: 93-96).

When an open economy with a role for government is considered, then the conclusion that investment generates savings has to be modified and the basic equation becomes the following: investment is equal to domestic savings plus government savings (taxation minus expenditure) plus foreign trade deficit (imports minus exports). Hence, an increase in investment expenditure can now be seen to generate some combination of domestic private savings, government savings and a trade deficit.

When there is full employment of the labor force, then the growth of the economy is effectively constrained by the growth of the labor force plus technical progress (Sawyer 1985: 241-46). This growth rate, which is designated r_f is equal to p+n, where p is the growth of productivity (arising from technical progress) and n the growth rate of the labor force. The rate r_f corresponds to the growth rate described as the natural growth rate in neoclassical growth theory. In circumstances of full employment, the equality of the growth rate given by (1) and by r_f requires that:

$$p+n = (i/k) - m (a - u)/k$$

Kaldor, Robinson, and Pasinetti all emphasized that in the long run, savings are brought into line with investment spending through variations (or changes) in the income distribution. Their analysis assumes different propensities to save out of profits and wages and implies a conflict between economic growth and distributional equity.

Robinson (1956) began by using some fundamental variables judged relevant to the determination of the rate of growth given the initial stock of capital goods and the state of expectations formed by past experience: technical conditions, investment policy including a Keynesian ex post savings equal to investment assumption, and financial conditions (Robinson 1956: 31-36).

Robinson (1962) argued (in response to the neoclassical adjustment mechanisms of variations in interest rates and the capital-output ratio) that, "there is nothing in the laws of nature to guarantee growth at the natural rate, but if entrepreneurs wish to invest sufficient to grow at the natural rate then saving will adapt, subject to an inflation barrier."

When a steady rate of growth appears then the share of savings adapts to it. In effect, the actual growth rate "pulls up" the warranted growth rate by forcing saving. Saving adapts to investment expenditure through the dependence of saving on the share of profits in income which rises with the level of investment relative to income in the way that has already been described (Robinson 1956; Chick 1983). Profits in turn depend on what happens to real wages when the system is out of equilibrium.

The basic equation of Robinson's model is the distribution equation:

$$PY = wL + \pi PK \qquad\qquad (1)$$

where π is the gross profit rate R/K, P is the price level, Y is income, w is the wage rate, L is labor's share and K is the quantity of capital. Dividing through by P, and rearranging the above equation to obtain an expression for the profit rate, gives the following:

$$\pi = (Y/L - w/P)/(K/L) = (R/L)/(K/L) = R/K \qquad (2)$$

Given the capital-labor ratio, the rate of profit depends on the relationship between output per head and the real wage. If all wages are consumed and all profits are saved, the rate of profit gives the rate of capital accumulation and the rate of growth. This follows since $S = I = \pi K$, and $\Delta K = \pi K$, hence, $\Delta K/K = \pi$. If the capital-output ratio is fixed, then,

$$\Delta K/K = \Delta Y/Y \text{ therefore, } \pi = \Delta K/K = \Delta Y/Y$$

Variations in the rate of profit and corresponding variations in the real wage provide the mechanism which equilibrates plans to save and invest and the actual and warranted growth rates. If the actual growth rate equals the natural rate, then the warranted and natural growth rates will also be equalized (Robinson 1962: 47-49).

Kaldor (1956, 1957) evolved a Keynesian model of growth and income distribution where shifts between wages and profits adjust the savings ratio (until this becomes the one required to equate g_w and g_n). In Kaldor's model of growth, saving adjusts to the desired level of investment through a rise in the share of profits in national income. The crucial feature of the Kaldorian model is that the saving ratio is flexible, so a steady state of economic growth can be obtained.

I/K is the rate of growth of capital stock and, in a situation of steady growth at full employment, it would equal the natural rate of growth. If one assumes that the natural rate is exogenously given, then the rate of profit in a state of balanced growth is determined by the propensity to save from profit income. A similar result was noted by Kalecki (1971: 13): "Thus, capitalists, as a whole, determine their own profits by the extent of their investment and personal consumption. In a way they are masters of their own fate."

Within certain limits (stemming principally from the fact that P cannot exceed Y), a ratio of profits to income P/Y exists and this ensures that the overall propensity to save is exactly that required to equate s/v to n (where v is the capital-output ratio and n the growth rate). Moreover, Kaldor has repeatedly argued that there are reasons to believe that the appropriate value of P/Y will, in fact, emerge: "the warranted and the natural rates of growth are not independent of one another; if profit margins are flexible, the former will adjust itself to the latter through a consequential change in P/Y" (Kaldor 1956: 93).

A higher level of investment may raise the rate of capital accumulation by raising the profit rate and the share of saving in total income. Therefore, the rate of growth is given by the rate of profit, which is determined by the profit earners' propensity to save. In short, Kaldor's work on distribution and his case for the inherent stability of economic growth depended on changes in the Keynesian marginal propensity to save (consume) as real income rises or falls. He also introduced the following proposition:

> The reinvestment of the profits of business enterprise always has been, and still
> is, the main source of industrial capital accumulation. This is an important pro-
> position because the rate of growth of particular sectors (and the profits earned)
> is often a function of the rate at which new technologies are being absorbed.[4]

Pasinetti's contribution was originally motivated by a desire to correct what he called a "logical slip" in Kaldor's theory but, in so doing, he developed what is a very general model incorporating a surprising and, perhaps, paradoxical conclusion. Pasinetti mentions this logical slip in Kaldor's argument when he observes that although Kaldor had allowed workers to save, he did not permit these savings to accumulate and generate income.

Pasinetti pointed out that "in any type of society, when any individual saves a part of his income, he must also be allowed to own it, otherwise he would not save at all" (Pasinetti 1962: 270). By working explicitly in terms of a division of society into capitalists and workers, it is clear that some part of total profits must accrue to workers as a result of their past savings.

Pasinetti reformulated Kaldor's model so as to reflect this observation but his systems of equations are rather similar to Kaldor's. The basic equation in Pasinetti's model is $r = n/s_c$, which shows that the balanced growth rate of profit is simply the ratio of the labor force growth rate to the capitalists' saving propensity. This result is similar to that obtained by Kaldor on the assumption that the propensity to save from wage income is zero; consequently, Pasinetti's remarkable conclusion:

> Without making any assumption . . . on the propensities to save of the workers, in the long run, workers' propensity to save, though influencing the distribution of income between capitalists and workers, does not influence the distribution of income between profits and wages. Nor does it have any influence . . . on the rate of profit. . . . The irrelevance of workers' propensity to save gives the model a much wider generality that was hitherto believed. Since the profit rate and the income distribution between profits and wages are determined independently of s_w, there is no need for any hypothesis whatever on the *aggregate* savings behavior of the workers. . . . The relevance of the capitalists' propensity to save . . . uncovers the absolutely strategic importance for the whole system of the decisions to save of just one group of individuals: the capitalists. The post-Keynesian theories . . . seemed to confirm that the relation between capitalists' savings and capital accumulation depended on particularly simplifying and drastic assumptions about negligible savings by the workers. The novelty of the present analysis has been to show that the relation is valid . . . whatever the saving behavior of the workers may be. (1962: 272-75)

In other words, on a steady-state growth path, the profit rate depends only on the growth rate and the propensity of capitalists to save; it is independent of workers' propensity to save.

A different approach to development and growth are the neo-Marxist and Dependency views of development/underdevelopment in which the expansion of the capitalist system is seen as an aspect of the movement of capital into areas of potentially high profits. Within the radical political economy tradition, this set of views finds expression in terms such as "dependency," the generation of "underdevelopment" and the relationships between the center and the periphery.

The discussion of Dependency theory and the related unequal exchange theory by analysts such as Baran, Samir Amin, Frank, Cardoso and Faletto, Emmanuel, Wallerstein, and others, is based upon the concept that the world economy is divided into a "core" of dominant nations and a "periphery" of dependent ones. These theories share the common feature that they emphasize the unevenness of development, and that the relationship between the more developed and the less developed countries is one of dominance of the former over the latter. As Baran argues, "The economic development in underdeveloped countries is profoundly inimical to the dominant interests in the advanced capitalist countries" (1957: 28).

Radical analysts have long emphasized structural rigidities and market failure due to social, institutional, and political factors which usually act as bottlenecks to the process of development (their advocacy of state intervention and regulation of foreign trade and investment as a way out of these bottlenecks is well known). It is not just a case of more developed economies having higher income levels than the less developed ones, but it also includes economic, political, and cultural domination. Dependency theorists have stressed that "dependency on foreign interests and foreign economic penetration keeps the state weak and prevents it from effectively playing its necessary role in protecting domestic industry and fostering economic growth" (Barrett and Whyte 1982: 1072). As a state's contact with the world capitalist economy grows, we might expect to see the government participating less in its economy.

Fel'dman's model and Perroux's theory of "growth poles" are two other important contributions within the radical tradition. Fel'dman's model (1965: 174-99) is based on the Marxist view of the macroeconomy and yet it generates results which, in the long run, are qualitatively similar to those of the Harrod-Domar approach to economic growth.

The division of an economy into two sectors (categories) is common for economists who follow the Marxian framework of thought and Fel'dman used this division and utilized it for his own purposes. In the Fel'dman model of growth, the overall growth rate of national income will not, in general, be equal to the growth rate of total investment output. The simple conclusion which follows from the Fel'dman model is that an increase in the proportion of current capital goods allocated to producing more capital goods eventually increases the growth rates of consumption and investment and output over what they would otherwise have been (Fel'dman 1965: 174-99).

Perroux (1988: 54-57) is best known for his theory of "growth poles" which is a theory of polarization. Economic development does not spread itself evenly throughout space, so, the spatial distribution of economic activity does not fluctuate around a long-term equilibrium norm, but tends to promote the concentration of growth in some areas at the expense of others. The growth-inducing investment (the initial investment expenditure is assumed to be growth-inducing; in other words, to be capable, under given conditions, of generating other induced investments) generates the following four effects (Perroux 1988: 70-72):

1. *Investment effects.* The total investment in a system or sub-system is the sum of the growth-inducing investment and of the induced investments.
2. *Production effects.* Every investment is affected by a coefficient of efficiency, the approximate expression of which is the inverse of the capital co-

efficient, and yields a product. The total incremental product is the sum of the products obtained from the initial induced investments.

3. *Income effects*. The incremental wages and the incremental profits generated by the incremental product can be obtained by applying to the latter the appropriate coefficients, which vary according to economic sector and over time. Similarly, the application of this incremental income of the coefficients of propensity to consume gives the savings generated by these incremental wages and profits.

4. *Balance of trade effects*. The incremental product increases the total product. By applying two coefficients to this increase, the additional imports and exports can be obtained and, hence, by reference to an initial position, the net effect on the balance of trade.

Perroux's main explicit policy conclusion was that governments need to establish "counter poles" to those which had been established in faster growing regions through the free working of the market and, in due course, hope to harness polarization in favor of less developed regions.

In sum, the study of growth dynamics in the post-Keynesian theory is of paramount importance. Central to this analysis is that growth is tightly linked to distribution and capital accumulation. Distribution, along with investment and technical change, is an important determinant of economic growth. The radical political economy tradition is concerned with the development and underdevelopment of real economies as they operate in actual/historical time.

RECENT THEORETICAL ELABORATIONS TO GROWTH AND DEVELOPMENT

Neoclassical Recent Contributions

The neoclassical growth theory is based on extensions of the traditional Solow growth model (Solow 1956, 1982; and 1991) or on recent "endogenous growth" models (Romer 1986; Lucas 1988). Growth, productivity and human capital studies can all be organized into a single theoretical package. The broad theme is the "endogenous" determination of the long-run growth rate through aggregative increasing returns to scale induced by human capital accumulation. The viability of perfect competition is maintained by making the stock of human capital into a "social factor of production," which influences the productivity of all. Solow had in his mind,

> The integration of equilibrium growth theory with medium-run disequilibrium theory so that trends and fluctuations in employment and output could be handled in a unified way. [Given the known neoclassical assumptions], capital deepening in the neoclassical growth models occurs when the stock of capital grows more rapidly than the labor force. The optimal path is the perfect fore-

sight competitive equilibrium path. All solution paths tend to a steady state in
which the ratio of capital to effective labor is constant. (1991: 394)

The Solow growth model states that the long-run growth rate of output per
worker is given by the rate of labor-augmenting technological progress, which it
treats as exogenous. Countries that are still fairly close to their initial conditions,
having started with lower ratios of capital to effective labor than they will eventually achieve in the steady state, will grow faster than countries that are further
along in that process ("catch-up thesis").

Thus, there will be permanent differences in levels of productivity, either
because some countries have faster population growth or lower savings rates
than others or perhaps because of deficiencies in climate or other factors not
accounted for in the model. However, "it is the expected convergence of growth
rates that really matters in the very long run" (Solow 1991: 398).

Romer (1986) and Lucas (1985; 1988), who focus on possibilities of divergent growth paths between countries, consider that the national accumulation of
knowledge, technology, and R&D is basically endogenous, so countries build
their own technological capabilities (i.e., Schumpeterian "creative dynamics").

All national economies do not have access to (or appear not to share in the
advance of) new technology in any effective sense. Political instability, social
institutions, tax systems, religious beliefs, etc., are more or less incompatible
with the successful practice of a changing, high-technology industry. Similarly,
private and/or public corruption might be a similar obstacle.

The endogenous growth theory also supports the view that all these apparently exogenous obstacles reflect, at a deeper level, a deficient formation of human capital. Romer goes one step further and assumes that capital (human capital in his case) has increasing marginal productivity. Consequently, as Solow
argues:

> [Because] the operative mechanism [of the neoclassical competitive equi-
> librium analysis in its optimizing version] is the increasing marginal productiv-
> ity of capital, increasing returns to scale make increasing returns to capital eas-
> ier to come by. . . . The human capital mechanism gives rise to an equilibrium
> in which consumption per capita grows without bound, even in the absence of
> exogenous technological progress. Without the human capital externality and
> the resulting increasing returns, the optimizing version of the neoclassical
> growth model without technological progress would lead to a finite-valued sta-
> tionary state for consumption and output per head. (1991: 400-402)

For Lucas, the neoclassical growth theory is treated as a positive theory of a
competitive economy with foresight. The supply of raw labor is allowed to grow
at a constant rate, and investment in physical capital is taken explicitly into account. The accumulation of human capital is introduced in a way that makes it
"a little more like the acquisition of skill and a little less like research" (Solow
1991: 402). In Lucas' formulation u is the amount of effort devoted to production of the single good and 1-u is the accumulation of human capital by a
worker already embodying human capital at level h. Thus,

$$h^{\cdot}/h = \delta(1-u) \tag{1}$$

According to Lucas, effort and know-how are very important and the growth rate of human capital is proportional to the time spent in training. Lucas uses the Cobb-Douglas production function including human capital in the productive technology for goods. The production of goods is thus given by the following equation:

$$Y = AK^b(uhN)^{1-b}H^\gamma \tag{2}$$

where A is a constant, K now stands for the stock of physical capital, N is the per firm supply of raw labor and H is the economy-wide average level of human capital. Also, the notation in (2) already embodies the assumption that the market for labor clears; in this formulation there is no presumption of increasing marginal product of human capital.

Lucas obtained rather similar results from a different source, that is, the absence of diminishing returns in the creation of human capital. Even if the human capital mechanism $h^{\cdot}/h = \delta(1-u)$ is regarded as "the moral equivalent of technological progress, the eventual per capita growth rate depends on all the parameters of the model" (Solow 1991: 404). This model determines the paths of two stocks, K and *h*. Therefore, according to Lucas, in a steady state, an economy beginning with low levels of human and physical capital will remain permanently below an initially better endowed economy.

Romer (1987) treats effort and knowledge as two important inputs into the production of knowledge and his research produced new results which were exactly the same as in Lucas' model (equation 1 here). In addition, Becker et al. (1988) and Azariadis and Drazen (1988) offered similar contributions to the above literature by building growth models which were capable of several equilibrium paths while focusing on human capital investment. Solow (1991: 404) concluded that "the models have something to say about the large and persistent disparities that separate rich and poor countries."

When discussing the role of international trade, Solow (1991: 407) argued that: "Under . . . exogenous technological progress, national boundaries have no particular significance for growth theory. . . . Anything that enlarges the market can increase the level and rate of growth of output." In this direction, Lucas worked out a particular model to illustrate "the endogenous progress of comparative advantage" and identified goods which are human capital intensive (i.e., high-technology products). The allocation of comparative advantage depends on the initial distribution of human capital. His particular model suggests that the countries specializing in high technology grow faster than others and, thus, reinforce their comparative advantage.

Krugman (1990) added to these studies of endogenous innovation and concluded that international integration may encourage innovation and accelerate growth. In addition, Grossman and Helpman (1988, 1989a, b) adopted the technological specification proposed by Romer (1986) and examined the impact of the comparative advantage in R&D relative to intermediate goods.

Studies by others such as Jones and Manuelli (1988) showed that many of the desired results–endogenization of the growth rate and its sensitivity to permanent influence by government policies or accidental disturbance–can be achieved without increasing returns of scale or externalities simply by relaxing one of the conditions and assuming that the marginal product of capital is bounded away from 0 as capital accumulates indefinitely.

Therefore, the neoclassical theoretical background of recent studies is either an extension of the traditional Solow model or the endogenous growth models. The former, the traditional view of differences in growth rates, suggests that the less advanced countries catch up to the leading ones and thus enjoy a faster rate of technological progress and growth. The latter supports the view that countries follow their own national growth paths and try to build their own technological capabilities with little tendency for convergence in income or productivity levels.[5]

It is worth mentioning that there may be some room for state intervention in order to improve human capital, R&D and innovation. This kind of intervention and government spending on human resource development and R&D may be acceptable by endogenous growth analysis.

The After-Cambridge (UK) Contributions

The link between growth and income distribution continues to be central to the post-Keynesian analysis. Recent developments have been concerned with exploring how the Cambridge (UK) school model can be extended with different kinds of government intervention so as to avoid a trade-off. Pasinetti (1989: 26-36) started from his first formulation (in 1962) and simply added government spending (G) to consumption (C) and investments (I) in the equation for national income (Y):

$$Y = C + I + G = W + P_w + P_c \tag{1}$$

where the right-hand side represents the income distribution aspect and all the distributive variables are gross of taxes. Government spending also has to be put into relation with government revenue (i.e., with the proceeds from taxation).

Denoting total taxation by T, the equation can be written as:

$$G = (1 - s_t)T \tag{2}$$

where s_t represents the proportion of total taxes that is not spent–a sort of government propensity to save. Thus $G < T$ or $G > T$ can be represented by $s_t > 0$ or $s_t < 0$, respectively; while $G = T$, the case of a perfectly balanced government budget, when $s_t = 0$. The saving functions for the various categories of savers are, thus, as follows:

$$S_w = s_w(W + P_w - t_w W - t_p W_w) \tag{3}$$

$$S_c = s_c(P_c - t_p P_c) \qquad (4)$$
$$S_G = s_t T \qquad (5)$$

where S_w is workers' savings net of both wage and profit taxes; S_c is capitalists' savings net of profit taxes; S_G is saving by the government; t_w is the proportional direct tax on wages, and, t_p is the proportional direct tax on profits. The overall direct tax on wages, and, t_p is the proportional direct tax on profits. The overall savings (S) will be the sum of (3), (4) and (5):

$$S = S_w + S_c + S_G \qquad (6)$$

where S_G positively adds something to total savings only if $s_t > 0$. If on the other hand, $s_t < 0$, government expenditure, by being in excess of taxation revenue, has the overall effect of destroying part of private savings (public dis-savings).

Pasinetti (1989: 28-32) distinguishes the following two cases:

Case 1: The case of *a balanced government budget*. This is the simplest case. In this case, government expenditure is exactly covered by explicit taxation. The relevant relation between savings and capital ownership is given by the following equation:

$$S/K = S_w/K_w = S_c/K_c \qquad (7)$$

By using the usual I = S equilibrium relation and by substituting from (3) and (4), and since S_G is equal to zero, the usual Cambridge equation can be obtained:

$$R = g_n/s_c(1 - t_p) \text{ or, } r (1 - t_p) = (1/s_c)g_n$$

which states that the long-run rate of profits r is determined by the natural rate of growth divided by the capitalists' propensity to save, which is now corrected by the taxation parameter, independently of anything else. In other words, in its original form, the Cambridge growth equation holds with reference to the rate of profits net of profit tax.

Case 2: The case of *a government budget deficit* (or *budget surplus*). In this case, the government spends more (or spends less) than it raises from taxation. Pasinetti wrote as follows:

> The model would not be the appropriate one to use if we wanted to consider an economic system that sometimes has a government budget surplus and sometimes has a government budget deficit. However, the case of a permanent government deficit (or surplus) is not inconsistent with the present model, provided that the deficit (or surplus) grows steadily at the same rate as that of all other magnitudes. But, finally, the validity of Kaldor's theory of income distribution and of the Cambridge theory of the rate of profits seems to go beyond the case of taxation with balanced budgets and extend to the case of government deficit, whether financed by monetary means or by a public debt, provided that the Ricardian Equivalence holds. The relevant step, both in Kaldor's theory and in Ricardo's, is taken at the point where, with government taxation (and a balanced budget), a process is envisaged through which the share of profits in Kal-

dor, and of wages in Ricardo, remains unaffected, as the burden of taxation is fully shifted to the other category of income. When this is granted, then if government expenditure goes beyond the constraints of taxation—but the conditions are satisfied under which taxation and deficit spending (through either monetary or debt financing) come to the same thing—it should be obvious that the original results could not but remain unaffected. (1989: 33-34)

It has been shown by Steedman (1972: 1387-95) that the existence of certain kinds of taxation and government spending will not affect the nature of a Pasinetti equilibrium, with a net rate of profit determined solely by the natural rate of growth and the savings ratio of capitalists.

Fleck and Domenghino (1987: 22-36) concluded that Pasinetti's paradox dissolves itself in a system with state activity: the workers' propensity to save remains a determining factor of the long-term distribution of income as well as a determinant of the long-term rate of profit.

Denicolo and Matteuzi (1990: 339-44) have shown that the Cambridge theorem can be extended to the case of government budget surplus (the net rate of profits is given by $r_n = (1 - t_p)P_c/K_c$) or budget deficit (the net rate of return on public debt equals that on private capital, that is $i = (1 - t_p)P_c/K_c$), even when the conditions on which the Ricardian Equivalence Theorem rests are not satisfied. They concluded that the natural rate of growth and the capitalists' propensity to save determine the net rate of return on capitalists' wealth, independently of anything else. Thus, the net rate of return on capitalists' wealth is completely independent of fiscal policies.

According to Fazi and Salvadori (1981; 1985) the Kaldorian model can determine the functional income distribution between wages and profits, the overall profit rate, the capital-output ratio and the capitalists' profit rate. Therefore, in Kaldor's growth model, the basic properties of the model are unaltered (Fazi and Salvadori 1981: 155-64).

Pattenati (1967) has shown how a theorem similar to Pasinetti's can be formulated on the basis of the distinction between households and companies which is closer to the reality of neo-capitalism than the distinction between capitalists and workers. Pattenati (1974) presented two models which are Post-Keynesian, since the distribution (not the level) of income is the variable that equates savings to planned investment. The economy can grow with a constant proportion of unemployment, which depends—among other things—on the government's fiscal policy. The whole burden of the adjustment falls, thus, on fiscal policy (Pattenati 1967: 97-126).

Finally, Chiang (1973: 311-13) made a simple generalization of the Kaldor-Pasinetti analysis of profit rate and income distribution by considering a model with three distinct saving propensities, s_{ww}, s_{pw}, and s_{pc}, each of which is associated with a different income claim (the first subscripts refer to the income source, and the second subscripts to the income class).

In concluding this section, it may be said that the Cambridge equation forms the basis of much of post-Keynesian analysis of growth, with various extensions to allow for fiscal policies (i.e., whether or not the conditions on which the Ricardian Equivalence Theorem rests are satisfied). Some showed that the Kaldorian model is logically consistent with the structure of a two-class economy while others offered support to Pasinetti's paradox. Taking into consideration that the actual rate of economic growth usually deviates from the warranted growth rate (which is not usually associated with full employment), fiscal policies really do matter—indeed, they matter a great deal.

CONCLUSION

A common complaint of orthodox economic theory in general (and theories of growth in particular) is that it is unrealistic and, by implication, of little use. Criticisms vary, but they mostly seem to stem from a distrust of the role of assumptions since assumptions or postulates of theoretical views and models are frequently criticized for being unrealistic. For some, the real world is much too complex and cannot be analyzed successfully by views such as "factor and resource endowments," "factors coming as manna from heaven," or "the dreams of perfect heavens."

Economic policies should not only try to promote higher growth paths but should also keep economies on a steady growth path because of the threat of instability (i.e., Harrod's "knife edge"). On the other hand, market forces tend to promote the concentration of economic growth in some areas at the expense of others. The unevenness of development and growth in all capitalist economies over time is matched by an unevenness between different geographical areas, regions and nations.

Moreover, state intervention or government involvement has been necessary in the process of growth and development. The state has a significant role to play but whether it intervenes, and in what form, depends on circumstances, given that every country has its own economic, social, political, and cultural characteristics. These notions form the subject matter of the following chapters.

NOTES

1. Kalecki pays special attention to various problems and incentives of expanding agricultural production (1976: 26-27; 31-36).

2. But the general equilibrium theory of Leon Walras and his followers never raised the question of what determines the total output in a state of general equilibrium.

3. For example, Alfred Marshall introduces his model with two driving variables, the rate of saving and the rate of increase in the size and efficiency of the work force (see Marshall's *Principles*: 10-11).

4. See Kaldor: "Capital Accumulation and Economic Growth" in Lutz and Hague, eds. (1961): 177-222.

5. Although standing on different theoretical premises, the endogenous growth theory comes close to the conclusions of Myrdal (1957) and Kaldor (1966; 1978) on "cumulative causation" and the possibilities of divergent growth.

Chapter 2

The Developmental State View

INTRODUCTION

The first part of this chapter is devoted to a discussion about the successful development experiences of Japan and Newly Industrialized Countries (NICs). The underlying purpose is to elaborate on the theoretical framework of the Developmental State and to examine this concept, bearing in mind that the nature of the Developmental State can only be seriously examined in the context of the relevant theoretical framework. A number of issues related to a new role for the government will be identified and examined as some future requirements arise from present economic and social problems.

During the past two decades, there has been a tendency among orthodox economists to minimize the role of the state in contemporary Japanese economy. This trend seems to be closely connected to the general revival of support for the ideology of free market forces with its consequence of rolling back the growth of the state. Although, "the main thrust of the analysis which pictures Japan as the 'epitome' of a liberal free market has come from the USA, this interpretation is also popular among Japanese commentators" (Eccleston 1989: 89).

Recent attempts to show that Japan's industrial experience illustrates why interventionist policies are not necessary for rapid economic growth have tended to focus the debate fairly narrowly on industrial policy. But nurturing the expansion of new industrial sectors and smoothing the decline of others is only one element of economic policy making and the whole array of government management activities also need to be considered. In this vein, the Japanese state should be seen as both a planner and an investor.

Japan has never experienced a laissez-faire stage of economic development, and "its recent history has been marked by more cooperative relations between the government and private business" (Eccleston 1989: 91-92). Clearly, even with less direct state spending, there is still a determination to promote a more orderly adjustment than the market would produce if left to itself, and the Japanese state has been an active participant rather than a passive umpire (Eccleston 1989: 122).

Finally, we need to ask in what sense the Japanese government is less interventionist than in other Western economies? Quantitative measures provide ambiguous evidence because, although the Japanese state does indeed consume a smaller proportion of GDP in spending on public administration, defense, health care or housing, public investment is actually the highest in the OECD area. Placing more emphasis on Japan's high rates of saving and investment (percent of GDP) also begs questions about how these high levels have been maintained during approximately the last four decades.

JAPAN AND NICs:
A NEW DEVELOPMENT EXPERIENCE

Japan and the Newly Industrialized Countries offer a new and different approach to the promotion of industrial development. The spectacular growth of East Asian economies is well known, even though they have experienced difficulties in the last few years.[1] In fact, their experience has overall shown that there exists a pattern of general development direction as they moved towards a more industrialized stage (i.e., they have followed similar economic development and trade policies).

Japan

At the end of World War II, Japan (a country composed of four islands) was a relatively less-developed economy with massive structural damages from atomic bombs and severe economic problems. According to available statistics (OECD: various), in the 1950s, the Japanese economy produced around 5 million tons of steel and 50,000 cars. Comparatively, Japan produced less steel and fewer cars than countries such as Brazil, Mexico or India do today and exported only textiles, rice and light manufactured goods. On the other hand, the U.S. economy at the same time was producing around 100 million tons of steel and 6 million cars every year.

However, almost three decades later, Japan produced more steel, cars and electronics than the United States, and had become a technological leader and a major world competitor in high technology goods. In the 1980s and 1990s, enterprises from the United States, the EEC and Japan are competing at the edge of the astonishing pace of technological innovation in the world markets.

Retrospectively, in the post-World War II era, trade policies in East Asian economies (except Hong Kong) began with a period of import-substitution; however, export-push strategies were enacted in Japan and other NICs in the 1960s. The governments of these countries helped to build up and protect the production power of domestic industries (i.e., plan-rational, production-oriented capitalist economies). In this connection, although Japan has never been a command economy, the Japanese government has managed to continually lead the process of industrial development, and industrial policies always emerged after tough bargaining and compromise between the government and targeted sectors (Nester 1991: 29). Despite conflicts among various interest groups within its political system, and competition among firms within its economy, "extensive economic and political agreements have been as important to Japan's economic dynamism as competition" (Nester 1991: 57).

Since the initial stages of the industrialization process, the Japanese government adopted a production, capital accumulation, and innovation-oriented approach. As a result, the Japanese economy achieved a competitive advantage by improving human capital and industrial learning, and building production capabilities for core industries. Innovating firms at the beginning of the product cycle crossed the technological frontier by investing in R&D, building skills, shaping demand for new products on world markets, and selling them under financial conditions that make production and further innovation possible.

Furthermore, the relations between the Japanese government and private business have been governed by recognition of a common interest. Strategic industries in Japan are targeted for export-oriented development and declining industries for protection, and both the former and the latter are nurtured through a dynamic mixture of cooperation and competition (Nester 1990: 167-70; 1991: 29). This mixture of a creative and dynamic cooperation and competition has produced efficient industrial policies and prosperous industrial sectors (Nester 1991: 29).

Indeed, the cornerstone of the successful Japanese industrial development was state involvement in promoting R&D and innovation of certain specific industries that were considered to be vital for the rapid growth of productivity and per capita incomes. On the other hand, "as Japan's productive capacity expanded sharply, expenditures on the output it generated necessarily increased. Among the components of aggregate demand, investment and exports played key roles in the rapid expansion" (Ito 1992: 50).

Maddison (1965) attributes the success of the Japanese developmentalist policy to the following factors:

1. government commitment to the promotion of industrialization;
2. a high savings and investments ratio and a relatively high rate of economic growth; and,
3. state efforts to transfer and develop a technology suitable to the Japanese conditions (the role of R&D, innovation, and human capital formation was very important).

The allocation of investment funds and the direction of industrial development have been guided by the state. Yet, direct participation by the state in the allocation of savings to industry has been very important in both qualitative and quantitative senses. Household savings in Japan have been approximately 75 percent higher than in the West over the past forty years, and the state has transferred these savings into investments by the public and private sectors.[2]

The central mechanism for this transfer is the Fiscal Investment and Loan Program (FILP), which lends at lower than market interest rates to a variety of public agencies. Public corporations, in turn, lend funds to private firms and, consequently, all Japanese industries have direct or indirect access to FILP. Banks play a vital role in that process by financing expansion on the basis of a very long time horizon.

Therefore, the state has played an important role in mobilizing and spending investment funds. Indeed, the biggest source has been the accumulated savings of households, which, since 1975, has been supplemented by substantial issues of government bonds (Eccleston 1989: 99; Ito 1992: 120-21). Savers have been able to accumulate several tax-free accounts and the government has, to a large extent, placed emphasis on government bonds, which are not completely free from regulation in Japan and are issued at a negotiated yield (Ito 1992: 120-21).

Rapid capital accumulation–high investment rates have been achieved for sustained periods by Japan and the NICs of Asia.[3] In fact, a high investment rate was possible in part by the high saving rate of the household sector and fiscal investment has played a major role (see table 2.1).[4]

Cowling (1990) and other commentators on the Japanese production system have ascribed its success to the existence of strong quasi-state institutions such as MITI, etc. which have played a very crucial part in promoting supply-side improvements. Hashimoto and Raisian (1985), and Mincer and Higuchi (1988) observed high levels of investments in human capital in the Japanese industry.[5] The R&D agencies and public corporations of Japan's technology policy "stress the priority of knowledge-intensive industries to Japan's industrial economy and future" (Best 1990: 202).

TABLE 2.1
Average Gross Saving (percent of GDP) in the EC, the United States, and Japan: 1960-1990

Country	1960-67	1968-73	1974-79	1980-90
EC average	24.7	25.5	22.6	20.5
United States	19.9	19.6	19.8	16.3
Japan	33.6	38.5	32.8	32.1

Source: OECD, Historical Statistics 1960-1990 (1992).

Japanese enterprises are capable of competing strategically on new grounds (i.e., ability to design, produce, shape demand for, and retail on national and, especially, world markets sophisticated manufactured goods and services on the basis of price, product quality, technological process, or product innovation). These firms are organizations that are continuously learning and creating new productive services by teamwork and experience and interfirm relations can be cooperative or market oriented. Thus, "strategy-culture-productive organization" (through the elimination of wasteful practices, "right-on-time automation") are basic principles for Japanese firms (Best 1990: 138; 166).

South Korea, Taiwan, Singapore, and Malaysia

The competitive success of leading, large Japanese firms has been successfully imitated by South Korea, Taiwan, Hong Kong, Singapore, and Malaysia. The NICs' governments have been particularly successful in achieving high rates of growth through thorough export-oriented industrialization strategies; in establishing key government organs to direct outward-oriented economic development; in amas-sing capital for producer goods (e.g., iron or coal); and in fostering import-substitution industries. Yet, East Asian economies caught up by breaking into markets of established producers and achieved full control over the value-added chain of manufactured products in export markets.

Furthermore, the NICs' states have pursued macro-level economic policies designed to influence private economic decisions, economic sectors, whole industries and individual firms within industries in ways that these governments deem desirable and developmental (i.e., comprehensive state intervention, which has loomed large in the economic restructuring of recent years).

Particular attention is drawn to a highly active state technology policy within which the role of the government has not been simply to finance R&D, but also to direct and coordinate the R&D efforts of private industry. Indeed, while most of the government's R&D spending is directed towards creating a more internationally competitive industrial structure (and reducing internal competition) by giving a lead to certain firms or by financing projects whose development costs are very large and may be risky, some of it is also prompted by the divergence between public and private costs and benefits in certain areas. Thus, public agencies play a vital role in technology transfer from the lab to the industry, which is often viewed as a costly and time-consuming process.

The relative weight of the South Korean industrial sector grew markedly from the 1960s to the 1980s, and the thoroughly planned structural transformation in the manufacturing sector was also impressive (see table 2.2). In addition, in many sectors, state-owned (public) enterprises and banks have been used as the chosen instruments for a "big push." However, private firms have not been left alone and, in many cases, are exposed to discretionary government influence, taking the form of what in Japan is called administrative guidance (Wade 1990: 110-11).

TABLE 2.2
South Korea: Sectoral Distribution of GDP (percent), 1962-1995

	1962	1970	1980	1995
Agriculture	40.0	29.8	14.2	6.7
Industry	19.0	23.8	37.8	30.5
Services	41.0	46.4	48.1	62.8

Source: World Bank (1997); Asian Development Bank (1997).

Kang (1989) attributes the industrial development of South Korea to the following factors:

1. *export orientation:* large expansion of exports;
2. *state planning:* overall programming of infrastructure development, social development, current research, external relations planning, and financial planning (thoroughness of planning);
3. *technology acquisition from abroad* (industrial know-how); and,
4. *the high-technology push into electronics* (as well as steel, construction, and automobiles).

The South Korean state may be seen as an "effective planner" and R&D has been supported by the government and institutions created by leading dynamic firms to import new foreign technology. A higher level of education, training, and learning-by-doing have also been key determinants and built the necessary human capital for the developmental process in South Korea. With respect to its integration with the world economy, South Korea was able to achieve a high growth (8.5 percent in the 1960s, 9.6 percent in the 1970s, 9.4 percent in the 1980s, and 7.2 percent during 1990-97 according to the World Bank) with significant import controls and thorough guidance of foreign direct investment.

Likewise for Taiwan, Wade (1990), among other scientists, documents the widespread and intensive use of active industrial policy and state-directed technological learning to guide the market economy purposefully (Singh 1998: 68).

Singapore is also an example as a country where strategic planning (i.e., control over key macroeconomic variables, and a systematic effort to coordinate public-private investment decisions and attract private investment) succeeded. Indeed, state planning played a vital role in Singapore's endogenous development, as the country's dependence on the outside world and imports was considered excessive and hence a danger.

State-owned enterprises constituted a fundamental departure towards planning. Besides, sustained rapid growth, sharply increasing export orientation, high savings (through social security and private sector capital accumulation schemes) and investment spending in infrastructure and the "modern factors of development and competitiveness," and structural transformation characterized Singapore's economic development since the 1960s (see table 2.3).

TABLE 2.3
Singapore Macroeconomic Indicators

	1960-69	1970-79	1980-89	1990-97
Real GDP growth [a]	8.7	8.9	7.1	8.3
Saving ratio [b]	11.5	28.8	40.6	47.7
Investment ratio [c]	20.7	40.5	41.8	36.4

Source: Singapore, Department of Statistics (1988, 1994, and 1999); Ministry of Trade and Industry (1990, 1994, and 1999).
[a] Annual real GDP growth rate.
[b] Gross national savings (% GDP).
[c] Gross capital formation (% GDP)

Manufactured exports became the engine of Singapore's economic growth. The share of manufacturing in total output grew from 16.6 percent in 1960 to 29.4 percent by 1979. In 1997, manufacturing contributed 27.4 percent to GDP and accounted for 23.3 percent of employment. The other major structural change was the increasing importance of services: financial and business services; communications and transport; and public administration, community, social, and personal services. Yet, Singapore's development as an international financial center emerged as an engine of growth after 1978, and was the economy's fastest-growing sector (Singapore: Department of Statistics; Ministry of Trade and Industry, various years).

Interventionism in Singapore was organized around government directives and plans, which set the broad objectives, targets, and strategies that guided its national development. The planning system was described as "a high degree of good and eclectic steersmanship."[6] Singapore planners took a view of the future; nevertheless, planning for manufacturing development in Singapore never got involved with the operational detail, and the incentive structure was continually revised in light of planning objectives.[7] As Singapore's *Strategic Economic Plan* observed: "State planning has played a very significant role in the development of Singapore for more than thirty years" (Singapore, *Economic Planning Committee* 1991: 14).

Malaysia is also regarded as one of the miracle economies of the world, where both poverty and inequality declined. Growth was not merely rapid and persistent; it was also equitable (World Bank 1990; 1993). As a rapidly growing economy, Malaysia exhibits high savings and investment ratios. The 1971-80 average savings and investment ratios were 29 percent and 25 percent respectively; these ratios increased to 33 percent and 31 percent on average over the period 1981-90. This rapid growth has occurred within a context of significant structural change. Indeed, the output share of the agricultural sector has fallen from 23 percent in 1980 to 16 percent in the early 1990s while the share of industry has increased from 36 percent to 44 percent over the same period (Asian Development Bank 1994).

Malaysia's industrialization process dates back to the 1960s when import-substitution industries like food, beverages and tobacco, printing and publishing, building materials, chemicals and plastics were established. Prior to that, the economy was largely dependent on rubber and tin. In time, agriculture began to diversify to include other crops as well as the processing of raw materials.

In the late 1960s, as the limited domestic market placed constraints on the rapid industrial development coupled with growing unemployment problems, the Malaysian government began to encourage the development of export-oriented and labor-intensive industries. Additionally, in the move towards an industrial-based economy, efforts were made to increase the supply of skilled manpower (pursuit of excellence, diligence, commitment and integrity, i.e., positive work ethics).

In the early 1970s, the rapid inflow of foreign investments resulted in the development of electronics and textile industries. Since 1981, the promulgation of "Heavy Industries Policy" aimed at developing a more balanced, integrated, and coherent national economy and industrial sector (e.g., the production of iron, steel, cement, small engine parts, and cars). The growth of these industries led to multiple developments and further growth of the manufacturing sector.

In the mid-1980s, the government realized that the manufacturing sector needed new impetus for growth and undertook more aggressive strategies and programs to develop this sector. In 1986, the government launched the *First Industrial Master Plan*, which was the blueprint for the further development of the manufacturing sector over a ten-year period (1986-95).

The Industrial Master Plan reinforced Malaysia's thrust for an outward-oriented industrial strategy based on (both) the intensive development of the resource-based industries and the diversification of non-resource based industries for higher levels of exports. The successful implementation of these industrial strategies enabled the manufacturing sector to be the leading sector in the economy.

Malaysia has already reached the stage where export-oriented industries have become the main vehicle for the country's drive for accelerated industrial development. The successful growth and diversification of Malaysian exports have propelled the country to be among the world's top trading nations.

Keeping abreast with global trends, the industrialization phase in Malaysia is recently focused upon the development of high value-added and high technology industries. With that, a major shift has begun from labor-intensive industries to capital-intensive and technologically sophisticated industries, while government planning (e.g., National Plan of Action for Industrial Technology Development) provides a clear thrust and direction for the development of a strong technological foundation for industrial and economic growth.

The Malaysian government is also assuming an active role in technology development, particularly in the development of key and emerging technologies. These essential technologies have been identified for the purpose of building the indigenous competency and innovativeness as well as for developing niche areas for domestic firms. It is envisaged that the further development of technological capabilities will provide the catalyst for further deepening and broadening of the country's technological base and industrial competency, which are essential for maintaining the competitiveness of domestic industries in the dynamic global market. Furthermore, a major policy objective is towards creating a knowledge-based workforce, and the thrust is directed at the upgrading of labor force skills, the promotion of improved managerial competence and initiative as well as the advancement of scientific and technological expertise.

To facilitate efforts in increasing the technological competitiveness of Malaysian industry and assist Malaysian investors to acquire new technologies, fiscal incentives are provided to encourage R&D efforts and various schemes have been launched for product design and development, productivity and quality improvements, market development, research, marketable new and emerging technologies, and industrial skills training. In addition, various institutions have been formed to accelerate technology development (i.e., joint ventures between the government and industry) and facilitate the introduction of strategic technologies from abroad.

Malaysia's *Second Industrial Master Plan* covers the period from 1996 to 2005. While the first Industrial Master Plan focused on further diversification and deepening of the resource-based industries, the second Industrial Master Plan requires the development of an integrated industry-wide vision embracing both manufacturing and business support services (like R&D and design capability, packaging, distribution and marketing activities), where each dynamic sector has the potential to be developed into a "cluster" (i.e., aggregates of more diverse sectors) (Mahathir CEO Malaysia, 1999).

Moreover, Information Technology (IT) has been recognized as a strategic tool to support the growth of the Malaysian economy. Substantial investments were directed towards laying the basic IT infrastructure as a step towards establishing a sophisticated network of facilities and services in order to improve efficiency, productivity, and overall competitiveness.

Theoretical Views—Controversial Issues

Some contend that East Asian economic success is ascribed to openness and small government, and see efficiency in resource use as the principal general force for the growth and transformation of these economies. Consequently, these countries built their own technological capabilities and overcame the limitations of small domestic markets by exporting manufactured goods at competitive prices. Other interpreters argue that state intervention was an important factor but only insofar as it offset market failures and promoted exports, through subsidies, etc., in order to assist domestic firms and industries in capturing gains from foreign competitors.[8]

However, both neoclassical and neoliberal views have a difficult task in accommodating the facts of pervasive interventions of the East Asian states in their internal and external economies, with the theoretical and policy framework used in such analyses. Some have even argued that these countries would have grown faster still if the state had not intervened in these economies (Lal 1983).

Others have suggested that the essential reason for the state's success in these countries is that it has followed the market rather than leading or guiding it. Such arguments have been carefully analyzed by Amsden (1989), Wade (1990), Chang (1994), and Singh (1994), among others, and found to have very little merit (Singh 1998: 71).[9]

Additionally, when discussing the successful development experience of East Asian economies, the recent neoclassical and neoliberal assertions (by IMF, World Bank, and WTO) with respect to the role of openness, external competition and closer integration with the world economy do not appear to stand up to serious examination either at a theoretical level or empirically. According to these assertions, the greater the degree of international economic integration, the better it is for any particular economy or for the world economy as a whole. A corollary of this line of argument is that the less the distortions from international competitive prices in an economy, the greater would be its economic growth (Singh 1998: 63).

Contrary to the neoclassical/neoliberal homilies about the virtues of "free mobility of capital and labor," "free entry and exit of firms," "reluctant market-conforming state intervention," and the importance of competition in the domestic market (which constitute the main policy gospel for developing countries), the practice of the successful East Asian economies has been rather different.

The unorthodox line of argument holds that East Asian success story should be ascribed to state as principal director or "government leadership and steerage of the market system," and is in harmony with Keynes' conclusion that planned economic development is the "most efficient" alternative that combines plan and market in a creative partnership. Therefore, strategic state intervention was the most powerful engine of that progress and in particular of the long run expansion of total output.

The necessary condition was the promotion of certain specific (targeted) industries of high potential. The working of industry-specific incentive systems as part of a thorough industrial strategy and the concomitant government guarantees and support to exporting firms, including the conglomerate nature of these firms having close links to premier banks, resulted in the creation of dynamic industries and prosperous sectors.

Indeed, the strong government goal of these economies in the earlier decades had served to reconcile private goals with social objectives, oversee the individual firm strategies, and combine them with a broader sector or national development strategy. In this respect, this "new" type of state (i.e., the Developmental State) is organized and concerned with promoting an aggressive industrial strategy while, at the same time, purposefully guiding the market economy.[10]

As in relation to the question of integration with the world economy, these countries appear to have taken the view that from the dynamic perspective of promoting long-term production-oriented intensive growth, investment, and technical change, the optimal degree of competition is not perfect or maximum competition.[11] The governments in these countries have managed or guided competition in a purposeful manner; it has been both encouraged but notably also restricted in a number of ways (Singh 1998: 83-84).

Clearly, the successful East Asian economies had sought a "strategic" or "managed" but not a "close" integration with the global economy—that is, "they integrated up to the point where it was useful for them to do so" for promoting industrial growth and endogenous competency (Singh 1998: 79). Therefore, the concepts of "guiding" the market and of "strategic" integration with the world economy are fully compatible with the unorthodox line of argument.

Selective intervention constitutes a fundamental characteristic of the Developmental State. In fact, the ability of the Developmental State to undertake selective, strategic intervention is based on the existence of a "strong" state structure and "strong" administrative capacity. Such states "concentrate considerable power, authority, autonomy and competence in the central political and bureaucratic institutions of the state, notably their [developmental elites, or] economic bureaucracies" (Leftwich 1995: 420).

In terms of policy objectives, their attention has focused almost exclusively on increasing growth, productivity, and exports and restrict their intervention to the strategic requirements of long-term transformation. What differentiates the NICs' Developmental States from the generality of planning institutions in so many developed and developing countries appears to be their real authority-power and technical competence in shaping developmentalist policies, and their ability to use both "carrots" (incentives, subsidies, etc. to private industries) and "sticks" (punishments) to influence firm behavior (Singh 1995: 10).

Further, the bureaucracy is given sufficient scope to take initiatives and operate effectively. In this sense, the NICs' states have been powerful and have what political scientists often label greater "autonomy" than in many other countries (Amsden 1989; Wade 1990; Fishlow 1991; Onis 1991). Autonomy of the Developmental State means that there is state-private cooperation in which the government (and the bureaucratic elites) independently develop national goals, and translate these broad national goals into effective policy action.

In some countries (such as India, Mexico, and bureaucratic authoritarian regimes of some countries in South America), the state's goals are reducible to private interests. However,

> The pattern of MITI's (or its Korean and Taiwanese counterparts') involvement in the economy was consistent with both the economic logic of selective industrial policy . . . and the logic of finding an equilibrium between bureaucratic autonomy and effectiveness, on the one hand, and bureaucratic power and accountability, on the other (i.e., correspondence between "state autonomy" and "state capacity"). (Onis 1991: 115)

Therefore, the strong NICs' Developmental States have had relative autonomy from dominant classes and interest groups, and the state technocracy (i.e., well-educated, well-trained and efficient technocratic planners) has played an active and important role in export-oriented development. Indeed, the generally positive strategic roles that the NICs' states have played in their production-oriented industrial growth cannot be explained solely in terms of "strength" (power) or "relative autonomy," but by their strong commitment to industrial development and economic growth.

If we suppose that a government which uses its military power or a military government is at one extreme (although a military government may not necessarily be a "strong" state) and a weak state influenced by interest groups is at the other (Myrdal 1968), then the nature of the Developmental State should be somewhere between these two extremes. Its relative position is, indeed, a reflection of and/or depends on the relative strength of the existing political forces (social classes, interest groups, local governments, trade unions, etc.).

The recent East Asian financial crisis has led to a further questioning of the developmental role of the state.[12,13] There are arguments that the "Asian Miracle" was only a mirage, or that the region's problems can be seen as consequences and penalties that it had to pay for deviating from the "disciplines" of the free market system.

Yet, it is known that economic growth based on expansion of inputs, rather than on growth in output per unit of input, is inevitably subject to diminishing returns. In this respect, the original Krugman (1994) argument is a rerun of this simple hypothesis, where economic growth faltered because of declines in factor efficiency. When one accounts for the role of efficiency in explaining growth in East Asia, Krugman's findings were that the contribution was also negligible.[14]

Others contend that financial deregulation undertaken by East Asian governments removed or loosened controls on firms' foreign borrowing, abandoned coordination of borrowings and investment expenditure, and failed to strengthen bank supervision (Wade and Veneroso 1998: 9). Consequently, suggestions have been made for a more active and interventionist role for the government in tackling the financial sector crisis. It is believed that this will alleviate the financial constraints on the real sector and hence stimulate the recovery process.

In this sense, the Asian model of development with strengthened governance systems could provide the most effective means of taking Asian economies back on a high and sustained growth path. Further reinforcement of government involvement—along with qualitative state intervention—and a long-term close and transparent working relationship between firms, banks, and the state (as well as other socioeconomic segments) is warranted to address market imperfections.

To sum up, Japan and the NICs did all the things that a "market-friendly" approach to development and growth (i.e., trade liberalization, private enterprise and a restricted role for the state) is not supposed to do (Singh 1995: 9). What is clear from the above discussion is that the state needs the market and private enterprise needs the state; due to their strategic partnership, substantial industrial development and intensive growth has occurred in places where this has happened. What really matters is not the extent of government intervention but the quality of such intervention.

DEVELOPMENTAL STATE: THEORY AND POLICY

Three desirable notions or key elements are of great importance in discussing the concept of the Developmental State:

- the role of the market and the state;
- emphasis on government investments; and,
- strategic planning.

These notions are discussed further below.

Market-State and the Developmental State

The conflict between the market and the state has always been at the heart of major debates in economic theory. Anglo-American economic analysis has focused on the essential opposition of market and plan. Within the market failure approach of Anglo-American industrial economics, there is a sharp division between government and industry, in which their roles are quite different (Sawyer 1992a: 54). The role of government is seen to be one of control and regulation rather than of aiding industrial development and of creating new opportunities for private business, which would not otherwise exist (Sawyer 1992a: 56-57).[15]

Further, the New Right schools support the view that state action almost always limits the effectiveness of markets, while the market failure approach suggests that governments should, and do, restrain and correct the operations of the market system. In complete contrast, the Developmental State analysis suggests a developmental role for the state which involves the active promotion of industrial development, with the state setting the general developmental framework within which firms operate and seeking to aid firms to fulfil the developmental strategy (Sawyer 1992a: 56-57).

As was stated before, Japan and the NICs have done all the things that free market policies to development are not supposed to do. The government in these economies has played a vigorous role, guided the market toward planned structural changes and followed a highly active industrial policy (Singh 1995: 9).

The Developmental State of these countries has been absolutely different from the state-"night watchman" (according to the Austrian view) and the state-"Leviathan" (according to the monetarist approach), and has had nothing to do with the interaction of voters, politicians, and bureaucrats that according to the Public Choice analysis, produces a bureaucratic state with significant weaknesses. These approaches (i.e., the New Right views) suggest cuts in public expenditure on education, innovation, R&D, training, infrastructural investment, etcetera, in the name of fiscal prudence and widening individual choices (which actually damage the long-term growth prospects of any economy) and, therefore, preclude any discussion about the range of government economic policies which may prove useful in the encouragement of industrial development.

Orthodox economic analysis draws a sharp division between state and industry and focuses on the essential opposition of market and government. In sharp contrast, the developmental role of the state mostly involves the active promotion of industrial development and competency under which the state adopts an entrepreneurial role, either in its own industrial operations or in its promotion of private business, and creates opportunities that would not otherwise exist (Sawyer 1992a: 56-57).

The successful Japanese state supported and promoted certain specific dynamic industries (of high potential) that required intensive employment of capital and new technology, industries (like car industry or electronics) that would be the most inappropriate for the industrial development and intensive growth of Japan if comparative costs of production were taken into consideration.

According to the neoclassical marginal analysis, which usually adopts short-term perspectives in policy decision making, the cost-side of these industries (spending on R&D, innovation, technology, human resource development, etc.) is high whilst the potential benefits are intangible and not direct. Investment expenditure in machinery or human resource development can be adversely affected by uncertainty about the future, which may be exacerbated by the short-termism of an unfettered market system. R&D may also be inhibited by a significant divergence between private and social returns and by long-term and uncertain pay-offs.

Consequently, from a short-term, static point of view, encouragement and support of such firms would not seem to be a rational development policy; but from a long-term viewpoint, these are precisely the industries that are capable of competing strategically on new grounds, on the basis of rapid technical progress, high labor productivity, product quality or innovation. Moreover, government expenditure on learning, skills, R&D, etcetera, financed projects whose development costs are very large and/or risky, and the difference between private and social returns could lead firms to underinvest.

Therefore, the experience of Japan and the NICs provides a strong argument against laissez-faire and in favor of government involvement for guiding the market system. In the case of all these countries, the governments have played a positive enabling role in the economy and, indeed, there is,

> A degree of complementarity between the market mechanism and an "active" state. The complementarity arises from the government setting the framework within which firms operate, and seeking to aid firms to fulfil the developmental strategy. The potential complementarity between them implies that the state adopts an entrepreneurial role and is thereby able to create opportunities which would not otherwise exist. If successful, the operation of the state enhances the operation of markets. Moreover, a variety of relationships between firms themselves and between firms and the government can be involved, with substantial differences emerging as between different economies. (Sawyer 1992a: 56-57)

Emphasis on Government Investments

The state as a direct player in the organization of investment was very much at the heart of Keynes' thinking and constitutes an explicit long-term policy proposal to be found in the *General Theory*. Following the Keynesian ideas, the state can take the responsibility for directly organizing investment and/or regulating the funds of public and semi-public bodies for more socially desirable investment purposes, and public capital expenditures would be more closely tailored to the needs of the private sector and significant enough to stabilize overall inve-stment.[16] As Seccareccia (1994: 376), drawing from Keynes, argues that,

> In . . . a speculative economy, entrepreneurs have generally lost their "sponta-neous urge" to invest in longer-term projects (their "animal spirits") and have themselves developed a rentier-like appetite for liquidity and short-run capital gains. The only logical alternative, then, is to view the state, which is in a posi-tion to calculate the marginal efficiency of capital-goods on long views and on the basis of the general social advantage, taking an ever greater responsibility for directly organizing investment. (Keynes 1973: 164)

Further, investment not only creates additional income but also increases and improves the productive capacity (i.e., it helps the supply side). If the level of investment is higher, then the rate of capacity utilization is higher, which implies that the level of total output is higher. Investment expenditure, which is en-couraged by high demand and profits, eventually adds to the productive poten-tial of the economy and is linked to expected output growth. Thus, capital accu-mulation is central to technical progress as it adds to both demand and capacity.

However, the formulation of a meaningful and coherent investment policy should take place within the framework of a development plan. As a minimum, the plan should provide an outline in the volume and pattern of production and demand as well as of the requirements for productive capacities, including labor and raw materials inputs.

Investments have to take place in order for technical change (i.e., either new products or new processes) to be brought into effect. The Kaldorian view is relevant here:

> It is the "technical dynamism" of the economy . . . which is responsible, in a capitalist economy, both for making the rate of accumulation of capital and the rate of growth of production relatively small or relatively large. . . . Technical progress is infused into the economic system through the creation of new equipment, which depends on current (gross) investment expenditure. (Kaldor 1978: 37, 54)

Indeed, technical change/progress can be expected to influence the volume of investments and open up new and more profitable opportunities for expansion. Profitability depends upon technical progress, and the rate of technical change can influence both economic growth and capacity utilization. The growth of capital stock depends on investment expenditure, which depends on profit and growth expectations.[17] Furthermore, faster technical change requires more and better new capital equipment for its implementation and relies on a higher rate of investment.

Strategic Planning

The strategic planning aspect seeks to explain some essential requirements for such a supply-side strategy. It builds mainly on the Japanese experience and tries to offer some suggestions. Mainstream analysis does not identify a central role for strategic planning within economic policy making. Cases are made for intervention, but these are seen as responses to imperfections in the market.

Previous state intervention has usually been of a microeconomic nature, with the state working at the edges of the market system, and has taken the form of various measures dictated by the pressure of events (e.g., unemployment). Direct state action in practice tends to be dictated by short-run, often highly partial, considerations and short-term measures that are often in contradiction to long-term strategic objectives. As Cowling argues:

> The market could not be relied on since, within the market, there are vicious and virtuous circles of cumulative causation. This short-termism of the market does not give proper attention to longer term considerations and crowds out long-term issues. So, fundamental changes, involving leaps in product, process or structure will not be handled well. (1990: 12)

Therefore, it is the government that can look ahead of the market when drawing up long-term parameters of a developmental intervention, which actually does not deny the importance of the market operating within this overall strategy. In its developmental part, the state takes a leading and proactive role and the market works within the long-term parameters set by government at various levels, for example, local, regional, and national (Cowling 1990: 32). Hence, one can put forward the case for state intervention in a modern context and suggest an essential role for effective, democratic public agencies in guiding the long-term evolution of growth and development with particular regard to industrial competency.

Cowling (1990: 12-15) supports the view that a coherent, national strategic planning system is an essential element of any efficient economic system for three fundamental reasons: transnationalism, short-termism of the market system, and centripetalism. The operation of unfettered market forces generates uneven development since the forces of cumulative causation (Myrdal 1957) and centripetalism (Cowling 1987) are involved in the operation of the market and sustain, exacerbate, and perpetuate inequalities and disparities between regions and nations.

The forces are strong and, thereby, the spending and other powers of government are reduced in the less successful firms, regions, and nations. These forces and the three central tendencies (mentioned above) within modern market economies "point to the requirement for national/community planning in order to achieve efficiency in the allocation and utilization of national/community resources" (Cowling 1990: 15).

Consequently, the Developmental State should be concerned with offsetting regional disparities and the lack of capital equipment, training, education, and social services. Public support is forthcoming for productive activities at both national and local levels, for the promotion of research, technical development and innovation, and for skill development and training.

Obviously, increasing and improving capital equipment and infrastructures, improving R&D status or pursuing a restructuring strategy for regions takes a long time. The government sector is involved in picking short- and long-term developmental plans. Government investments in both improving, renewing, and extending physical, business and social infrastructure, and technological and mechanical equipment, can increase the productive capacity of an economy.

Public investment in regions and rural areas is designed to add to the sum total of investment capital, training, R&D, technical development, and services available, and can add to the opportunities for local development and social welfare. The enhancement of decentralized activity should be considered here in terms of the expansion of local authority economic strategies. Local economic restructuring should be related to the following (Martin 1989: 41):

1. the need to support and develop indigenous resources, firms and industries;
2. the growth of concern with the quantity and quality of employment through training, education and workplace experience programs;
3. an increasing direct involvement of local authorities with local industry and trade unions; and,
4. the desire of local authorities to increase democratic control over work and the economy.

A planned developmental strategy should be based on a complete knowledge of the resources and needs of regions (particularly of those which provide the locations for such a strategy) with the development of indigenous resources be in the foreground. In fact, the formulation and implementation of such planning by developmental and public agencies and local actors within regions would allow concrete linkages between industrial and regional policies.

The Developmental State can successfully contribute to long-term supply-side initiatives aimed at shaping the industrial landscape and establishing growth poles in order to counterbalance the "power of attraction of the center" (Myrdal 1957: 26) and, hence, at restructuring or promoting the activities of particular industries, sectors, and regions, particularly those where resources are inefficiently utilized, or underutilized, which would aid overall national growth.

A government might adopt a growth pole strategy, since potential growth and further development can be stimulated by state intervention. A growth pole/center policy would create greater external economies, and economies of scale could accrue as a result of investments, mainly in R&D, by the government sector and by firms or industries. Obviously, the larger and more powerful the center, the greater the external economies. The existence of these external economies would make the growth poles more attractive for new industrial development, and create conditions and opportunities conducive to faster growth of existing and incoming industry.[18]

Obviously, the benefits of a growth or development pole can be felt in the surrounding areas: the maximum utilization of investment expenditure; an improvement in the range of services likely to be available to people and to industry; the exploitation of external economies; the spatial diversification of economic activity; and, the capacity to withstand the effects of future structural changes and cyclical downswings.

The effectiveness of such a comprehensive policy is a solution in the long term. However, if one talks about "a polycentric system of intervention with a diversified innovation and restructuring strategy for regions" (Martin 1989: 41), such a strategy would have to place emphasis on information, technology complexes, science parks, research, technical education, and training.

The promotion of technology transfer from public sector education bodies to private enterprises is also of great importance, especially for those industries characterized by small firms, each of which is too small to undertake its own research and development. Technology resource centers and public sector bodies can provide access to high technology plants which are normally beyond the reach of smaller firms. Furthermore, Cowling (1990: 19-20) suggests that:

> [A proactive Developmental State will] give priority to those industries, both old and new, which appear viable and indeed strategically important in a long-term perspective, but which are vulnerable in the short or medium-term without significant intervention. Such industries have to be provided with the resources and commitment to allow them to grow and mature, so that in the longer term the degree of intervention can be progressively reduced and the focus switched to other industries which have emerged as new priorities.[19]

Therefore, the Developmental State has not only to select sectors and industries for government attention and support—often described as "picking winners," but also to "create winners" while improving their developmental environment. However, the transfer of industrial strategies to new environments may be self-defeating in the absence of Developmental State policies required for its effective implementation.

Active state policies, such as investment expenditure on, and comprehensive strategies for the modern factors of development and competitiveness, are needed to complement a highly interventionist industrial strategy. In fact, a qualitative turn is needed: instead of placing emphasis mainly on consumption expenditure and transfer payments, the state should also consider government investments, especially on the accelerators of development, as very important. In other words, governments should rely heavily on state investments which are both production-increasing and productivity-increasing expenditures.[20]

Clearly, policy initiatives would appear to be necessary on the international-national-local interplay. Indeed, the first of these is necessary because of the international focus of strategically important activities. National-level policy initiatives are also important because the detailed characteristics of socioeconomic norms and structures are nationally based. Finally, the idea behind regional and local initiatives is to improve the capacity to supply goods and services by exploiting particular competitive advantages and needs (Albrechts et al. 1989: 8).

CONCLUSION

This chapter has briefly presented the successful developmental paths of Japan and NICs, and particular emphasis has been placed on the role of public investments. State policies usually encompass a large number of targets or multidimensional targets, and a large number of important activities can only be administered by governments and cannot be achieved in practice by private business.

Hence, governments can contribute to economic growth and development by increasing their production-increasing and productivity-increasing investment spending; by curtailing policies and practices that create inefficiencies; and by pursuing appropriate fiscal policies as well as regional policies, industrial policies, etcetera.

The most important theme developed in this chapter is that of the Developmental State based on qualitative state intervention. Reasons for the belief in its importance stem from the ample evidence of market imperfection. Although demand management policy is clearly necessary for GDP growth and good economic performance, the Developmental State can improve the longer-run supply potential of any economy and can play an active role in it.

NOTES

1. The picture appears to have changed in the 1990s, and even these economies have experienced difficulties during the last five years or so due to the downgrading of demand management and other Keynesian policies by Japanese and NICs' policy-makers; this has brought about slowdown in GDP growth, higher levels of unemployment, and other economic difficulties.

2. See, for example, OECD, *Survey on Savings* (1985); OECD (1986); as well as more recent OECD publications.

3. Capital accumulation and productive investment spending on the modern factors of industrial development and competitiveness have been of great importance; options available for rent-seeking and speculation have been seriously restricted.

4. Individual income tax and corporate income tax are major sources of revenue for the Japanese government. Each of these two taxes accounted for about 35 percent of the total tax and other revenues of the national government in 1988.

5. In Japan, a high ratio of the labor force has received some formal training. In a 1989 survey, about 32 percent of the workers at the firm went through a formal training program. To some extent, this has also happened in Germany and France since 1980. In contrast, very few American youths have been in jobs where formal training had been provided (Lynch 1991).

6. The Lee Governments focused on the building of a technocratic state, such as the decisive role of a determined developmental elite and technostructure in economic and social planning coupled with centralization and consolidation of state power.

7. Some combination of incentives, disincentives, commands, and controls.

8. Such assistance entailed government support for certain domestic strategic industries. According to the strategic trade policy view, government policy can alter the terms of competition to favor domestic firms over foreign ones and shift economic profits in imperfectly competitive markets from foreign to domestic companies.

9. The East Asian economic progress (for example, the introduction of new methods of production) is hardly conceivable with perfect—and perfectly prompt—competition from the start; indeed, it is incompatible with such an analysis. What has to be accepted is

that strategic state intervention was the most powerful and effective engine of that progress and, in particular, of the long-term expansion of total production.

10. Moreover, the current debate has focused on cluster-led industrial development. See, for example, *World Development* 27, no. 9 (September 1999).

11. Even neoclassical scientists (e.g., Krugman 1987; Rodrik 1992) now accept that the optimal degree of openness for an economy is not close integration with the global economy through free trade (see also Singh 1998: 83).

12. In some cases (e.g., Indonesia), the problems arose in countries that we would not consider to be Developmental States. In others, the collapse of the asset price bubble, difficulties in the financial sector, and the foreign exchange problems contributed to the difficulties, rather than the developmental role of the state.

13. It is worth mentioning that the financial crisis did not affect these economies evenly.

14. Most of Krugman's ex post analysis also stresses the problem of "moral hazard" rather than efficiency growth (see also Roubini 1998).

15. For a complete discussion see Sawyer 1992a: 54-57.

16. The proposal in favor of government investment deals with the composition of government expenditures and not whether the share of total government outlays (percent of GDP) should rise so as ultimately to monopolize all investment spending in the economy.

17. The dependence of profits on investments arises from the Kaldorian theory of income distribution. Also Kalecki (1933: 42-46) argues that the level of investment determines the total profit (under certain assumptions) and that the logical link between the variables of investment, profits and national income operates in the following direction:

Investment → Profits → Profit margin → National Income

18. Perroux (1968) made considerable use of the concept of external economies as a vehicle for spreading the possibilities of growth into many sectors, and stressed the vital role of propulsive industries in growth pole theory.

19. The notion of strategic global repositioning is also very important and relevant here.

20. Private investments on the modern factors of endogenous development and competitiveness are also essential and desirable.

Chapter 3

The "Better Father"

THE SCENARIO

Once there were two fathers (the state) each of whom had kids (the private industry/business). Father$_1$ gave his kids lollipops and sweets (financial incentives, subsidies, and other forms of financial support to industries) at their request, and father$_2$ gave lollipops and sweets to his kids occasionally. Father$_1$ spent a substantial amount of his earnings on lollipops and sweets, as an incentive for his kids to work hard, whereas father$_2$ spent very little of his earnings on sweets and lollipops; instead, he gave his kids sound advice and direction (long-term strategic program) to help them to be successful.

The kids of father$_1$ grew up to be insufficiently educated, lacking special skills, welfare-reliant, and found difficulties in facing life (the international competition). The kids of father$_2$ grew up, became well-educated scientists and well-trained technicians and, therefore, were able to face life successfully and reap the rewards of their hard efforts. The name of father$_1$ is "Mr. Mainstream" and of father$_2$ "Mr. Developmental State."

The above scenario illustrates two different attitudes and raises some very simple questions: who is the "better father"? Whose father's love was thorough? Whose father's attitude was successful? This chapter offers suggested answers to these questions.

SOLUTIONS

The Mainstream Theory

The orthodox theory deals with an advanced capitalist world of perfect markets, price adjustments, equilibrium outcomes in product and resource markets, and decisions made on the basis of marginal, private profit and utility calculations. It assumes economic "rationality" and a purely materialistic, individualistic, self-interested orientation toward economic decision making.

Neoliberalism focuses on the unquestioning exaltation of free markets and the rhetoric of business which invoke perfect competition as bringing benefits for the economy. Free markets alone are efficient, product markets provide the best signals for investments in new activities, labor markets respond to these new industries in appropriate ways, firms know best what to produce and how to produce it efficiently, and product and factor prices reflect accurate scarcity values of goods and resources now and in the future (Todaro 2000: 96).

Competition is effective, if not perfect; technology (as well as the change of technology) is freely available and costless to absorb, and information is also perfect and costless to obtain. Under these circumstances, any government intervention in the economy is distortionary and counter-productive. Hence, the conclusion is that "minimal government is the best government" (Todaro 2000: 96).

Long-term relationships appear as rigidities in the sense that prices may not immediately respond to variations in demand or supply. Yet, the "New Right" schools of thought strongly support the view that by keeping resources locked up in declining sectors or inefficient activities, industrial policy reduces national income below what it would have been in its absence, and society bears an additional burden.

Therefore, the neoliberals argue that by permitting competitive free markets to flourish, privatizing state-owned enterprises, promoting free trade nationally and internationally, restoring investors' confidence, and eliminating the plethora of government regulations and price distortions in factor, product and financial markets, both economic efficiency and economic growth will be stimulated.

Recent endogenous growth models, nevertheless, discard the neoclassical assumption of diminishing marginal returns to capital investments, permit increasing returns to scale in aggregate production, and frequently focus on the role of externalities in determining the rate of return on capital investment. Although technology plays an important role in these models, it is no longer necessary to explain long-run growth (Todaro 2000: 100-101).

Unlike the traditional growth model, new growth theory seeks to explain technological change as an *endogenous* outcome of (government and private) investment expenditure in human capital and knowledge-intensive industries. Where complementary investments produce social as well as private benefits, governments may improve the efficiency of resource allocation. They can do so by providing public goods (infrastructure) or encouraging private investment in knowledge-intensive activities where human capital can be accumulated and subsequent increasing returns to scale generated (Todaro 2000: 101).

The "market-friendly" approach or the "middle ground" position of the World Bank in the 1990s is the most recent variant on the neoclassical counter-revolution.[1] This approach recognizes that there are imperfections in product and factor markets, market failures in investment coordination and environmental outcomes, and phenomena such as missing and incomplete information, externalities in skill creation and learning, and economies of scale (which are particularly endemic to LDC markets) (Todaro 2000: 96).

Therefore, governments do have a role to play in facilitating the operation of markets through "non-selective" "market-conforming" interventions—for example, by investing in physical and social infrastructure, health care facilities, and educational institutions and by providing a suitable climate for private enterprise.[2]

Heterodox Views

Government structure and management of development have been vitally important, and will continue to be so in the future. Indeed, the development process may be initiated and accelerated with the help of different forms of state intervention. Particular attention has been given to the role of politics in society, the interaction between the political process and the social structure, and decisive factors affecting state building, forms of regime, and political change.

Heterodox approaches rely heavily upon an assumption about the state being the most important engine of growth and structural transformation. These theories and strategies have adhered to conceptions of state-led or state-managed development, and in this context, emphasized the importance of economic planning (i.e., important initiating and coordinating functions in relation to the private sector). Planning came to be accepted, therefore, as an essential and pivotal means of guiding and accelerating economic growth.

Since the second half of the twentieth century, ample experience has suggested that the guiding and supportive role of the state has been the very foundation of successful development in countries which were latecomers to industrialization. State intervention created the initial conditions for industrialization through state investment in infrastructure, development of human resources and technological change.

In the early stages of industrialization, a key role of the state was the protection of infant industries. But in the later stages of industrialization, the nature of state intervention in the market must change and become functional, institutional, and strategic. Additionally, state policy and/or intervention may stimulate and direct private economic activity so as to ensure a harmonious relationship between the desires of private firm and the social and developmental objectives of the central government.

Indeed, the proper functioning of a market needs the support and guidance of the state, while conversely the state cannot do without the markets. As Best

(1990: 20) contends, "Plans and markets are alternative means of economic co-ordination. The purpose is not to substitute the plan for the market but to shape and use markets." Also Amsden (1989) distinguishes between state policy which is "market-conforming" and that which is "market-augmenting."[3]

Evidently, there are many cases (e.g., France, Italy, Japan, and NICs) where there has been a degree of complementarity between the market mechanism and an active state, and the government has played a positive role in the economy. The development experience of a number of countries (the successful Far Eastern experiences, among others) suggests the importance of the strategic partnership between the government and private sectors. These can cooperate in a variety of different arrangements—each contributing what it does best and both participating in the financial returns, within the context of a thorough development agenda. Such a close working relationship could be created with the help of political determination and comprehensive administrative reforms.

The states in the high-performing East Asian countries (i.e., Developmental States) in particular, have intervened to a such extent that they have "governed the markets" in critical ways (with only slightly different compositions of their policy instruments) and consciously promoted selective sector growth. Indeed, the East Asian governments have consistently and deliberately remedied market failures, provided both administrative and technical support, and altered the incentive structure to boost specific industries that would not otherwise have thrived (Amsden 1989; Wade 1990).

The capital markets of these countries have been controlled by the governments by means of both interest rate policies and direct control measures. In fact, these governments have issued direct instructions to the banks, closed off the options available for rent seeking, and guided investments by selective credit policies (e.g., "policy loans" carrying interest rates below the normal market rate and promoting longer time horizons).

Furthermore, the state authorities of Japan and NICs have systematically intervened in the market competition between national industries and forced upon them some form of coordination. Economic contests have been organized by the governments in order to avoid unnecessary competition among national industries with a view to combining the benefits from both cooperation and competition. In fact, the state has deliberately accelerated the process of industrial concentration as a basis for successful competition in international markets. Finally, over a long period, there have existed tight import controls and several restrictions on foreign investors and activities.

Therefore, the Developmental State–"New Competition" line of argument (as one of a high degree of government intervention) is strongly related to, and concerned with, strategic actions for achieving outward-oriented development, and can successfully contribute to long-run supply-side initiatives aimed at re-structuring or promoting the activities of prioritized sectors and industries (i.e., longer-run structural reforms instead of short-run measures). Obviously, the effectiveness of such a comprehensive strategy is a solution for the long term and would have to place emphasis on the "accelerators" of endogenous growth, industrial competency and competitiveness.

THE EXPERIENCE OF JAPAN AND NICs:
FACTS AND LESSONS

East Asia has realized a remarkable record of high and sustained export-led economic growth. As seen in table 3.1, from the 1970s to 1996, the major economies of East Asia grew more rapidly than the rich industrial countries. This is unusual among developing countries; others have realized rapid growth rates but not over the course of several decades. Moreover, it is generally viewed that Japan, South Korea, Taiwan, Singapore, Hong Kong, and Malaysia have such a pattern of relatively more equitable income and wealth distribution as their income has risen. In this regard, the East Asian countries appear to be unique in that they combined this rapid and sustained growth with highly equal income distributions. In particular, East Asian economies became known as the "East Asian Tigers," a tribute to their strong economic growth rates.

The initial years of high export growth had motivated Japan and the Asian NICs to invest further in capacity augmentation in steel, semiconductors, electronics, processing, and assembly industries. In addition, Japan and NICs have achieved high investment rates–rapid capital accumulation for sustained periods. State injections in the form of infrastructure and the modern factors of industrial competency and competitiveness were strongly complementary to the private sector and increased these economies' productive capacity as well as investors' confidence. As their productive capacity expanded sharply, investments and exports played key roles in these economies' rapid expansion while domestic savings rates remained substantially higher than global averages.

TABLE 3.1
East Asian Economies' Growth Rates, Annual Average (percent)

Country	1970-79	1980-89	1990-96
Hong Kong	9.2	7.5	5.0
Singapore	9.4	7.2	8.3
Taiwan	10.2	8.1	6.3
South Korea	9.3	8.0	7.7
Malaysia	8.0	5.7	8.8
Japan	9.5	8.4	4.3
China	7.5	9.3	10.1
Indonesia [a]	7.8	5.7	7.2
Thailand [a]	7.3	7.2	8.6
Rich industrial countries	3.4	2.6	2.0

Source: IMF, Press Release (June 1997).

[a] Although some would have considered Indonesia to have been a Developmental State in some respects under Sukharno (which was a rather corrupt regime), neither Indonesia nor Thailand is considered to be a Developmental State.

Table 3.2 presents data on the equivalent shares in some countries' GDP for the main categories of public expenditure in the years between 1960-86, while table 3.3 illustrates the uses of total government outlays in OECD countries during the period 1990-97. During the period 1960-86, Japanese government investment was about twice the level of other Western economies and, despite the cuts imposed on government spending in Japan during the mid-1980s and in the 1990s, the differential has remained significant. Nevertheless, Japan's larger share of government expenditure is devoted to government investment rather than consumption and appears to be quite different from the general OECD pattern (the state as investor). All the above are shown in tables 3.2 and 3.3 which follow.

TABLE 3.2
Uses of Total Public Expenditures (percent of GDP) in the
Largest Seven OECD Economies, Annual Average, 1960-1986

Country	Government Consumption	Government Transfers	Government Investments
United States	18.2	12.3	1.9
Japan	8.8	10.3	7.3
Germany	17.3	19.2	3.9
France	14.3	24.4	3.9
United Kingdom	19.2	18.0	4.2
Italy	16.3	20.3	4.2
Canada	18.3	15.3	3.7
Smaller OECD average	15.2	18.0	3.8

Source: OECD, Economic Outlook (December 1982 and 1987).

TABLE 3.3
Uses of Total Public Expenditures (percent of GDP)
Annual Average 1990-1997

Country	Government Consumption	Government Transfers	Government Investments
United Kingdom	19.9	12.2	4.0
Germany	18.4	15.3	3.4
France	18.0	21.4	3.7
Denmark	25.2	18.4	1.9
Sweden	27.1	19.7	2.3
Netherlands	14.8	26.3	3.9
Italy	17.3	18.0	4.9
United States	18.1	10.8	1.5
Japan	9.1	11.5	6.1

Source: OECD, National Accounts (1998 and 1999).

The figures in tables 3.2 and 3.3 reveal that industrialized nations have different priorities in their government spending. Sweden and Denmark favor government consumption and, to a lesser degree, government transfers. The latter have a much lower share in the United Kingdom, the United States, and Japan. The Japanese state has rarely consumed resources at more than half the level of the other major economies.[4] In complete contrast, government investment in Japan has consistently exceeded the average of the other six economies by an equally wide margin.

Japan has experienced the highest rates of government investment since the 1960s, and the government relies heavily on investment spending. Furthermore, direct participation by the state in the allocation of investments to industry has been important in both the qualitative and quantitative senses, and the Japanese government has played an important and active role in both mobilizing and spending investment funds.

In Japan and NICs, particular attention has been drawn to highly active state technology policies within which the role of the government has not been simply to finance R&D, but also to direct and coordinate the R&D efforts of private industries. This implies a key role for state planning in areas like physical and social infrastructure, and strengthening technological capacities and industrial competitiveness. In addition, the rate of industrial production growth in Japan was higher than in the United States and the EC/EU since the mid-1970s (see table 3.4).

TABLE 3.4
National Spending on R&D, 1995

Country	R&D per Capita	R&D (% GDP)	R&D(st)	R&D(ind)
Belgium	220	1.57	26.7	71.6
Germany	502	2.88	32.8	65.1
France	364	2.35	48.1	43.9
Denmark	288	1.55	45.5	46.8
Netherlands	297	2.17	41.8	53.5
Italy	177	1.25	49.5	46.4
Spain	67	0.72	48.8	47.5
Portugal	20	0.50	66.1	27.4
Greece	23	0.47	69.1	19.2
United Kingdom	299	2.25	36.5	50.4
EC average	276	2.04	47.0	52.0
United States	528	2.82	48.3	49.6
Japan	619	2.85	16.8	77.1

Notes: (1) R&D (st) and R&D (ind) are the percent of spending on R&D financed by the state and by industry respectively, and (2) R&D per capita is expressed in ECU.
Source: Eurostat (1998).

As can be seen from the above table, the EEC member states devote differing amounts to R&D, ranging from 2.9 percent of GDP in Germany to less than 1 percent in Greece, Spain, Ireland, and Portugal. France, the Netherlands, and the United Kingdom are fairly high on the list with a figure of roughly 2.3 percent. Belgium, Denmark, and Italy occupy positions in the middle of the table.

A similar disparity exists if the source of funding is considered. Of the total spending on R&D in Greece (69 percent) and Portugal (66 percent), it is the state which is the main supporter. Industry plays a particularly important role in both Belgium (72 percent) and Germany (64 percent). In the other EC countries, state and private funding is more evenly balanced.

In the EC/EU, public sources provide on average 47 percent of the funds devoted to research. This is higher than in Japan, where more than 75 percent of all research is funded by industry. Also, industry in the Community (which finances 52 percent) carries out 65 percent of all research—a figure which is slightly less than in the United States (72 percent) and Japan (73 percent).

In Japan and NICs, while most of their states' R&D expenditure has been directed toward creating a more internationally competitive industrial structure —and reducing internal competition—by giving a lead to certain firms or by financing projects whose development costs are very large and possibly risky, some of this government spending is also prompted by the divergence between public and private costs and benefits in certain areas.

Therefore, R&D has been supported by the state and institutions created by leading firms to import new foreign technology coupled with a higher level of education, training and learning, which have also been key factors in building the necessary human capital for the developmental process in these countries.

Comparison between Japan, the United States, and the EC shows that the growth rate in industrial production in the European Community was slower during the 1980s and 1990s than in the United States and Japan. Besides, the level of industrial employment in the EC has fallen steadily since 1974 and only started to stabilize at the end of the 1980s, while the situation remained stable in the United States after rapid expansion in 1984. Meanwhile, Japan was in a better position than the EC and the United States during the same period. The evidence suggests that the European Community (Union) has lost ground against the United States and particularly against Japanese industry (see table 3.5).[5]

TABLE 3.5

Value Added in Industry (percent of GDP): EC, United States, and Japan, 1974-1990

Country	1974	1980	1985	1990
EC average	40.0	37.5	35.1	32.7
United States	33.5	33.6	31.0	n/a
Japan	44.7	41.9	41.0	41.8

Source: OECD, Historical Statistics 1960-1990 (1992).

Moreover, there is no doubt as to the importance of the increasing openness of national economies to international competition along with rapid changes in technology. Factors such as R&D, skills, and innovation have been brought to the fore as national competitiveness advantages. In fact, the need for strategic global repositioning is derived from trends in the global economy. Such a purposeful direction combined with the cooperation of industries, government bodies and agencies, research institutions, and funding institutions can create dynamic competitive advantages.

Technology policies focused on strategic sectors, and close cooperation between government and the business sector can contribute to the development of internationally competitive firms. Simultaneously, it is recognized that the states must strengthen their capacity for planned interventions to support, rejuvenate, and reposition targeted industries and sectors and promote exports. However, the need to focus attention on the expansion of new exports for the global market should not diminish attention to other sectors and products.

Changes in the world economy and the enormous success of the Asian Tigers emphasize the need for producing competitive exports, especially, product/ service differentiation and niching. In the 1980s and 1990s, enterprises from the United States, the European Community, and Japan are competing at the edge of the astonishing pace of technological innovation in the global markets. These notions are borne out by table 3.6 which shows how rapidly exports and imports have grown over time for EC/EU member states, the United States, and Japan.

TABLE 3.6
The Increasing Openness of the Economies of the EC, the United States, and Japan: 1960-1996 (percent of GDP at market prices)

Country	Exports of Goods & Services				Imports of Goods & Services			
	1961-70	1971-80	1981-90	1996	1961-70	1971-80	1981-90	1996
Belgium	44.4	56.4	73.3	72.0	44.4	56.1	71.3	66.2
Denmark	28.6	29.2	34.9	36.4	30.4	31.4	33.1	30.6
Germany	19.3	24.2	30.3	34.7	17.3	22.0	26.5	25.7
Greece	7.5	12.1	16.5	18.1	16.3	21.7	27.3	28.0
Spain	10.5	14.2	19.5	25.1	12.4	15.9	20.2	24.5
France	13.5	19.4	22.3	23.0	13.1	19.0	22.4	21.2
Ireland	34.6	42.5	55.3	70.0	41.1	52.2	54.8	56.2
Italy	14.6	20.8	21.4	24.3	14.2	21.2	21.5	20.7
Luxembourg	81.3	89.4	97.2	87.3	75.7	83.0	96.4	88.3
Netherlands	41.1	46.6	54.9	52.6	41.9	45.0	50.8	47.0
Portugal	23.5	23.7	33.5	31.7	28.7	34.9	43.6	39.1
U. Kingdom	20.5	26.5	25.9	27.3	20.9	26.9	26.5	27.7
EC (12)	19.4	25.0	28.5	31.3	19.1	24.8	27.6	27.4
U. States	5.3	8.0	8.6	11.1	4.7	8.3	10.7	12.9
Japan	9.9	12.2	12.6	9.1	9.5	11.5	10.5	7.3

Source: CEC, European Economy: *Annual Economic Report for 1996* No. 59, Tables 38 and 42 (1996).

On the other hand, national economies always need to be ready to react to signals, incentives, and disincentives coming from the world economy.

When considering the recession element, it is understandable that any slow down in international trade would affect national economies more than the relatively insulated ones. In particular, the recent financial crisis of 1997 has adversely affected export recovery in Japan and East Asian economies as well. However, although U.S. firms have started regaining some of their lost market shares and improving their competitiveness over the 1990s, according to some observers, China gained market share in the United States and Japanese markets at the expense of these economies during the last three-four years.

To sum up, fundamentals of East Asian transformation and development have been the strong focus on industrialization and intensive long-term production-oriented growth, as opposed to considerations involving profit maximization and short-run capital gains on the basis of current comparative advantage.[6] The success stories of Japan and NICs clearly show that their governments pursued thorough knowledge-based, investment-led, outward-oriented policies using explicit strategic interventions within their industrial economies.[7]

FACING THE REALITY: POLICY CONSIDERATIONS

Market forces usually produce cumulative movements away from spatial equilibrium; once growth disparities occur, they tend to become cumulative and self-perpetuating. Production has become more complicated, more fragmented, more specialized, more related to and dependent upon other firms and accelerators (quick and reliable access to highly specialized firms, skills, R&D, communications, information, transportation, talents, etc.).

Changes in the structure of production increase the relative attractiveness of the more developed areas. Economies of scale and learning effects might lead (in certain sectors) to the domination of some firms. There might be sectors which are more profitable than others, which would mean that specialization does not benefit all regions or nations equally. For most, if not all, of the modern factors of competitiveness, the most developed countries or regions are better endowed than the lagging countries or regions. The countries or regions specialized in strategic sectors are likely to benefit more from trade and/or from increased trade than less developed countries. Therefore, the more developed countries or regions may reinforce their initial superiority thanks to trade.[8]

Approximately during the last two decades, free market policies have been overemphasized and presented as the panacea for further development, competency and prosperity, resulting in insufficient productive activity (e.g., through a lack of effective demand and inadequate levels of investment expenditure) and thus, not effectively tackling the scale and diversity of problems that face most countries. Despite this shortfall in endogenous growth, many still argue that the so-lution lies in laissez-faire policies; consequently, alternative development policy considerations have been virtually ignored.

Undoubtedly, the new millennium poses new challenges for development policy; two are fundamental. First, it is increasingly recognized that policy must be consistent, thorough and effective, and planning must be for the long-term as well as for the short- and medium-term. Second, government and private sectors together must set the development agenda of tomorrow to meet the diverse and changing needs of both consumers and producers (partly as a result of global competition). In this regard, the role of government in the "new liberal order" appears to be an interesting and challenging one.

Ideally, when the priorities are right, scarce productive resources will increasingly be allocated efficiently, more productive resources will be created through higher levels of investment, both productivity and profitability will increase, and industrial strategies will come to center stage, resulting in new and more attractive profitable opportunities for private firms. Hence, if the future of many countries needs to be very different from the past, it will require a much sharper focus on a radical development policy agenda.

When discussing the nature of state intervention, one may identify two roles for the state in a market economy: a regulatory one and a developmental one. The regulatory role is a traditional focus of state intervention in economies like the United States and the United Kingdom, and "policy in most Western countries tends to be ad hoc and reactive" because of suspicion of state planning (Cowling 1990: 18).

Consequently, traditional regional and industrial policies usually suggest micro-policy options (in order to reallocate capital and labor) and government intervention of a regulatory kind (in order to remove market imperfections and correct situations of market failure). These economic policies attempt to utilize only competitive and profitable industries and firms—which are adapted to some local characteristics—thus, seeking to pick winners and invest in success.

In complete contrast, Developmental State strategies seek to offset regional disparities, and the lack of human and material resources. In fact, investment injections can stimulate indigenous regional/local development (i.e., multiple effects of investment planning on regional/local restructuring and growth). More importantly, Developmental State action is directed toward thorough long-term strategies to mobilize market forces (and utilize the creative dynamics of the business sector), build up world-market-standard industries, and systematically develop efficient economic locations. Therefore, the Developmental State tries to create success and improve the functioning of the market.

Moreover, financial incentives and schemes, although they may have produced some short-term efficiency improvements in some areas, are often seen to be partial, inadequate, and thus unsuccessful measures for a successful regional growth and industrial development for the following reasons:

- inadequate demand management policies or limited supply-side policies;
- general and/or specific regional and industrial problems (which differ from one country to another);
- general and/or specific micro-problems (e.g., new technologies and equipment, profitability, employment, uncertainty, etc.);

- centripetal market forces;
- short-term policy decision making; and,
- strong competition (mainly international competition).

These traditional incentive policies (based mainly on market failure), as well as automatic stabilizers, often recommend some temporary assistance, offer only marginal solutions, and mitigate the effects of industrial and regional problems on incomes. But, although the aim should be commercial viability without extra state support in the long run, they do not get at the root of the problems. In contrast to this, particular emphasis should be placed on state investments such as government investment on information, technology complexes, science parks, research, training/retraining, education/technical education, and work-place experience programs.[9]

Instead of targeting particular industries for subsidization, the state can finance and direct the development of technologies that can be used by the prioritized industries in order to improve their efficiency, profitability, and competitiveness. Industries will therefore utilize the modern knowledge—such as ideas for raw materials, manufacturing processes, product designs, and ultimately, commercial products—and transform this knowledge into new technologies and pro-ducts. In addition to funding R&D, the Developmental State action includes state support of technical knowledge and new manufacturing techniques, especially to the small firms, which often lag behind in technological development.

These two opposite approaches (the orthodox and the Developmental State) to regional and industrial development are illustrated in table 3.7.

TABLE 3.7
Two Opposite Policies to Regional and Industrial Development

	Characteristics of Market-Based Policies	Characteristics of Developmental State Policies
Theoretical Framework:	• Neoclassical theory • Small state sector	• Post-Keynesianism • High quality state intervention
	• Free enterprise culture	• Supply potential and strategies
	• Deregulation, privatization	• Growth poles
Causes of Disparities:		
General	• Inefficiency in problem regions due to market rigidities	• Demand-based explanations incorporating the *cumulative causation* principle
Specific	• Lack of entrepreneurial culture	• Structural weaknesses
	• Excessive state intervention	• Drain of financial capital to prosperous regions

TABLE 3.7 Continued

Policy Implications:		
		• Low investment
		• Inadequate government participation in regional growth
Policy Implications:	• Micro-policy options	• Comprehensive policies
	• Reactive policies (e.g., correction of market failure)	• Proactive policies
	• Minimal public expenditure	• Aggregate demand management
	• Regulatory role for the state	• Industrial strategy
	• Financial incentives to overcome market failure	• Government investment in infrastructure and accelerators
	• Low tax	• Expenditure injections on regional-local growth
	• Selective assistance	
	• Deregulation of regional markets	• Decentralisation and Participation
	• Free trade, "close" integration, removal of distortions	• "Managed" trade, "strategic" integration

Source: Karagiannis (1996).

It is not the descent of the Schumpeterian "magic spirit" which builds skills and brings about innovation. There are many well known reasons why a free market system would not perform as well as one involving some forms of state intervention, and there are many well known examples where the difference between private and social returns could lead firms to underinvest. However, these are precisely the modern factors of industrial competency which the industries and firms need in order to be capable of competing strategically on new grounds on the basis of rapid technological change, innovation, high labor productivity, and product quality.

Government action may be able to aid supply of relevant labor skills or R&D and to reduce the extent of market uncertainty. Therefore, particular emphasis should be placed on mobilizing capital, upgrading technology, increasing labor productivity, and the human skills necessary for effective competition in the global marketplace.

An important point that mainly emerges from the New Competition view is the relevance of relationships between firms (as well as between firms and the government). General equilibrium analysis supports situations of perfect competition and, therefore, long-term relationships appear as rigidities.

However, technical inefficiencies and failures to adequately develop and use new products and processes often occur; but the nature and causes of the failure are usually unclear. It is not the traditional market failure which can be corrected by appropriate measures (like taxes or subsidies) or through regulatory policy. The solution is likely to require cooperation between firms and between firms and the state.

The pressure for interfirm cooperation and coordination across phases in the production chain comes, in part, from the competitive lead that accompanies problems solving at a time of rapid technological change. Indeed, the New Competition literature identifies the cooperation among firms, particularly the small ones, in these areas which are normally subject to fierce competition in order to "shape the rules of the market game and [to shape] complementary investment strategies" (Best 1990: 16-17).

The successes of small firms producing for niche markets in certain parts of the world, like Emilia-Romagna in Italy, Baden-Württemberg in Germany, in Japan, and a number of Pacific Rim countries, spawned the literature on so-called "industrial districts" and "flexible specialization." This has resulted from striving for size, consolidation, restructuring, and reorganization in preparation for more intensive competition in the global market, and has been an important source of industrial dynamism in these regions (Piore and Sabel 1984).

All of these experiences show that the economies which are able to generate more effective long-term-oriented cooperative arrangements, regarding technological and organizational learning and investment expenditure in human and physical assets, are likely to outperform the countries that largely rely on classic free market mechanisms (which depend on short-term, individualistic competitive forces).

Moreover, Developmental State action has not only to select sectors and industries for government attention and support (so as to raise competitiveness and efficiency), but also to create or improve their appropriate developmental environment. Therefore, cautious active state policies are needed to complement highly interventionist industrial strategies (e.g., government investment on, and technically proficient plans/strategies for, the accelerators of development and competitiveness).

However, the transfer of industrial strategies to new environments may be self-defeating in the absence of effective politico-institutional structures required for their effective implementation. Indeed, "good" public institutions and effective politico-institutional structures make the task of intervention easier; "bad" and ineffective ones more (or much more) difficult.

Mainstream economic analysis usually adopts short-term perspectives in policy decision making. Most government interventions have usually taken the form of actions directed toward a combination of removing so-called market imperfections and correcting market failures (the state acts as an adjunct to the market system). In complete contrast, the Developmental State theory (and the New Competition literature) is strongly related to, and concerned with, "long-term market-shaping activities [instead of] market-reacting responses" (Best 1990: 11).

The forces of cumulative causation as well as the three central tendencies within modern capitalist economies (i.e., short-termism, transnationalism, and centripetalism) point to the necessity for thorough strategic planning.[10] Indeed, a coherent national strategic planning system may be seen as "an essential element of any efficient economic system" (Cowling 1990: 15), and governments and businesses should rely heavily on strategic planning (i.e., dynamic industrial complex programming) in their effort to make the best use of natural resources, land, manpower, industrial, and commercial potential.

In this regard, the Developmental State is involved in picking short- and, especially, long-term developmental plans of the future by focusing on state investments on the accelerators of development and endogenous competency at the national and regional/local levels (as financial incentives provided by banks or the government have often been partial and unsuccessful measures). These technically proficient strategic plans must be designed to guide private firms so that their actions will serve national, social, and developmental goals.[11]

Clearly, the expansion of industry represents a net addition to the effective use of resources and can contribute to a higher degree of capacity utilization. For this reason,[12] industrial strategy should be an important part of government policy making. This requires that the state "adopt a strategic view of future industrial development in the economy concerned and provide a range of support mechanisms to those sectors deemed to have a key role to play in the future" (Sawyer 1992b: 8).

Therefore, the Developmental State can successfully contribute to long-run supply-side initiatives aimed at restructuring or promoting the activities of particular firms, sectors and regions. In its developmental part, the state acts to shape the industrial landscape taking a leading and proactive role in the industrial economy, and the market–which continues to play a substantial and crucial role–works within the framework set by the government at national, regional and local levels.[13]

Obviously, an old-fashioned protectionism is not recommended, which may not create competitive industries and sectors. Instead, a mixture of inward- and outward-oriented development strategy is suggested,[14] defined in terms of economic growth, productivity, industrial competency, and competitiveness, which should constitute the foremost priority of state action.

In this technological age, quality goods and services are strategically important to firms and to countries. Improved quality can lead to both increased market share and cost savings; both can affect profitability and productivity. Yet, inconsistent quality is an international concern, as irregularities in supply and inadequate marketing can be severe constraints on exports. For both industries and a country as a whole to compete effectively in the global market place, products and services must meet global quality and price expectations. Trade of superior products can increase firms' profitability, resulting in a positive impact on countries' balances of payments (Heizer and Render 1996: 79-80).

CONCLUSION

Most industrial policies have been based on mainstream or market failure analysis, and most state interventions have usually taken the form of ad hoc responses to pressing problems. Governments have often put great faith—perhaps far too much—in the ability of private firms and industries to achieve industrial growth and desirable industrial performance.

The forces of cumulative causation operate at the level of the firm and at the aggregate level of a region or nation breeding success and failure. Consequently, some nonmarket forces (i.e., government action) are required to offset these tendencies. The policy dilemma here is how to preserve the creative functions of markets along with thorough developmental strategies/policies while restraining their centripetal tendencies.

The Developmental State is concerned with offsetting these forces or tendencies toward disparities and the underutilization of productive resources while carrying out a wide range of policies. Therefore, there are many types of activity that should be undertaken by such a state.

The creation and/or promotion of business winner requires cooperation and/or complementarity between market and state, and investments on the modern factors of growth and competitiveness (investment spending in machinery and people, and technological change and its implementation). It also requires a strategic plan not only for private industries/businesses but also for the future development.

Contrary to the current orthodoxy, the desired industrial performance and development requires better state action, and this is most likely achieved from Developmental State policies. What really matters is not the extent of state intervention but the quality of such intervention. Thus, Mr. Developmental State is the "better father," as his "love" has been real, thorough, and successful.

NOTES

1. The middle ground position of the World Bank in the 1990s attempts to define the appropriate role for the state as one that limits it to always being, by and large, a pure facilitator of the private sector through its corrections of market failures in general. Such an approach, although it seems to be pragmatic, is quite conservative, highly partial, and passive and may be illustrated by asserting a "Geisha model" for the state: it is expected to know how to walk lightly, keep the man—i.e., the private sector—happy and stay subordinate in the relationship, playing little or no strategic agential role.

The World Bank's ideal for the role of government is clearly one of yoking of apparently unequals, and the relational model is a fairly strict division of duties or labor with little allowance for entrepreneurial action by the "Geisha state"—because of an expected show of "Geisha government" failure—and little encouragement is thus given to do otherwise than her narrowly circumscribed "Geisha government" role (Northover 2001: 10-11).

2. There has been the recent development of the new institutional economics–seen by its proponents as lying within the neoclassical school of thought–which pays particular attention to constitutional order and normative behavioural codes and has largely retained the view of an optimal set of institutional arrangements on the basis of efficiency considerations. In this regard, the vision for the "Geisha state" is very conservatively hedged in and even further rhetorically embellished by concerned admonitions on the nature of the

good "Geisha government" as expressed in notions of good governance (i.e., calls for good or democratic governance that focus on good administrative, judicial, and electoral practice) (Northover 2001: 11).

3. Dore (1986b) roughly classifies state interventions in the economy as follows:

- Regulation of individual transactions in order to make markets work more efficiently;
- Regulation of the structure of production and trade in order to prevent monopoly and oligopoly;
- Intervention to promote economic growth, of which there are two types: actions taken completely with regard to the domestic economy (i.e., "domestic developmentalism"); and, actions taken explicitly to promote the competitiveness of the nation in the global economy (i.e., "competitive developmentalism"); and,
- Pork barrel intervention–the use of state power to promote particular sectional interests, either for personal or electoral advantages.

Jacobson and Andreosso-O'Callaghan (1996: 276) classify active developmental policy strategies as follows:

- active negative (protection of traditional sectors);
- active positive (coordinating indicative planning); and,
- active direct (state as entrepreneur).

4. When considering the lower levels of government consumption in Japan, many economists often choose to exclude defense expenditure because of the constitutional limitations bequeathed by the U.S. occupation. Therefore, allowing for defense closes the gap in government consumption.

5. In addition, over the last two decades, the annual growth in the productivity of the EC industry was slightly higher than in the United States (3.4 percent as against 3.2 percent) but appreciably lower than in Japan (5.5 percent).

6. Some would question the possibility of Developmental State policies in a globalized economy, because Japan was able to protect its industries from competition with transnational corporations while they were built up.

7. There is an on going debate on the relevance of the nation-state in this global era, given the constraints that the global political economy imposes.

8. A report by OECD (1987: 256) points out that "manufacturing expertise grows by the cumulative effects of scale, learning, etc. and is–contrary to the assumptions of the orthodox theory of comparative advantage–geographically concentrated."

9. There are a number of reasons in favor of government investment; these may include the following:

- there is a strong and sufficient theoretical analysis related to state investment;
- investment spending is the only component of aggregate demand that seriously helps the supply side. Government investment is more reliable and, therefore, more preferable than the private investment for an investment-led developmental strategy;
- the evidence is quite supportive to the use of government investments; and,
- financial incentives and schemes have been partial, inadequate and unsuccessful measures for a successful regional and industrial development. Thus, there may not be any other (or any better) choice.

On the other hand, private investments on the modern factors of development are absolutely necessary.

10. For a more detailed discussion, see Myrdal 1960: 15-16.

11. Strategic planning, however, may involve considerable tension as private firms may not embrace policies that subordinate their profit-making to larger social interests.

12. Alongside many others already discussed.

13. Post-Keynesian and radical scientists argue that social efficiency is intimately bound up with economic democracy and the decentralization of political power (for further discussion, see Cowling 1982 and 1987; Sawyer 1992b, among others).

14. The relative weight of this dynamic mixture of inward- and outward-oriented development depends on the country's development situation.

Chapter 4

The Modern State Intervention

INTRODUCTION

What governments should or should not do, as well as the essential opposition between market and state, have always been at the heart of major debates in economic theory. The dividing line between those activities that fall in either the government sector or the private sector varies between different nations and at different times.

The twentieth century has seen some profound changes in thinking about the economic role of government. The first quarter century of the postwar period was largely characterized (at least among the OECD countries) by economic growth, high levels of employment alongside state activism, and a widely held belief in the beneficial powers of government.

The second quarter century in contrast has been characterized by much lower rates of economic growth in the OECD nations (though with rapid growth in the NICs), persistent or rising levels of unemployment, and a general decline of support for the role of government. In country after country the state is being rolled back, and "let the market decide" has become the main policy gospel for both developed and developing countries (Arestis and Sawyer 1998: 1).

Since the late 1970s, most OECD nations have undertaken a reassessment of the role of their states. The current debate on the role of government mainly concerns its economic aspects. The same broad debate may be behind attempts to reform public sector management and to control public expenditure better. But it would be undeniable that the intellectual and policy climate has shifted from one which saw an active role for state in economic and social matters toward a generally more skeptical view of the role of government.

In all parts of the world, people are legitimately questioning what their governments ought to do. All these important questions ultimately raise the most fundamental questions of political organization. At the same time, none of these issues can be decided on political principle alone, as the issues are both deeply philosophical and intensely practical.

This chapter discusses important features of the desirable modern state intervention. It is recognized that there have been some major and important changes in the industrialized economies that are often seen as changing the possibilities for government action. In particular, major shifts have been under way in the management of the public sectors around the world, although both the pace and extent of these shifts is greater in some countries than in others.

The first section discusses briefly the "era of change" while considering the changing role of government. The second part examines an institutional system that appears to have been used with enormous success—the "Developmental State": the case of state that takes on a central developmental role in the economy without directly owning most of the productive assets. The final sections pursue aspects of the Developmental State model and deal with key elements of the desirable modern state and its new role.

AN ERA OF CHANGE

Since the mid-1980s, the public sectors of Western developed countries have undergone major changes as governments try to respond to the astonishing pace of technological innovation, globalization, and international competitiveness. Indeed, the process of globalization has continued apace. This fact is reflected not only in the increased financial flows across the foreign exchanges, which have in fact increased dramatically in size, and higher levels of foreign direct investment, but also in the degree of integration between financial markets in different economies and in the organization of production on a transnational basis. These changes (alongside many others) may actually limit the ability of national states to pursue independent and effective economic policies, and make government control much more difficult than hitherto (Arestis and Sawyer 1998: 1-2).

Perhaps, it is self-evident that the capitalist systems of Japan, France, or Sweden are substantially different from those of the United States or the United Kingdom. Besides, the institutional arrangements are clearly different, no matter whether institutions are seen "in terms of norms and standards of behavior or in terms of organizations" (Arestis and Sawyer 1998: 3). Although the existence of institutional differences may seem self-evident, this notion stands in some contrast to the implicit view developed within the neoclassical analysis.

In this analysis, a perfect market economy in a position of general equilibrium is adopted[1] and the state is treated as a neutral agent acting in some social interest (as so often is the case in the neoclassical market failure theory). In this regard, state policy is directed at removing so-called market imperfections and correcting market failures (Arestis and Sawyer 1998: 5).

Additionally, there has been the recent development of the "new institutional economics" (Williamson 1985, among others) seen by its proponents as lying within the neoclassical school of thought, which has largely retained the view of an optimal set of institutional arrangements on the basis of efficiency considerations.

In contrast, the post-Keynesian and radical traditions support the view that institutional arrangements are relevant for policy and decision making, and economic performance. In fact, this analysis does not have any belief that optimal institutional arrangements will necessarily emerge and, consequently, would doubt that there is any single set of optimal arrangements.

The institutions of the government sector are important, according to the post-Keynesian and radical approaches, in numerous ways. This is not just a matter that the government sector is usually a major provider of important services (e.g., education and health) and infrastructure or that the central bank underpins the financial system; it is also that the public sector can play an important role in the molding of the institutions of the private sector (Arestis and Sawyer 1998: 4). However, features and specific institutional arrangements of one economy cannot be easily transplanted into another, especially where sociopolitical and cultural elements are involved.

In the late 1970s, a harder-edged set of views (i.e., the "New Right") was brought to general attention. The New Right is generally associated with laissez-faire and anti-big-government philosophy, a desire to avoid active government and a belief in the inherent stability of the private sector. New Right theorists claim that the growth of government results in significant reductions in long-term growth and employment, in addition to hurting overall economic performance. Hence, less government would improve aggregate welfare by improving economic efficiency. Instead of governments forcing people to do things through a state bureaucracy, markets were superior in every respect, with expressions like "freedom" or "choice" replacing the "serfdom" of government (Friedman and Friedman 1980).

In complete contrast, the post-Keynesian and radical analyses do not follow the New Right in believing that there is no constructive role for the state, and that state activity is detrimental to development and prosperity; hence, the free working of the market system is crucial for economic growth and prosperity. The experience of a number of NICs suggests the importance of the state as a powerful engine of that progress and, in particular, of the long-term industrial development and production-oriented economic growth. "At a minimum, the process of development requires the guiding hand of the state, and does not come about through the agency of the market alone" (Arestis and Sawyer 1998: 9).

However, since the early 1980s, there have been attacks on the size and capability, scale and scope, of bureaucratic government. For this reason, and perhaps for others, there has been a transformation in the management of the government sectors of a number of advanced countries. The rigid, hierarchical, bureaucratic forms of public administration based on Weber's ideas, which have predominated for most of the twentieth century, are changing to relatively flexible systems of public management.

These changes in the government sector may have occurred as a response to several interrelated imperatives. These include: first, modern developments in economic theory; second, various attitudes toward the bureaucratic state; third, the impact of rapid changes in the private sector, particularly globalization; and, fourth, rapid changes in technology and, especially, in information systems (Hughes 1998: 8).

History suggests that, unless pushed, public organizations and government-owned enterprises usually lag behind in technological progress and innovation. In a rather similar vein, the *Al Gore Report* argued:

> From the 1930s through the 1960s, we built large, top-down, centralized bu-reaucracies to do the public's business. . . . With their rigid preoccupation with standard operating procedure, their vertical chains of command, and their stan-dardized services, these government bureaucracies were steady–but slow and cumbersome. And in today's world of rapid change, lightning-quick informa-tion technologies, tough global competition, and demanding customers, large, top-down bureaucracies–public or private–don't work very well. (Al Gore 1993: 3)

Moreover, the new public management is not similar to public administration, and the change of concept (public management or entrepreneurial government instead of public administration) points to the same phenomenon: at the repla-cement of traditional government bureaucracy by a new model[2] based on better and more efficient state action. In fact, public administration is concerned with office management, processes and procedures, rules and regulations, usually ad hoc decision making, and with translating policies into action. It has an inward focus and short-term perspective.

In contrast, the new public management does include public administration, but also aims to achieve results and improve accountability and skills. It shows more concern with longer-term strategies and focuses on management and plan-ning, strategic goals, output targets and outcomes, performance appraisal and efficiency, and disaggregation of government bureaucracies into agencies. Fur-thermore, strategy considers the public institutions and/or government organiza-tions in their external environment functions, sets objectives, not just by politi-cians but by the agency and its various parts,[3] and addresses "a crucial concern: positioning the [public] organization to face an increasingly uncertain future" (Nutt and Backoff 1992: 58).

Perhaps, using longer-term considerations in the public sector is the best way towards reinventing government, and national governments are realizing that administrative competence can be a substantial competitive asset and are borrowing ideas from each other at an increasing rate. In a 1990 publication the OECD contends that "a shared approach can be identified in most developed countries in which a radical change in the culture of public administration is needed if the efficiency and effectiveness of the public sector is to be further improved" (OECD 1990a: 1).

This change in culture is indeed required to change state bureaucracies into results-based institutions in which managers, policy and decision-makers, technocrats, etcetera, are accountable for achieving targets and results. The OECD further argues that many of its members "are trying to make their public sectors more managerial" with a common feature being the introduction of a more discretionary and participative style of relationship: "between levels of hierarchy; between control agencies and operating units; and between producing units, be they public or private" (OECD 1991: 11). Instead of regulating administrative action by rules and hierarchical authority, many countries appear to follow two broad avenues.

First, they seek to raise the production performance of public organizations: improve the management of human resources including staff, development, recruitment of qualified talent and performance pay; involve staff more in decision-making and management; relax administrative controls while imposing performance targets; use information technology; and stress operations and service quality.

This avenue is aimed mostly inside the public institutions to improve skills, incentives and performance for civil servants, given that an important problem with government institutions is the incentive structure in which they operate. Indeed, civil servants or government employees find themselves in a situation in which the reward signals are perverse and their efforts are often misdirected. Therefore, the new public management is supposed to restore the incentives for efficient operation and quality products and services.

Second, most countries seek to make greater use and enhance the creative dynamics of the market system (even though the ways and methods vary from one country to another; there are, for example, high roads and low roads that modern capitalist economies can take). Furthermore, the debate over new public management and entrepreneurial state raises larger questions about the nature and role of the public service (and even the role of government in society).[4] As Harcourt argues:

> I do not wish to deny that there are aspects of the growth of bureaucracies and of the power and influence of policy makers that are disquieting, to say the least. Keynes' optimism that disinterested and highly intelligent persons desire the common good more than their own good (except indirectly by obtaining satisfaction from making the world more rational and just than they found it), has not always been borne out. The structures of many government departments —the hierarchies, the motions, that have to be gone through for promotion, the drive and ruthlessness needed in order to reach the top—are not necessarily the ideal incentives or channels for ensuring that altruistic, charitable, and tolerant people (as well as intelligent ones) make it to the top. Bureaucratic empires built for their own sakes, rather than to serve useful social purposes, are also not unknown. Those who favor intervention, as I do, and a flourishing public sector must seriously come to grips with these problems. (1997: 172-73)

It is worth noting here, however, that building bureaucratic empires for their own sakes is not limited to the public sector.

Public administration in developing and less developed countries is rooted in the colonial systems inherited from their colonial governments. These colonial systems were based on highly centralized authorities using bureaucratic means to administer their colonies.[5] Despite the different models of economic development followed in Africa, Asia, Latin America, the Caribbean, or in the Pacific, the familiar Weberian precepts were to be found.

Hence, the government sectors of developing and less developed countries can be characterized as following the traditional, bureaucratic model of public administration. Polices, rules, and regulations were formulated to standardize the system of administration throughout the colonies in Africa, the Caribbean and Asia. An elaborate system for documenting correspondence was devised, and the use of paper became fundamental in the administration and management of the colonial systems.

Nevertheless, this led to the compilation of volumes of paper into a filing system of enormous proportions as well as a number of problems: managers were poorly trained and lacked direction; there was an inefficient organizational structure with overstaffing common; weak oversight by the government; the opportunistic misuse of government-owned enterprises and harmful political interference (Jorgensen 1990: 62). But this system of documentation, in conjunction with the legal system, called for a highly literate and regimented officialdom.

Moreover, particularly in the period following World War II, development administration for less developed and developing countries was the most powerful institutional factor. The idea was "to apply to developing [and less developed] countries the administrative . . . procedures derived from the former colonial countries" to modernize their economies and accelerate development in order to catch up with the leading ones (Hughes 1998: 213). "This approach included the various features of the best administrative practice available in the developed nations and this, naturally enough, was the traditional model of public administration" (Hughes 1998: 213). In addition,

> The bureaucracy was the sole employer of professional experts, most often trained in the country of the former colonial master, and maintained sole ownership of technical knowledge in the various sectors from agriculture to mining and industry. As the sole source of knowledge, it is easy for the bureaucracy to assume that it knows best, that its experts need to be able to impose their solutions to the various problems of development. (Hughes 1998: 210-11)

As Smith (1996: 227) also argues, "Development planning has consequently tended to be highly centralized, technocratic and of the 'top down' variety, where the experts at the top make the decisions about what the masses need in terms of programs of development."[6]

Bureaucracies are particularly important in both less developed and developing countries, and are usually intimately involved in the economy and society. However, they often operated at a remove from their own societies and constituted an elite with more in common with their counterparts in the developed nations and with foreign corporations than their own people. Yet, in the less developed and developing world, most bureaucracies served themselves and often looked after their own interests first.

In fact, public administration itself has been susceptible to corruption because officials exercise a substantial amount of power. Although not part of the traditional model, corruption appears to have become endemic as public servants followed their own interests.[7] In addition, politicians quite often use jobs with the government sector and public enterprises to reward political friends, so payrolls swell with people whose qualifications for employment are principally political connections.

Consequently, the largest share of the government current expenditure has been dedicated to wages and salaries and debt repayments, whilst the level and share of government capital spending have been very low. Yet, to meet their interest obligations, countries mired in debt squeezed critically important programs in education, health, and infrastructure. According to Smith (1996: 221), public employment accounted for over 50 percent of nonagricultural jobs in Africa, more than 36 percent in Asia, and 27 percent in Latin America in the late 1980s.

In the 1970s and 1980s, and in response to the attack by economists on the role and size of government, many less developed and developing countries have sought to redefine the role of government and change its management. Some of this was in response to demands made by international agencies which required market reforms and public sector cuts. Less developed and developing countries found themselves undergoing various kinds of structural adjustment through international agencies, notably the World Bank and the IMF.

Financial assistance to governments "comes with a panoply of conditions; it is in no way a gift" (Haynes 1996: 84). The IMF requires debtor governments to take action in five main areas: firstly, trade barriers are to be reduced; secondly, various subsidies and price controls are to be cut or withdrawn; thirdly, financial systems are to be restructured by withdrawing controls on capital movements; fourthly, state-owned enterprises should be privatized and foreign investment controls cut; and fifthly, government intervention in both the management of the economy generally as well as in the provision of social services is to be minimized (Haynes 1996: 84).

However, the shift to less state did not work as intended. "One difficulty in the reform process has been that the advocates of reforms have assumed that 'one size fits all' and that any government could be improved by the institutionalization of their preferred new pattern" (Peters 1996: 17-18). The message of experience since then is rather different: the government is central to social and economic development as a partner, catalyst, and facilitator.

Markets require or need a competent and appropriate public sector to work at all. Consequently, what was more important was that government be efficient, facilitative, and appropriate to its circumstances rather than merely small. In addition, a major part of the new public management as applied to developing and less developed countries is the increased attention paid to what governments do.

In its 1997 development report the World Bank called for three fundamental building blocks. First, "strong central capacity for formulating, coordinating [and implementing] policy," including visions, goals, and strategic priorities on the place of politicians and the public service alike; secondly, an efficient and effective delivery system, setting the balance between accountability and flexibility on the one hand, and better performance and quality service on the other; and thirdly, motivated and capable staff, with incentive structures to motivate them to perform well (World Bank 1997: 81).

All these elements are to be found in the new public management approach, compared to that of the traditional model of public administration. As mentioned before, government strategy was not a matter for emphasis in traditional public administration, neither was performance nor incentives for staff to perform. The composition and complexity of the new public management will play a critical role in determining the rate and pace of development, and governments should increasingly become more concerned with providing a vision of future economic direction.

It is therefore fundamental that the public administrative system to be modified in order for countries to compete and exist in a rapidly changing global environment. Modernizing governments should also involve forging integrated and dynamic partnerships with the private sector, and limiting state action to the strategic oversight of development and growth. This is the main concern of the "Developmental State model," which is discussed below.

THE NATURE OF THE DEVELOPMENTAL STATE

The development experiences of Japan, South Korea, Taiwan, Hong Kong, Singapore, and, recently, Malaysia have shown overall that there exists a new kind of state intervention as they moved toward a more industrialized stage. In the transformation process, the state interacts with the rising enterprises, works with and often promotes the private sector (i.e., a plan-oriented market economy). "The intimacy of the Developmental State with the private sector and the intensity of its involvement in the market provide directional thrust to the operation of the market mechanism" (Johnson 1981: 9-10).

Indeed, Developmental States systematically guide the market as a means of long-term economic transformation, and create the conditions for endogenous growth and industrial adaptation without directly owning most of the productive assets. Direct government ownership and control of industrial production is of secondary importance as compared with the process of building up technological infrastructure and investing in human capital formation and research. The market, on the other hand, is employed as an instrument of industrial policy by exposing particular firms to international competitive pressures.

Therefore, the developmental orientation of such a plan rational state was different from both the plan ideological state in the Soviet-type command economies and the regulatory orientation of typical liberal-democratic states. In fact, the Developmental State has possessed considerable leverage over private industries in terms of securing compliance with its strategic choices and national purpose goals, while planning has been active, strategic, and selective, based on wide consultation and serious efforts to reach agreement on the form of intervention (Johnson 1981: 9-10).

Strategic industrial policy forms a central component of the Developmental State model, and was organized around government directives. But government planning for manufacturing development in East Asian Countries did not get involved with the operational detail. Well-educated, well-trained planners took a view of the future development and endogenous competency of these countries, and their incentive structures were continually revised in light of planning objectives. This planning system was described as a high degree of good and eclectic steersmanship (i.e., state capacity).

From a comparative perspective, Developmental States are characterized by relatively small scale, tightly organized bureaucratic structures with the Weberian characteristics of highly selective, meritocratic recruitment patterns and long-term career rewards, which enhance the solidarity and corporate identity of the bureaucratic elites. Highly meritocratic systems were designed so as to attract the best managerial talent available to the ranks of the bureaucratic elites and ensure a high degree of unity, capability, and professionalism. The size of the bureaucratic apparatus helped to consolidate the elite position of the bureaucrats in society, and achieve an equilibrium between autonomy and accountability (Onis 1991: 114; 124).

Furthermore, the strategic power of the East Asian Developmental State has depended on the formation of political coalitions with domestic industry, and government intervention has relied on organizational and institutional links between politically insulated state agencies and major private firms (i.e., the corporatist nature of the Developmental State). Indeed, the formulation and implementation of strategic industrial policy have been facilitated by specific politico-institutional arrangements. However, the Developmental State by its very nature involves an unusual concentration of state and private power, which would be hard to justify by the standards of Western pluralistic democracy.

The significant element of compulsion exercised by the bureaucrats in securing government/private partnership constitutes a distinctive feature of the Developmental State model. The extraordinary degrees of control exercised by the state over the financial system and the extreme dependence of individual conglomerates on bank finance have been instrumental in eliciting compliance with the requirements of strategic industrial policy.

Economic coordination and development in these states have been managed by specific institutions, whose task has been to organize the critical interactions between state and industry. These have been the core centers or pilot agencies (to use Johnson's term) of strategic economic direction (Johnson 1982: 26).

What differentiates these high commands in NICs' Developmental States from the generality of various planning institutions in so many developing and less developed countries appears to be their authority, technical competence, and professionalism in shaping development policy (although of course this, too, varies from state to state), as well as their ability to use both sticks and carrots to influence firms' decision making (Leftwich 1995: 412). Compared to a strong autonomous state, a weak state systematically underprovides economically desirable interventions, and systematically overprovides politically motivated and economically harmful policy actions.

Another striking element of the Developmental State is that this type of state has been autonomous enough in the policy formulation and implementation process, and has not been overwhelmed by special interest groups. In fact, both state power and autonomy were consolidated before national or foreign capital and interests became influential, and private economic interests were generally politically weak or insignificant relative to state power (Leftwich 1995: 416-17).

This relative autonomy has flowed from the political power and support of the central political executives. Politicians provide the space for the bureaucrats to take important decisions by holding off special interest groups who might deflect the state from its main development priorities, and also legitimate and ratify the decisions taken by the bureaucrats. On the other hand, bureaucrats are given the freedom of action necessary for effective policy intervention. Besides, the ability of the Developmental State to deal with both civil society and particular local and foreign interests highlights the need for state capability in shaping mutually advantageous economic relationships (Onis 1991: 115).

Therefore, Developmental States are distinguished by the character of their developmental elites as well as the relative autonomy of these executive elites and the state institutions that they oversee (even though the form and extent of relative autonomy has varied). The specific nature of this embedded autonomy however, "must be seen as the product of a historical conjuncture of domestic and international factors. It is an autonomy embedded in the concrete set of social ties which bind state and society and provide institutional channels for the continuous negotiation and renegotiation of goals and policies" (Steinberg 1989: 74; quoted in Onis 1991: 123).

In short, the common denominators in both the democratic and the authoritarian forms of Developmental State action are the unusual degrees of bureaucratic autonomy, and institutionalized public-private partnership (Onis 1991: 114; 119). The coexistence of these two conditions facilitates the process of policy formulation and execution. Moreover, Developmental States have generally been serious and effective in raising the quantity and quality of industrial investment. Therefore, the nature of the Developmental State may be defined by the following features:

- a relatively strong state;
- an effective and productive state-investor;
- a state which is not (over-)influenced by interest groups; and,
- a strategic state.

Like all states, Developmental States are not static. Various changes in their socioeconomic structures, politics, and international environments have brought about changes in their elite coalitions as well as the ideas, interests and institutions that bear on them, both national and foreign (for example, structural differentiation, increased international pressures, economic and political liberalization, globalization). All these significant changes may induce an important modification of the Developmental State model, given the very real constraints that the global political economy imposes (Leftwich 1995: 421).

In drawing on the comparative literature, it is thus the main purpose of this chapter to elaborate on elements of the desirable state intervention, based on developmentally driven political purposes and institutional structures. This notion forms the subject matter of the following sections.

ELEMENTS OF MODERN INTERVENTIONISM

The state can, and should, play an important role in improving the social and economic conditions of a society, and can actively and adequately contribute to development. This has been apparent, both in theory and in practice, since the writings of List and the German industrialization effort in the latter half of the nineteenth century. About a century of facts prove the historical involvement of the government sector in important development efforts. For example, a package that entails spending on roads, schools, and airports will certainly add to total output and current employment (even without multiplier or accelerator effects). Apart from the three traditional functions of the state and the fiscal budget—allocation, stabilization, and distribution—recent attention has been focused on its new developmental role; the quality of state intervention rather than the extent of such intervention.

But the view that the state remains the main engine of economic development, structural change, and the process of policy reform inevitably raises the important issue of state capability and capacity (Ahrens 1997: 114). As Evans argues, "The consistent pursuit of any policies, whether they are aimed at 'getting prices right' or implanting local industry, requires the enduring institutionalization of a complex set of political machinery" (1992: 141).

In the new millennium, therefore, the role of government in adapting to and managing the needed changes will be critical, even though state action will be constrained by the pressures of globalization and other forces. The search for the appropriate role of government needs to take into consideration the importance of institutions and the environment and incentives they create.

Besides international competition, it is the organizational design of, and the incentives within, the public sector and the institutions linking the public and private sectors (i.e., the politico-institutional environment) that are crucial to the developmental consequences of government policies (Ahrens 1997: 117).[8] In fact, effective economic policies "not only require credible commitments . . . but crucially depends on the administrative, technical, and political capacity and capability of policy-makers" (Ahrens 1997: 115). Moreover, "different kinds of state structures create different capacities for action. Structures define the range of roles that the state is capable of playing. Outcomes depend both on whether the roles fit the context and on how well they are executed" (Evans 1995: 11).

The outline of the above argument can be essentially recapitulated in four main points:

1. the ability to craft and adopt specifically tailored institutional structures is as important to effective governance as the formulation of policies;
2. effective governance structures and hence developmental outcomes depend on the roles that policy-makers pursue and the general character of state structure;
3. while the initiation of economic reforms may be facilitated by discretionary authority of government, elites, and political institutions that insulate policy-making from distributive claims of interest groups, their consolidation requires stabilized expectations regarding a new set of incentive structures and the confidence that these cannot be discretionarily altered; and,
4. policies need to match institutions and vice versa (Ahrens 1997: 118-19).

What will interventionism be like in the twenty-first century? Even if the goal now is to make government action better, through reinvention, the nature of government involvement has changed (and is likely to change further). Although prediction of any kind has its risks, there are several characteristics of the modern state intervention, which will probably be paid particular attention to in the next century, compared to the old one.

First, there will be increased focus on improving relations between the public and private sectors. More governments might seek to ensure the evolution of institutional frameworks characterized by integrated and dynamic public and private sector partnerships with the capacity to capitalize on strategic and tactical alliances. In fact, the public and private sectors can cooperate in a range of different arrangements, each contributing what it does best and both participating in the financial returns, within the context of socially defined programs. The complementarity between them can enhance the operation of markets, and can create opportunities which would not otherwise exist.

Second, modern intervention should be strategic. Traditional government bureaucracies required little conception of strategy and serious forward planning was either not carried out or carried out in rather limited ways. Hence, strategy of any kind would have been considered political, if thought of at all (Hughes 1998: 149).

The essence of strategy is to achieve results. The role of strategy is to try to specify what the results should be and to set out how achievements aggregate into the overall purpose (or national purpose in the case of Japan and NICs). Strategic planning gives direction and purpose to public organizations; without strategy, policy making is without direction.

In fact, it is the planning process not the plan itself which is more important; that is, the use of long-term parameters allows the public institutions from top management down to develop a shared vision for the future. Just as there are systemic arguments for relying on the creative dynamics of the market forces to play a centrally important role in modern economies, there are parallel arguments for imposing on these market forces coherent strategies, within which they are allowed to operate (Cowling 1990: 11-12).

Furthermore, strategic planning may be seen as essential for efficiency, but the nature of planning is all important. In this regard, Bozeman and Straussman (1990: 54) argue that there are three major features of a strategic approach: defining clear goals and objectives; developing an action plan that mediates between public institutions and the environment; and designing operational methods of effective execution on the basis of the organizations' capacities.

Nevertheless, state planning should not get involved with the operational detail (as comprehensive centralized planning is infeasible and undesirable). In fact, state planning must be strategic and proactive rather than passive; selective rather than comprehensive; but wherever possible based on some notion of consensus (Cowling 1990: 16-17).

Third, a system of accountability should be required by any government, as the two forms of accountability, political and managerial, are tightly related, even though this link has quite often been problematic. Indeed, "the system of accountability is what ties the administrative part of government with the political part and ultimately to the public itself" (Hughes 1998: 225).

In the traditional bureaucratic administration there is some form of accountability which relies upon the formal links provided through the hierarchical structure. It is accountability for avoiding errors rather than achieving outcomes (Hughes 1998: 233). Hence, improving accountability should be a specific aim of the move toward entrepreneurial intervention. The public institutions would then be responsible for the effective implementation of strategic plans and monitoring the progress of these plans, as well as for their own performance. In fact,

> Institutions can formalize the commitment to such [strategies], and their structure, procedures and personnel can act to ensure that such commitments cannot easily be reversed, but they are simply ratifying [plans] already established. The history of planning [in many countries] shows how fragile was the commitment, despite the creation of many new institutions, [and the lack of teeth of these institutions was obvious]. With clear goals, and a determination to pursue them, institutions with teeth should be forthcoming. (Cowling 1990: 23)

Fourth, quite often, government sector reforms and capacity-building programs have been introduced in many countries without the benefit of systematic and disciplined diagnoses of institutional capacities. This has resulted in wasted investments, inadequate levels of skill and competence, ineffectiveness and performance shortcomings.

In contrast, the economic success of Japan and NICs could not have been achieved without the decisive role of their competent technostructures and their determined developmental elites in economic and social planning. Indeed, an important feature of these technocracies has been their technical competence, and many of the top officials of both Japanese and East Asian countries have received advanced training abroad.

Obviously, capacity building and competence might be important strategic goals that will determine the extent and pace of fundamental changes within the public sectors, within institutions. Strategic human resource management and planning coupled with investments in human resource development (i.e., high quality and timely education, training, and the continuous development of scientific manpower) should be strongly linked to the modernization process of the public sector and institutions toward better and more effective state action.

Furthermore, competitive wages for well-educated, well-trained technocrats can attract more talented individuals and increase integrity and professionalism. On the other hand, external pressure on appointments and patronage should be eliminated.

Fifth, modern interventionism and new public sector management require increased attention on better use of resources. This involves directing resources to emphasize those programs that most assist the attainment of strategic objectives. It also involves more public spending on infrastructure and the modern factors of development and competitiveness, and less spending on unnecessary and nonessential kinds of government expenditure (i.e., an appropriate redistribution of available funds from government consumption to government investment).

Furthermore, with the advent of modern information technology, the need for a highly centralized public administration with paper as the focal point of communicating became obsolete. With the computer, fax machines, electronic mail, satellite transmission, and the internet, new types of communication tools are widely used. This is expected to lead to reductions in clerical staffing levels and/or dislocations in the workforce of both the public sector and public institutions.

These reductions and dislocations may be inevitable, but should be based on rational, efficient, and effective human resource management and planning. For instance, less employees (but well educated and well trained) may replace those civil servants who retire or resign. Such a decision and policy action is expected to bring about two benefits: (1) it will improve skills, efficiency, effectiveness, competence, and operations quality, especially when combined with better utilization of modern technology; and, (2) it will release resources for higher levels of government investment, which will improve the environment for productive activities to take place.

These important notions and policy suggestions, along with decentralization and participation which are discussed in the following section, have attracted the support of many, if not most, governments of countries in all stages of development, and are probably irreversible. However, the wider effects of modern interventionism on "not only the public sector [and institutions] but the entire political system still have some distance to travel" (Hughes 1998: 261).

DECENTRALIZATION, PARTICIPATION, AND REGIONAL POLICY

The concept of decentralization that is considered here is one of governance between levels of central and local government (i.e., to shift responsibilities downward from central levels to local authorities). The notion of decentralized government is often based on the belief that there is a systematic relationship between the quality of administrative performance in state activities and local government efficiency.

Decentralization may increase the accountability of political decision makers and make their commitment credible. In fact decentralization can be a means of overcoming the severe limitations of central administration, and can lead to more flexible, innovative, and creative administration. Consequently, the efficiency of a central government could be increased through decentralized forms of governance.

Decentralization can also facilitate coordinated planning between the various government departments and/or agencies and make plans more relevant to local needs (i.e., the demand for decentralization to regions). Whatever its ideological foundation or level of intervention, the contemporary state must localize its governmental apparatus.[9]

According to Smith, the following facts may result from decentralization:

1. Decentralization to regional or local levels allows officials to disaggregate and tailor development plans to the needs of heterogeneous groups and regions. Democratic decentralization is an effective way of meeting local needs and can result in a variety of public policies, as there is an imbalance of resources and requirements between levels of government. Decentralized structures may be favored because they promote diversity in public policies, and may allow better political and administrative penetration of national government policies into rural areas.

2. Decentralization may lead to the development of greater administrative capability among local governments and private institutions in the regions. The role of local governments can be quite supportive and facilitative through local infrastructure, environmental improvement, and by increasing and improving the provision of public goods and social services at local levels (i.e., the developmental role of regional and local authorities). It can generate additional resources, encourage more efficient use of existing resources, and give local authorities the opportunity to improve and expand the infrastructure in regional and rural areas (i.e., local development and regional growth).

3. Local government can identify and even define service requirements and deliver, plan, or regulate public services. By reducing diseconomies of scale, decentralization can increase the number of public goods and services, and the efficiency with which they are delivered, at a lower cost. On the other hand, the main sources of revenue available to local and regional governments are taxes, charges, grants, and loans. But tax decentralization (its concept and measurement) is not straightforward because it involves subnational controls over all aspects of tax policy. This does not imply a denial of a useful role for active local participation in the administration of policies to assist the poor (i.e., wel-

fare policies); to promote regional and industrial development; and to improve R&D, innovation, etcetera.

4. Decentralization can increase participation in planning and development, and may also allow greater representation for various political and social groups and unions in development policy decision making that could lead to greater flexibility in the allocation of government resources and investments. If political decision making is decentralized among subnational units, each unit may tailor its tax and expenditure package to the preferences of its citizens. Efficiency and social welfare are therefore likely to be maximized under highly decentralized political structures. Decentralized structures of government require political choices, and the governance values might justify whether and to what extent the political decision making is centralized or decentralized. Decentralization is desirable because by devolving real decision making to local levels, higher levels of interest and participation in local government result. It also provides for greater speed and flexibility of decision making, as regional/local development requires such flexibility (Smith 1985: 47-52).

Obviously there is a strong link between decentralization and participation, which may be considered as a requisite for high quality government polices. Participation in the design and implementation of work can improve efficiency. Uphoff and Esman define participation as: "before-the-act involvement in [both] the choices and efforts producing benefits" (1984: 13).

In order to make government action more effective, the state's institutional capability needs to be invigorated by establishing effective and transparent rules and procedures, better operations quality and increased participation while being relatively independent of societal pressures and rent-seeking activities. In fact, with more participatory systems of public administration and management, governments can become more open and manage better public responses to new initiatives while restraining arbitrary action and corruption.

Participation in policy decision making can take many forms, and state-business-society relations at all levels establish the participatory component of the desirable Developmental State. Democratic participation clearly requires a decline in the power of central administration. In this regard, the Developmental State view should be concerned with fuelling institutional change in order to facilitate the emergence of development plans in a decentralized way.[10]

Such a radical approach may pay particular attention to the enhancement of democracy in at least two dimensions. First, it argues that participation by local authorities, unions, etc. can improve the organization of production. It can also contribute to a less inequitable income distribution among its goals, to more efficient economic and social development, to substantial regional development and regeneration, etc., and hence, social efficiency may be intimately bound up with democratic participation (i.e., the active involvement of all the social partners). Besides, local authorities and trade unions should be fully involved in the formulation, evaluation and implementation of proposals.

Secondly, a more open and transparent style of government action can help restrain the power of small groups who have access to government decision making, and can discourage these groups from certain activities or operations.

BUILDING THE TECHNOSTRUCTURE

It has been often argued that Developmental State policies are concerned with promoting domestic development (especially industrial development). However, it is unlikely that significant state intervention would be warranted given that there are major constraints on developmental policies (e.g., the nature of the civil service, its outlook, etc.) and that public institutions are limited in their abilities to perform certain tasks (e.g., the ability to react to changing technology and hence the adoption of the appropriate technology in a changing environment).[11] For this reason, the pursuit of a Developmental State strategy requires specific politico-institutional structures, whose task would be to organize the critical interactions between state and industry.

To implement its industrial policies in manufacturing industry, the Japanese State has relied heavily on the Ministry of International Trade and Industry (MITI); indeed, MITI was a necessary—but not sufficient—condition for its economic success. Although the Japanese institutional structure cannot be easily transplanted, something akin to MITI will have to be instituted in any country seeking a successful, proactive developmental role for the state (Cowling 1990: 19).[12] What is important to learn from the Japanese experience is the approach to the problem (Cowling 1990: 18).

First of all, a central core is absolutely essential, a Bureau of Industry and Trade (BIT) composed of a small, entrepreneurial team of well-educated, well-trained and efficient technocratic planners. This executive new look elite should be organized around the requirements of a dedicated, determined, and efficient Strategic Planning Agency (SPA), with a long-term commitment, the independent capability and the powers to implement the interventionist strategy. This embedded autonomy (to use Evans' 1995 term) may represent the institutional basis for effective government involvement. With the assistance of consultants from leading corporations, banks, trade unions and universities, such an institution can form a consensus on the best policies to pursue (Cowling 1990: 24-25).[13]

Sectoral Agencies (SA) should also be part of the BIT, close to the firms and industries with whose future they will be intimately concerned and responsible for the strategic direction in their specific sectors. Therefore, the sectoral agency will perform a key role in the industrial regeneration of the region. "The process could be started off by the SPA within the BIT" identifying sectors in which strategic intervention is warranted and advantageous. Besides, the act of putting the strategic decision-making machinery within the regions would allow officials to disaggregate and tailor development plans to regional/local needs (Cowling 1990: 27).

While having a strong core, the approach is clearly entrepreneurial, and the proposed type of planning should be neither comprehensive nor centralized. Loose and transparent links between the core planning agency and government ministries and departments involved in the industrial strategy (e.g., treasury, education, training, etc.), and sectoral agencies and regional authorities/boards would decentralize much of the work of the central bureau.[14]

"To be successful our planning must be democratic, and our institutional structure must allow for participation at all levels" (Cowling 1990: 28). Indeed, participation by the social partners can improve the organization of production and help restrain the power of small groups which have access to government decision making.

Therefore, such a network of institutions, as advocated before, must be derived from a prior commitment to fundamental changes in policy making. Indeed, institutions with a strategic planning role are necessary, and short-term perspectives should be replaced by long-term ones that are much more favorable to productive investments and production-oriented sustained economic growth.

Furthermore, the institutional structure must provide continuity, consistency and commitment to the direction and pace of development. This may require a high degree of incentive-compatibility of state policies and development and economic performance, as well as the creation of institutional arrangements that constitute a stable economic and political environment—in which consensus building concerning developmental strategies works (Ahrens 1997: 119; 126).

Without such vital commitments, embedded autonomy, accountability, effectiveness, seriousness, competence and capacity, the Developmental State policy making will founder on: short-term expedients; the power of transnational and other capitalist interests; the conservatism, ineffectiveness and inefficiency of the civil service; or the resistance of the people (Cowling 1990: 23).[15]

CONCLUSION

In most capitalist economies, the state undertakes a number of functions. Its role can be defined either in terms of institutions or in terms of its functions. But in both cases, the government has a certain role to play with substantial effects on the economy and society. There are also many cases where the range of state activities extends beyond the passage of laws and the levying of taxation; from facilitating and/or promoting industrial growth to its direct involvement in the productive process.

From a comparative perspective, the ability of the Developmental State to undertake selective strategic intervention was based on the formation of strong administrative capacity, and the system was designed in such a way as to attract the best managerial talent available to the ranks of the bureaucratic elite, which in numerical terms was quite small by international standards.

In fact, the consolidated strategic power of the East Asian Developmental State has relied on both bureaucratic autonomy and close government-private cooperation. It is quite obvious that, unless the autonomy and cooperation requirements are satisfied, attempts to implement Developmental State policies may prove to be counterproductive. In such an environment, the inability of the state elites to discipline private firms in exchange for subsidies may lead to a situation where selective subsidies can easily degenerate into a major instrument of rent seeking by individual groups.

A central lesson that emerges from this new experience is that the transfer of specific Developmental State policies and strategies to new environments will be self-defeating in the absence of the political and institutional conditions required for their effective implementation.

An important question concerns the lesson to be drawn from the East Asian development experience which can subsequently be generalized to and applied in other developing countries. In fact, the available evidence demonstrates quite conclusively that the East Asian Developmental State model is the product of specific historical circumstances with the logical corollary that there may exist major constraints on its transferability to and/or replicability in different or alternative national contexts. What is important to learn from the East Asian case is the approach to the problem.

Another fundamental question centers around the compatibility of the Developmental State model with political liberalization and democratic forms of governance; whether the transfer or replicability of the Asian Developmental State forms is compatible with widespread political participation. Hence, the question whether East Asian type political economies can coexist with a liberal Western type political system emerges as a central problem for comparative political economy during the next decade.

However, calls for "good governance" or "democratic governance"—which focus on good administrative, judicial or electoral practice—seem to entirely miss the point: few societies in the modern world will be able to resolve deeper development problems or make speedy transitions from poverty without active state intervention which approximates the model of a Developmental State (ideally, but not necessarily, the Western democratic type). Contrary to the current orthodoxy, developmentally driven institutional structures and political purposes can better be achieved from Developmental State policies.

NOTES

1. Provided that imperfections which restrain perfect competition were removed.

2. The "market supremacy" views emphasize the notion that the "collective good" could be better served by introducing private management styles, lock, stock and barrel into the public sector domain.

3. In many countries, politicians now demand that public institutions and agencies should consider the longer-term implications of programs and policies even though this involves them in political matters. On the other hand, public institutions and agencies themselves seek to "develop [long-term] objectives and priorities rather than assuming policy only derives from politicians" (Hughes 1998: 150).

4. Obviously, the specific type of approach should seriously and thoroughly consider the conditions and requirements of the specific public sector.

5. The Weberian bureaucracy was a successful export to developed and lesser developed countries alike.

6. Some of these problems occur in developed economies too, particularly where bureaucracies involve technical experts.

7. While not unknown in developed countries, problems of corruption appear to have been worse in less developed and developing ones (Hughes 1998: 214; Huque 1996: 23).

8. See also Evans 1995; World Bank 1997; and Stiglitz 1998.

9. The localized state is a controversial topic. Liberalism argues a normative case for political democracy at the local level on the basis of a political model of man. Neo-classical view predicts behavior under specified conditions on the basis of an economic model of man, though providing some analytical confirmation of some of the positivist elements in liberal theory. Neo-Marxists are concerned with social movements and collective interests within specific historical circumstances.

10. The Japanese state tried to create "winners"; thereby there was centralization and consolidation of state power. On the other hand, the Korean state has not been so democratic.

11. The inadequate capacity and competence of state institutions.

12. The Japanese planning, its various instruments, institutions and mechanisms are a product of its own history and culture. However, different countries are characterized by "quite different historical and cultural circumstances," (quite) different socio-political elements (Cowling 1990: 18).

13. As Cowling argues: "Economic policy will be built around the twin pillars of Treasury and Industry; the former with a relatively short-term demand perspective, the latter with a longer-term supply perspective" (Cowling 1990: 24).

14. This approach allows "considerable autonomy in determining the mode of operation, and adjusting it as experience accumulates." The main objective is "a dynamic economy rather than sticking to a set of rigid rules imposed by a central bureaucracy." We must avoid squandering people and resources (Cowling 1990: 25).

15. Some theoretical issues in this section have been previously discussed; however, due to their importance, they are reiterated here.

Chapter 5

EC/EU Problems and Government

INTRODUCTION

An outstanding feature of the real world is the existence and continuation of a variety of economic and social problems, of inequalities and disparities. There are, of course, important differences between nations or regions but they are differences of degree rather than kind. The main aim of this chapter is not to fully describe these problems but rather to provide adequate evidence for their existence and persistence, which leads to differences in policy recommendations that can only be understood by reference to the underlying view of the economy which is adopted.

The various policies that have been adopted in the EC area do not seem to provide sufficient response to regional decline, while market-friendly policies cannot contribute to substantial and important solutions. The patterns of production and exchange that characterize the EC/EU seem to bring both gains and losses. It is possible to argue that measures and instruments evolve over time within nation states, and that we should not be surprised at slow progress with the EU. Progress toward European integration is checked by the absence of fiscal coordination and of high quality public policies and state intervention.

The first section of chapter 5 provides the main theoretical approaches to regional development, discusses the regional problem in the EC and evaluates European regional policies. The following sections discuss some other economic and social problems in the EC area with respect to state involvement (such as unemployment and slowdown in GDP growth). Finally, special reference is made to Japan and the United States, and comparisons are made between them and the EC.

THE REGIONAL PROBLEM OF THE EC/EU

Theoretical Perspectives to Regional Development

It is possible to distinguish the following two main and very different approaches to regional development: the neoclassical view; and the post-Keynesian and radical analysis based on the principle of "cumulative causation" (Myrdal 1957) with the important contributions by Kaldor (1971; 1978) and Cowling (1987; 1990).

The neoclassical school of thought suggests that, in equilibrium, there is an equalization of returns to each factor of production. In the short run imbalances may exist; therefore, resources may be unemployed because of unforeseeable random events or because market participants speculate that by holding resources off the market system today, they will get a better return tomorrow (i.e., failure of prices to adjust).

Such events cause prices and quantities to deviate from their long-run equilibrium values. The geographical dimension of this view is based on the internal mobility of resources and implies that each region tends to specialize in producing what it is comparatively good at producing.

The neoclassical approach focuses on the idea of marginal substitution between different factor inputs in response to relative prices. A depressed or underdeveloped area would face a low demand for labor and, consequently, would provide low wages. The equilibrating mechanism would include the movement of labor out of the depressed region in search of high wages elsewhere and the inward movement of firms attracted by the low cost of labor.

These movements would be expected to continue until wages were equalized across regions and, in effect, full employment restored through wage flexibility and factor mobility. Therefore, resources are viewed as moving in response to price signals, with resources moving into areas of high rewards and away from areas of low rewards (Sawyer 1989: 420-21; 451).

Neoclassical theorists believe in the natural disappearance of spatial disparities. They generally assume perfect mobility of production factors between the regions of a given country or between nations. Wages will tend to equalize over regions or countries. A similar simple reasoning can be applied to capital movements, which will tend to equalize returns on capital over space.

Therefore, in the neoclassical analysis there is no room for spatial disparities, and disparities that may have occurred occasionally will be wiped out by movements of factors of production.

A similar result will be achieved even if factors of production are not mobile provided there is trade, that is, trade can replace mobility of factors with respect to prices. In Heckscher-Ohlin view, exchange of goods between countries or regions leads to factor income equalization. Eventually, in the absence of labor or capital migrations, wages and capital income between countries or regions will be equalized. Trade will provide convergence. This analysis assumes that all countries or regions have equal access to technology and the rate of change of technology.

In the traditional trade theory, regions or countries specialize in sectors and benefit equally from this specialization, since all sectors are equally good for the economy. The new trade theory has provided a new argument for industrial targeting and added a concept of importance to this discussion: the notion of "strategic sectors" or "strategic trade" theory (Dixit 1986; Krugman 1986; 1991).

The "cumulative causation" process is associated with the name of Myrdal (1957). Basically, it is a hypothesis of geographic dualism, applicable to nations and regions within nations, which can be advanced to account for "the persistence of spatial differences in a wide variety of development indices including per capita income, rates of growth of industrialization and trade, employment growth rates and levels of unemployment" (Myrdal 1957: 38).

Myrdal argued that in the context of development both economic and social forces usually produce tendencies towards disequilibrium, and that the assumption in orthodox economic theory that disequilibrium situations tend toward equilibrium is false. Thus, the free working of the market mechanism promotes an imbalance in regional resource use as "the play of forces in the market normally tends to increase rather than decrease the inequalities between regions." Not only trade but labor and capital are also attracted to some favored areas in what Myrdal describes as "the power of attraction of a center" (Myrdal 1957: 26-27).

Myrdal considered the hypothesis in the context of a geographically dual economy describing how, through the media of labor migration, capital movements and trade, the existence of this dualism not only retards the development of the backward regions but can also retard the development of the whole economy. According to his view, both economic and social forces tend to strengthen the disequilibrium situation by leading to cumulative expansion in the favored region at the expense of other regions, which then become comparatively worse off, thus, retarding their future development.[1]

In the centers of expansion, increased demand spurs investment which, in its turn, increases incomes and demand and causes a second round of investment, and so on (Myrdal 1957: 27, 38). Instead of leading to equality, the forces of supply and demand usually interact with each other to produce cumulative movements away from spatial equilibrium.

The final result in the expanding region can include improvements in education and health care facilities, transport and communications, etc., improving productivity and efficiency and widening further the competitive advantage of the growing region over the lagging regions. The process is cumulative, not in the sense that all market forces influencing the spatial distribution of factors of production work in the same direction, but that an initial push or pull of factors to one region or area rather than another will tend to move factors increasingly toward them and away from others.

In order to explain the diverse trends of development between different regions, Kaldor (1978) focused on the movement of the "efficiency wages" (i.e., the index of money wages divided by the index of productivity) in one region relative to other producing regions. Indeed, this movement is the result of two elements: the relative movement of money wages and that of productivity. If this relationship moves in favor of an area it will gain in competitiveness and vice versa.[2] In Kaldor's own words:

> "Efficiency wages" will tend to fall in regions (and in the particular industries of regions) where productivity rises faster than the average. It is for this reason that relatively fast growing areas tend to acquire a cumulative competitive advantage over a relatively slow growing area; "efficiency wages" will, in the natural course of events, tend to fall in the former, relatively to the latter—even when they tend to rise in both areas in absolute terms. . . . It is through this mechanism that the process of "cumulative causation" works; just because the induced changes in wages increases are not sufficient to offset the differences in productivity increases, the comparative costs of production in fast growing areas tend to fall in time relatively to those in slow growing areas; and thereby enhance the competitive advantage of the former at the expense of the latter. . . So the principle of cumulative causation leads to the concentration of industrial development in a number of successful regions. (1978: 148)

Finally, Kaldor concludes that:

> This principle of cumulative causation—which explains the unequal regional incidence of industrial development by endogenous factors resulting from the process of historical development itself rather than by exogenous differences in "resource endowment"—is an essential one for the understanding of the diverse trends of development as between different regions. (Kaldor 1978: 148)

Cowling (1987; 1990) extended the above concept on the effects of cumulative causation into the social and political arena. According to the author, inequalities in economic terms—due to the process of cumulative causation—generate inequalities in political power, cultural domination, etc. A region that is relatively prosperous does not only have more economic spending power but may be politically more powerful and exert cultural dominance over the less prosperous regions.

The phenomenon of cumulative causation at the level of the firm leads to industrial concentration. Centripetalism arises from the interaction of firms and markets and "relates to the tendency for higher level activities and occupations to gravitate to the center—to be lost to the regions; to be lost to the periphery" (Cowling 1990: 15). Furthermore, Cowling argues that:

> Strategic decisions with major implications for many local, regional and national communities are being made outside those communities. This is the reason that has led to the loss of a substantial degree of local, regional and national autonomy. The same centralizing forces imply a transfer of resources to the center, which reduces the capacity of the periphery to sustain its own economic, political and cultural development on which future self-determination is based. Centripetal economic tendencies become centripetal political and cultural tendencies and the community enters a vicious circle of relative decline. (Cowling 1990: 15)

The central area is more economically advanced and has a higher income level than the periphery. The prosperous and successful regions at the center always have economic power over the unsuccessful and depressed regions at the periphery.[3] Hence, production in the periphery may be controlled by the center.

Further, this economic power is allied with political and cultural power and this cultural power can, to some degree, be imposed on the periphery as a consequence of the economic power. Thus, it is useful to think in terms of a division between the center, or core, and the periphery, whereby the core is not only economically and technically advanced as compared with the periphery but is also able to exercise political and cultural domination over the periphery.

Regional problems are basically problems of spatial economic imbalance—geographical disparities of material well being and growth rates of income and employment within a nation, or between different areas and/or different nations. Depressed regions are considered to be the materially worse-off areas. Resources in the less developed areas have usually been underutilized, and the growth of resources has been slower than elsewhere (Sawyer 1992a: 69).

Moreover, modern capitalist economies do not conform to perfect competition, and full employment is not a usual outcome from the operation of markets. The trouble with the neoclassical analysis is that, in a world of static comparative advantage, free trade favors the rich and the strong (whether firms or regions). Consequently, the allocation and reallocation of resources (and, especially, the creation of them) between sectors, between industries, between regions and between nations cannot be explained successfully by neoclassical equilibrium analysis.

Lastly, the cumulative causation argument relies on some degree of increasing returns to scale. In contrast, a great deal of the neoclassical analysis rests on the rejection of any assumption of increasing returns to scale, and the technical possibilities, the economic structures and the social and political environment are not taken into account.

Regional Disparities and Problems in the EC/EU

Some regions experience more severe fluctuations in employment and income than others. The rate of activity varies widely from one region to another, depending mainly on the economic situation in each region. In rural areas, the economy is still largely dependent on agriculture; such areas tend to have low-income levels, especially in the less developed countries. Further, regional disparities in employment growth lead to corresponding regional disparities in unemployment.

In 1990, agriculture accounted for only 2.9 percent of Community GDP compared to 5.1 percent in 1974. In the EC as a whole, 6.5 percent of persons employed were working in agriculture in 1990 compared to 11.7 percent in 1974. There seems to be a steady fall in the agricultural labor force in all of the EC/EU countries. The move out of agriculture (due to technological change which led to a sharp reduction in the need for agricultural labor) and toward industrial and tertiary activities is a process that all EC countries have experienced. The difference is particularly noticeable in the south of the Community, where labor productivity in agriculture is lower (OECD 1992).

Moreover, the regional problems of the EC/EU countries have been allied with structural problems. But, on the other hand, various structural problems and changes in the socioeconomic environment have affected most (if not all) regions in the EU. During the last two decades, although there have been fundamental changes in the structures of all the Member Countries, regional disparities have shown no tendency to decline.

The regional (and rural) areas have a poorly developed infrastructure, an insufficient provision of social services and generally lower levels of living standards than those in urban areas and large cities. A high level of unemployment is only one indication, and other features include the lower-than-average earnings received by workers in these areas and a serious lack of job opportunities for both men and women.

In addition, apart from measures of household welfare associated with employment prospects, there are other aspects of regional depression which also affect the living standards of people who live in these areas. For instance, in some regions the environment has suffered from the excesses of periods of industrial expansion which have left them despoiled and polluted.

In other areas, apparent regional or rural tranquillity often conceals a neglect of the necessary infrastructure associated with the agricultural sector of an economy. In both cases, there is frequently a large proportion of low-quality housing and a poor transportation network. Besides, the people in these regions tend to receive less in the way of social service provision, and standards of health care and education may be low. Thus, the north-south disparity applies in the overall activity rate not only between different regions within a country but also between different countries.

Regional growth disparities may be shown by disparities in GDP or GDP per head. Disparities in levels of GDP are measured here in terms of Purchasing Power Standards (PPS). Evidence on this indicator shows that although the position of some regions improved during the 1980s, regional disparities have in general shown no tendency to decline.

Twenty percent of the EC population still live in regions where the per capita GDP is less than 75 percent of the Community average, and inter-regional disparities in the European Community are at least twice as great as those in the United States (CEC 1991c). Per capita GDP in the top ten regions in the early 1990s was more than three times greater than that of the bottom ten regions (see tables 5.1, 5.2, and 5.3).

As can be seen from these three tables, there is little or no tendency for convergence in the regional per capita PPS (or GDP) in the EC area. The gap between EC/EU countries remains wide and does not appear to be narrowing in spite of the higher growth rates recorded by most of the poorer countries. PPS trends over the 1980s do not show a convergence toward the EC average in all countries, possibly because of the exception of Ireland, Spain, Portugal, and Greece.

TABLE 5.1
Country-Level per Capita PPS, 1980-1990 (EC = 100)

Country	1980	1990
United Kingdom	97	101
Germany	119	117
France	114	112
Denmark	106	107
Ireland	61	68
Luxembourg	115	124
Belgium	106	105
Netherlands	108	101
Italy	102	102
Spain	72	75
Portugal	53	56
Greece	52	47

Source: Eurostat (1993a) and (1993b).

TABLE 5.2
Regional per Capita PPS, 1980-1990 (EC = 100)

Country	1980		1990	
	Lowest	Highest	Lowest	Highest
United Kingdom	74	154	74	137
Germany	85	187	81	183
France	87	182	79	166
Belgium	83	166	78	166
Netherlands	87	208	82	135
Italy	58	135	61	135
Spain	45	91	49	98
Portugal	44	69	35	76
Greece	35	71	34	58

Source: Eurostat (1993a) and (1993b).
Note: Ireland, Luxembourg and Denmark are classed as single regions.

TABLE 5.3
GDP per Head, 1992 (EU$_{12}$: 100)

Country/Region	EU: 100	Country/Region	EU: 100
Belgium	**110**	**Ireland**	**77**
Vlaams Gewest	111	**Italy**	**106**
Region Wallonn	88	Nord-Ovest	120
Bruxelles	175	Lombardia	135
Denmark	**108**	Nord-Est	120
Germany	**108**	Emilia-Romagna	129
Baden-Wurttemberg	132	Centro	109
Bayern	127	Lazio	121
Berlin	96	Campania	73
Brandenburg	44	Abruzzi-Molise	92
Bremen	156	Sud	72
Hamburg	198	Sicilia	73
Hessen	150	Sardegna	80
Mecklenburg-Vorpommern	41	**Luxembourg**	**131**
Niedersachsen	106	**Netherlands**	**103**
Nordrhein-Westfalin	114	Noord-Nederland	104
Rheinland-Pfalz	103	Oost-Nederland	90
Saarland	110	West-Nederland	110
Sachsen	42	Zuid-Nederland	98
Sachsen-Anhalt	44	**Portugal**	**67**
Schleswig-Holstein	105	Continente	69
Thueringen	38	Acores	41
Greece	**50**	Maderia	44
Voreia Ellade	47	**United Kingdom**	**99**
Kentriki Ellade	48	North	88
Attiki	56	Yorkshire-Humberside	91
Nisia Aigaiou, Kriti	44	East Midlands	93
Spain	**78**	East Anglia	101
Noroeste	64	South East	116
Noreste	89	South West	94
Madrid	98	West Midlands	91
Centro	63	North West	89
Este	90	Wales	84
Sur	61	Scotland	97
Canarias	75	Northern Ireland	80
France	**113**		
lle de France	170		
Bassin-Parisien	103		
Nord-Pas-de Calais	90		
Est	104		
Ouest	94		
Sud-Ouest	97		
Centre-Est	107		
Mediterranee	97		

Source: CSO, Regional Trends (1995).

Within the EC nations, regional disparities and inequalities are tending to widen rather than converge. Only 40 percent of EC regions in 1990 had a per capita GDP that was closer to the Community average than it had been in 1980 (CEC 1991c). There are various studies that confirm increasing levels of income disparity in the Community (for example, Ben-David 1992a).

Moreover, some social indicators used to measure living standards conceal many disparities between different EC member states, different regions, urban and rural districts, and sectors of activity (this is the one part of the regional problem). With the exception of Ireland, the countries of Northern Europe, which are more industrialized, better equipped with the modern factors of industrial competitiveness and infrastructure of all kinds, and thus richer, generally have a higher living standard than those in the south (this is the other). Hence, the regional distribution of resources as well as social services is highly uneven (Eurostat 1992; 1999).[4]

Regional Policies in the EC Area

Most government economic policies are aimed at addressing the regional problems through the stimulation of investment in the following: (1) new production techniques aimed at productivity improvements at the expense of employment; and (2) new activities usually belonging to sectors with high technology products and advanced producer services (Lipietz 1986; Scott 1988; Sabel 1989; Hirst and Zeitlin 1989).

Regional policies can have some influence on the regional distribution of economic activity. In spite of the great diversity of national and regional conditions within the EC/EU countries, similar experiences exist in terms of both types of policies pursued and their results.

Clearly, this uniformity of experience has been shaped by the dominant paradigm of development pursued for almost fifty years following World War II (Albrechts et al. 1989: 6-7). In fact, it was influenced heavily by mainstream economics and by the increasing operation of free market forces. Hence, regional policy characteristics were directly related to the development approaches which were based on mainstream economic theory.

Among European countries, British governments pursued regional and industrial policies aimed at reducing the degree of spatial socioeconomic imbalance in the country, and eliminating the disparities in economic performance and employment opportunities between the depressed north and west on the one hand, and the more prosperous and dynamic south and Midlands on the other. In fact, these policies sought to redirect investment expenditures and redistribute economic activities and jobs from the growth regions to the depressed areas as the main mechanism for promoting greater regional balance.

Italy provides the highest levels of fiscal transfer (percent of GDP) in the Community in order to support the weaker regions, but this seems to be a product of greater diversity in regional income. For Italy and Germany, low income tends to go with trade deficits . . . [and] fiscal transfers [tend to go] to regions with trade problems. The region that fails to develop or loses its export base automatically receives a degree of protection from the tax and welfare system. Standards in [various] declining areas are protected by [the redistribution of] income and by [the maintenance of a certain] level of public services. In Italy (as well as in all EC countries), low-income regions usually enjoy fiscal gains (they pay less in taxes than they receive in services and benefits) [with] high-income regions providing the support. (MacKay 1994: 576)

In the French case, comprehensive economic policies aimed at developing the local economy exist;—economic policies whose objective is to speed up the automation process and the introduction of new technologies. Growth coalitions and the development agencies (as they operate in France) play their own important role and try to encourage local development (Clout 1987: 171-91).

One major aspect of French planning is regional development planning which was carried out as a "pilot program" in Greece. Clearly, Greek regional development policy has not been wholly French in either its theory or its practice, and the Greek state authorities themselves usually bear ultimate responsibility for plans and their implementation (Carter 1987: 427-29).

The problem of regional disequilibrium in Greece is bigger than in any other EC/EU country. The regional development effort has been directed toward an integrated growth of the less developed regions of the country. The effort undertaken by the Greek government to eliminate the obstacles which hinder a balanced growth among the regions of the country is directed at both furthering the development of immediately productive activities and securing the formation of the required fixed social capital in the various areas.

Greece and the entry of Portugal and Spain in 1986 add to regional inequality and imply larger transfers between different parts, if inequality is to be contained.[5] Integration seems to take a notably different form, since the EC/EU usually gives freer play to market forces. Table 5.4 presents the different types of regional incentives of the EC countries and Sweden, relative to the role of the government, in the 1960s and 1970s.

TABLE 5.4
Main Regional Incentives: Distribution by Country and Incentive Type

Country	Incentive
Belgium	Interest subsidy
	Capital grant
Denmark	Investment grant
	Municipality soft loan
United Kingdom	Regional development grant
	Regional selective assistance
Germany	Investment allowance
	Investment grant
	Special depreciation allowance
	Regional soft loan

TABLE 5.4 Continued

Country	Incentive
France	Regional policy grant
	Regional employment grant
	Local business tax concessions
Ireland	Standard capital grant
	Selective assistance
Italy	Capital grant
	National fund scheme
	Social security concession
	Tax concession
Luxembourg	Capital grant/interest subsidy
	Tax concession
	Equipment loan
Netherlands	Investment premium
Greece	Investment grant
	Interest rate subsidy
	Increased depreciation allowance
	Tax allowance
Portugal	Financial assistance
	Tax concession
Spain	Regional investment grant
	Official credit priority
Sweden	Location loan
	Location grant
	Employment grant

Sources: OECD, *Restructuring the Regions: Analysis, Policy Model, and Prognosis* (Paris: 1986); and D. Yuill and K. Allen, *European Regional Incentives* (Glasgow: European Policies Research Center, 1987).

Table 5.4 clearly illustrates that the mainstay of most regional incentive packages in Europe is the capital grant. Loan-related schemes are fairly common but are generally only of secondary importance. As for fiscal aids, these are found in seven of the thirteen countries covered; the majority of them take the form of tax concessions rather than accelerated depreciation allowances. Finally, labor-related subsidies are found in around half the countries (Allen and Yuill 1989: 119).

The trend in recent years in terms of the incentive types on offer has been toward

> Grants and away from soft loans. [Moreover, where such loans have been maintained] the trend has been towards interest-related subsidies rather than providing both subsidies and loans. A further trend has seen a move away from regionally targeted tax concessions and, indeed, this trend has been quite significant in recent years. Finally, and as already mentioned, there has been a growing interest in labor-related subsidies (Allen and Yuill 1989: 119-20).

Besides, some expenditures, particularly grants, may be more redistributive than others, while also being acceptable from an allocative viewpoint.[5] Some types of tax, particularly corporate income taxes, may also be more redistributive than others. Thus, it is clear that different incentive types and policies have different advantages and disadvantages, as they are concerned with different economic structures, different state priorities and policies, different types of industries and activities.

Clearly, traditional regional policies have not been successful in terms of lessening the regional disparities and contributing to substantial regional development. The regional policy of the EC/EU in the 1980s and the 1990s is basically related to this past unsuccessful approach to regional growth. It emphasizes the following five priority objectives (CEC 1991):

1.   to promote the development and structural adjustment of underdeveloped regions, that is, regions whose economy is largely dependent on agriculture, and which have relatively low levels of income, high unemployment and a poorly-developed infrastructure (e.g., roads, railways, social services, etc.).

2.   to redevelop regions, border regions or areas within regions seriously affected by the decline of industry (i.e., shipbuilding, iron and steel, coal, and textiles).

3. & 4. to combat long-term unemployment (unemployed persons aged over 25 in particular) as well as to facilitate the integration of young people into working life.

5a. & b. to adapt production processing and marketing structures in agriculture and forestry and to promote the development of rural areas.

Objectives 1, 2, and 5b are the only ones of a specifically regional nature; the others have some direct relevance to regions experiencing economic and social problems. Objective 1 covers those regions whose per capita GDP is less than 75 percent of the Community average. These are peripheral regions with relatively little industry (the whole of Greece, Ireland and Portugal, about 70 percent of Spain, the Italian Corsica, Mezzogiorno, and the French overseas departments and Northern Ireland in the United Kingdom). Around 21.5 percent of the EC/EU population lives in these regions, and the development policy priorities include the modernization of R&D, communications/telecommunications infrastructures, vocational training, business services, etcetera.

Objective 2 covers sixty regions or areas within regions in nine different Member States with a total of forty eight million inhabitants. The priority in these regions is given to employment and the quality of the environment, the redevelopment of industrial sites and the renovation of buildings, the promotion of new activities, economic restructuring and the improvement of the region's image, training, R&D, forging closer links between universities and industry, etcetera.

Objective 5b covers fifty six regions or areas within regions in Germany, France, Italy, and Spain with a total of fifteen million inhabitants according to the number of persons working in agriculture, the level of socioeconomic development assessed on the basis of per capita GDP, etcetera.

An Evaluation of Regional Policies

In the last five decades or so, regional policies were often considered minor complements of standard national macroeconomic policies and were limited to the selective promotion of activities (usually the promotion of R&D) in lagging regions. Traditional regional policies were designed to affect the geographical distribution of economic activity by restraining growth and development in fully employed regions and encouraging expansion in problem, underdeveloped areas through financial inducements and schemes to the private sector and the correction of micro-imperfections or a differentially high rate of public spending to improve the infrastructure. Such economic policies were followed in the majority of OECD and all of the EC countries from the 1960s onward.

The EC usually reallocates market areas and redistributes production in favor of the most efficient and best situated firms and industries. Economies of scale and learning effects usually lead in certain sectors to the domination of some firms, as these sectors are generally more profitable than others. Consequently, geographical specialization and a concentration of production are more likely to benefit the core, "the power of attraction of a center," than the periphery of the Community (Myrdal 1957: 26-27).

A relatively recent OECD report notes that manufacturing expertise and industrial skills "grow by the cumulative effects of learning, scale, etcetera, and are—contrary to the assumptions of the orthodox theory of comparative advantage—geographically concentrated" (OECD 1987: 256). In fact, internal and external economies of scale and scope develop in particular locations, and concentration provides its own momentum with benefits unevenly distributed. Thus, economic disparities, far from being self-correcting, are rather self-reinforcing.

This geographical specialization and concentration of production may be seen as a consequence of the issue of transnationalism and one of its systematic features. At the same time, the dominant transnational corporations are internationalizing their economic activities and drawing the control of the use of an ever-increasing share of the world's economic resources into the ambit of the key areas or cities of the world (Cowling 1990: 15).

The European Community/Union is not a homogeneous region; spatial differences within the EC/EU are significant. There are great differences in output, in income, or in unemployment between member countries; between the regions of each member country; and between the various regions of the Community as a whole.

The EC's major regional problems are concentrated in the south. Italy, Portugal, Spain, and Greece suffer from severe income and unemployment disparities—the existence of backward agricultural/rural areas characterized by low productivity, heavy emigration, and low participation rates.

In the United Kingdom and Belgium, income levels do not appear to differ much across regions, but unemployment rates differ sharply due to the run-down nature of important industries which happen to be regionally concentrated. In France and Greece, the presence of one hypertrophied capital region monopolizes each country's activities. In Germany, regional problems seem less serious than elsewhere in Europe.

On the whole, various findings confirm the view that the regional problem tends to become more acute as one moves away from the center of Europe (Clout 1987: 24-37). The emergence and persistence of various regional problems, can be traced to "the process of development itself," and within this, to shifts in technology, R&D, and the pattern of demand (Kaldor 1978: 148).

The move away from agriculture and toward industrial and tertiary activities is a process that all EC countries have experienced. Technological change has led to a sharp reduction in the need for agricultural labor force, thereby "exacerbating the effects of shifting demand" (Kaldor 1978: 146).

In the past, the industrial and tertiary sectors were seen as not providing sufficient employment opportunities. This is in part a reflection of the general unattractiveness of agricultural problem regions to industry due to factors such as a lack of resources and human capital, an underdeveloped infrastructure, etcetera.

While intervention by regional governments and local authorities can have some beneficial effects, a distribution of resources in favor of the "losers" (firms or regions) and, especially, state investments in regions and rural areas are also required in order to: support and develop indigenous resources, firms and industries; to add to the sum total of investment capital, industrial competency and services available; to create or enhance the opportunities for regional/local restructuring and economic development; and to improve social welfare.

In the last five decades, regional policies have tended to be centralized and state-sponsored. Regional policies based on government subsidies, grants, loans, and tax concessions are usually limited in terms of regional differentiation and, consequently, often achieve little in the way of restructuring or directing the transformation of the socioeconomic base that is required in most regions in crisis (in general, the narrower the industrial sector considered the more difficult it is to find a useful and effective way of dealing with short-term problems).

Geographical concentration can turn industrial problems into regional problems. The types of labor most in demand elsewhere may migrate, leaving a less adaptable work force in the region. Also, the development of public services and other facilities may lag behind those in other regions which, in turn, may discourage the influx of new investment.

Tax incentives and credit policies may have a useful role to play. They are offered to industries going to specified areas or development regions. But these generally have rather less immediate and less sharply focused effects than those that can be achieved by direct budget spending. This is why there have been calls for improved monitoring of the role of the state in reducing regional disparities through its own procurement and expenditure policies. It may also, at times, be preferable to employ direct investment subsidies or public capital improvement programs (Allen and Yuill 1989: 119-20).

In some cases it may be useful, in order to increase a region's industrial attraction, to develop its infrastructure in advance of the need, or to select it as the site for public enterprises. In the case of southern Italy, which lags behind in social capital, services and innovation, the Italian planners counted heavily on public investment in the impulse sectors to generate the private investment spending needed to attain employment and output targets. This remark may distinguish the market failure Anglo-Saxon analysis (the United Kingdom and the United States) from the developmentalist policy (France and Italy).

From the 1980s onward, dissatisfaction arose in part from the gap between the needs of the problem regions and that which policies could achieve. In general, the policies did not encourage decision making in the region or enhance indigenous development which may have led to self-sustained growth from within the area. Rather, the start up of new small firms distorted the occupational structure toward lower skilled workers, leaving those with technical, professional, and managerial skills to seek jobs in more prosperous regions (Moore and Rhodes 1987: 116).

Another point of criticism is that too much emphasis has been placed on attempting to influence the geographical distribution of manufacturing industries that have been in decline or growing relatively slowly, and too little emphasis has been placed on encouraging business services to move to the depressed areas. Whereas in the past, manufacturing has been the focus of regional development, it has been shown that services and inter-sectorial linkages at the regional scale are increasingly being considered crucial (Moore and Rhodes 1987: 116; Martinelli 1989: 20-21).

High technology is often considered as a single panacea for industrial policies and adopted as a fashion instrument. However, the determinants of overall patterns of industrial growth and competitiveness are clearly more complex, and may depend on many other factors than technological innovation. Consequently, technological complexes may prove insufficient in themselves to solve the broader problems of regional development and innovation.

The regional policy of the EC/EU in the 1980s and the 1990s has been confined to generalities. The role of the state, the different instruments, and the kinds of different strategies have not been specified. Obviously, the state of each individual EC/EU country needs to play its own specific role as different countries have their own specific problems.

Therefore, the governments of each EU Member should adopt different development strategies and different policy priorities. However, the coordination of these policies within the EC/EU should be taken into account. Indeed, to effectively combat the different economic and social problems requires action by individual national governments as well as collective action within the European Union.

Moreover, some support supply-oriented disparity-reducing policies–which place the emphasis on the reduction of disparities in output and income–and point out that redistributive policies might slow down rather than facilitate the adjustment process of low-income areas; they might reduce incentives to migrate, to work, to innovate, to take risks, and thus create welfare-reliant, inefficient societies. Others suggest demand-oriented disparity-reducing policies, which put the emphasis on the reduction of disparities in disposable income and in public service levels by means of transfers. According to this view, transfers in the area of welfare payments often contribute greatly to increasing the income of people living in poorer areas. As MacKay argues:

> The Community Budget remains below 1 percent of Community GDP, provides no automatic response to regional decline [and, therefore,] has no strong redistributional role between richer and poorer parts of Europe. . . . It is not strongly redistributive, it is not highly sensitive, it does not act as a built-in stabilizer. The Structural Funds and the Community Budget do not provide anything which remotely resembles built-in stabilizers. At the moment the Community Budget has at best a weak redistributive effect. MacDougall (1977) estimates that with a Community Budget of the order of 2 to 2.5 percent of GDP it would be possible to reduce inequalities of regional per capita income by 10 percent, while a budget of 5 to 7 percent of GDP would achieve a reduction of 40 percent in inequalities. [Thus,] Community expenditure would have to be strongly redistributive and highly sensitive to cyclical changes in economic fortune. (MacKay 1994: 572, 578)

Evidently, market forces left to themselves are not seen to eliminate regional inequalities and disparities; consequently, spatial disparities in the EC/EU, between countries and between regions–in the absence of strong public finance policies–are likely to increase. A strong EU public finance policy–which implies a substantial increase in the size of the EU budget and a redistribution between Member Countries–is a necessary, not a sufficient, condition of a reduction in disparities.[6] Indeed, a much larger fiscal budget, a more proactive fiscal policy, and fiscal redistribution within the EU is necessary to protect weaker regions against cyclical effects (MacKay 1994: 578).

Automatic fiscal stabilizers are a Keynesian response to a weakness of market systems; without fiscal transfers, cumulative forces of decline may be set in motion. Within the EU, real compensation and redistributive fiscal policies are required. A key question for the EU however, is whether economic integration leads to the reduction of regional income inequalities as well as other regional disparities. The political drive to unite Europe has taken insufficient account of the problems posed by regional disparity and, therefore, "efforts to encourage convergence are in effect attempts to impose uniformity of economic performance. Attempts to create a unified Europe have not addressed the question of fiscal transfer adequately. Transfers have an economic as well as a political role" (MacKay 1994: 584).

In order to hold the whole EC/EU together, economic gains must be widely distributed. But, in the long run, problems of political will are important and might frustrate attempts at fiscal transfer. Designing budgetary actions and policies that will at the same time reduce spatial disparities within the EU and be politically acceptable will be very difficult.

UNEMPLOYMENT IN THE EC/EU AREA

A Brief Theoretical Review

The two main approaches related to unemployment shall now be briefly presented: first, the neoclassical, and second, the Keynesian.

Neoclassical analysis strongly suggests that with price flexibility, a market economy can operate in an efficient manner with full employment of resources, including labor. The neoclassical approach assumes a clearing of the labor market, and that wage adjustment and labor mobility are a feature of both the short and long run.

The market system tends to eliminate involuntary unemployment through eventual changes in price levels. But neoclassical theorists go further and advance the proposition that markets tend to be in equilibrium; that recorded unemployment is thus always voluntary; and that any government attempts to reduce unemployment must inevitably result in higher inflation (Davies 1985: 13). The regional dimension of this view supports the proposition that in the short run, regional wage flexibility clears the labor market which then induces interregional movements of labor and capital, until eventually, in the long run, a new equilibrium is reached.

The Keynesian approach suggests that the volume of employment is a function of the level of effective demand. It further suggests that left to themselves, market forces do not generate full employment. An appropriate level of aggregate demand is a necessary condition for economic growth, higher levels of employment, and good economic performance. Therefore, government intervention can affect employment through aggregate demand management policies. On the other hand, supply-side policies are also important and may themselves be influenced by demand.

Discussion of the Problem

Most EC countries have experienced high levels of unemployment during the last two decades, and this problem may rise further. The ratio of recorded unemployment in the EC in the mid-1990s was more than three times as high as it was twenty years previously, and this position (or worse) has prevailed consistently for several years. In the late 1990s, more than fifteen million persons in the European Community/Union were unemployed (OECD 2000).

Unemployment is one of the most worrying aspects of the labor market, affecting 8.4 percent of the active population and usually women more than men. Youth and long-term unemployment remain high, although unemployment rates vary widely from one member state to another. In 1990, Luxembourg had the lowest rate (1.7 percent), while Spain (16.1 percent) and Ireland (15.6 percent) had the highest rates. The rates in the other EC member states vary between 4.5 percent and 10 percent (CEC 1991c; OECD 1994).

Regions also vary widely in their unemployment levels (i.e., the regional dimension of the unemployment problem) and the overall employment figures hide substantial disparities at the regional level. Regional disparities in employment appear to be wider than those in GDP; unemployment rates range from 1.5 percent to 29 percent.

During the first half of the 1980s, regional disparities widened because of job losses, especially in manufacturing. In the second half of the 1980s, this trend began to be reversed. Yet, technological change has reduced the demand for unskilled labor; this may be witnessed by the relatively low education standards and skills of long-term unemployed people. During the last two decades, fewer jobs were created in the poorer regions of the European Community, and unemployment was caused by the decline in the agricultural sector (CEC 1991c; 1999).

The variations in employment growth, labor force growth, and unemployment rates in the EC are described in table 5.5, and regional disparities in unemployment rates are illustrated in table 5.6.

TABLE 5.5
Employment Growth, Labor Force Growth, and Unemployment Rates
EC, United States, and Japan: 1982-1990 and 1991-1997

Country	Employment Growth		Labor Force Growth		Unemployment Rates	
	1982-90	1991-97	1982-90	1991-97	1982-90	1991-97
Belgium	0.6	-0.5	0.2	0.6	11.3	11.1
France	0.4	-0.5	0.5	0.4	9.5	10.8
Germany	0.8	-0.5	0.8	0.5	7.4	9.0
Denmark	0.8	-0.2	0.8	0.3	9.1	11.4
Ireland	-0.2	-0.1	0.1	1.9	15.5	18.1
Luxembourg	2.3	2.3	2.3	2.5	1.5	1.6
Netherlands	1.6	0.7	1.3	1.2	9.8	7.9
Italy	0.6	-0.1	0.8	-0.2	10.9	10.9
Spain	1.4	-1.4	1.3	0.5	19.0	19.9
Portugal	1.6	0.8	1.3	0.9	7.1	4.5
Greece	0.7	0.1	0.9	1.0	7.4	9.4
United Kingdom	1.5	-1.7	0.9	-0.6	9.7	9.8
EC average	0.9	-0.1	0.8	0.8	10.2	10.3
United States	2.1	0.7	1.6	0.9	7.1	6.9
Japan	1.3	1.2	1.3	1.4	2.5	2.3

Source: OECD, Employment Outlook, Tables 1.2 and 1.3 (July 1993 and July 1998).
Note: Columns 1 and 3 show average annual percentage rates of change between 1982 and 1990. Columns 2 and 4 show average annual percentage rates of change between 1991 and 1997.

TABLE 5.6
EC Unemployment Rates, 1992 (percent)

Country/Region	EC: 9.2	Country/Region	EC: 9.2
Belgium	**6.7**	**Ireland**	**15.3**
Vlaams Gewest	4.9	**Italy**	**8.5**
Region Wallonn	9.5	Nord-Ovest	6.5
Bruxelles	9.0	Lombardia	3.4
Denmark	**9.1**	Nord-Est	3.7
Germany	**6.4**	Emilia-Romagna	3.6
Baden-Wurttemberg	2.8	Centro	6.0
Bayern	2.9	Lazio	8.3
Berlin	9.9	Campania	17.2
Brandenburg	12.7	Abruzzi-Molise	9.9
Bremen	7.6	Sud	13.3
Hamburg	5.3	Sicilia	17.5
Hessen	3.6	Sardegna	15.0
Mecklenburg-Vorpommern	16.2	**Luxembourg**	**2.1**
Niedersachsen	5.3	**Netherlands**	**5.6**
Nordrhein-Westfalin	5.5	Noord-Nederland	7.6
Rheinland-Pfalz	3.6	Oost-Nederland	5.3
Saarland	6.0	West-Nederland	5.4
Sachsen	12.4	Zuid-Nederland	5.2
Sachsen-Anhalt	14.1	**Portugal**	**3.8**
Schleswig-Holstein	4.5	Continente	3.8
Thueringen	13.8	Acores	3.2
Greece	**7.8**	Maderia	3.2
Voreia Ellade	6.7	**United Kingdom**	**9.8**
Kentriki Ellade	8.0	North	10.9
Attiki	9.7	Yorkshire/Humberside	9.8
Nisia Aigaiou, Kriti	3.6	East Midlands	8.6
Spain	**17.8**	East Anglia	7.6
Noroeste	16.6	South East	9.5
Noreste	15.3	South West	9.0
Madrid	12.5	West Midlands	10.3
Centro	18.4	North West	10.5
Este	14.9	Wales	9.5
Sur	25.9	Scotland	9.9
Canarias	24.7	Northern Ireland	15.4
France	**10.0**		
lle de France	8.2		
Bassin-Parisien	10.1		
Nord-Pas-de Calais	12.9		
Est	7.7		
Ouest	10.1		
Sud-Ouest	10.3		
Centre-Est	9.7		
Mediterranee	13.2		

Source: CSO, Regional Trends (1995).

Most regions of high unemployment in the EC/EU are either depressed (in which activity rates tend to be low) or have traditional industries in decline. European unemployment has been accompanied by a relatively rapid decline in manufacturing employment in the EC area. The share of employment in manufacturing fell in the 1980s from 22.1 percent to 18.0 percent in the United States; from 24.7 percent to 24.1 percent in Japan; and from 27.5 percent to 23.2 percent for the EC. This relative decline represented an absolute fall for Europe of almost 5.5 million jobs.

Of the former EC(12), the only countries to avoid a fall in manufacturing employment were Portugal and Greece, with the United Kingdom experiencing the most extreme cut of 16 percent, representing more than 2 million jobs. Furthermore, the loss of manufacturing jobs in the EC has been accompanied by an increasingly adverse balance of trade in manufacturing and by a rise in unemployment.

Employment in the manufacturing industry has continued to decline, while service sector employment, particularly part-time employment, has grown rapidly. This also implies further long-term unemployment, which has a considerable structural component. In most EC countries, labor force growth has outpaced employment growth during recent years and, as a consequence, the unemployment rates have risen dramatically. High unemployment, especially long-term and structural unemployment, continues to be a major social and economic problem in the European Union and, as has been previously noted, unemployment rates rose in almost every EC and OECD member state in the 1980s and early 1990s.

The rise in recorded unemployment is concentrated more among men and has remained persistently high so that rates of over 10 percent exist in a number of EC/EU countries. The sharpest relative increases have occurred in two countries, Ireland and Spain. With the jump in the unemployment rate, the number of unemployed people in the EC area in the mid-1990s exceeded eighteen million–an increase from 1991 of over three million (OECD 2000).

A more disturbing picture of the EC's comparative record emerges when Japan and the United States are chosen as reference points. In fact, the unemployment rate in Japan has remained very low, averaging around 2.5 percent throughout the 1980s and 2.9 percent during the last decade.

The government sector takes part in labor market programs in all the EC countries. But government spending on labor market programs by most EC governments was higher in the mid-1980s than in 1990 and in the mid-1990s. In contrast to this position, Denmark had the largest rates of public expenditure on labor market programs in the EC/EU and OECD area which varied from around 5 percent in 1985 to more than 6.5 percent in 1995 (OECD 1991; 1997).

These short-term policies are mainly based on subsidies and grants, and some governments have adopted training grants in an attempt to encourage industries to invest more in training. However, as structural unemployment grows from the gap between the pressures on economies to adapt to change and their ability to do so, adaptation is vital to progress in a world of new technologies, globalization, and international competition. This is why labor market programs need to have a thorough long-term perspective, as unemployment is a very serious and complicated problem.

To combat unemployment successfully, an appropriate macroeconomic policy is required, which needs to focus on faster non-inflationary growth of aggregate demand. This was recently recognized by some OECD (and EC) countries (see, for example, OECD 1994: 31-44). However, the majority of EC/EU governments seem to have taken insufficient account of the problems of employment and unemployment.

OTHER EC/EU PROBLEMS

Slowdown in GDP Growth

Economic activity in the EC has slowed down considerably during the last two decades. Real GDP in the EC area grew by only 1.4 percent in 1991 and 1.1 percent in 1992, decreased slightly by -0.4 percent in 1993, and grew by 1.8 percent in 1994. The picture is not much different in the late 1990s. Economic growth has been uneven and relatively weak and the slowdown in economic activity has not been uniform across all the EC (and the OECD) countries. The variation in growth rates of GDP in the EC countries, the United States, and Japan is described in table 5.7.

TABLE 5.7
Real GDP Growth in the EC, the United States, and Japan: 1982-1994

Country	1982-90	1991	1992	1993	1994
Belgium	2.4	2.0	0.8	-0.7	1.2
France	2.5	0.7	1.3	-0.7	1.5
Germany	2.8	3.7	2.0	-1.9	1.4
Denmark	2.4	1.2	1.1	0.7	2.8
Ireland	3.9	2.2	2.7	2.6	3.4
Luxembourg	4.4	3.0	2.4	1.2	1.8
Netherlands	2.7	2.2	1.5	-0.3	1.4
Italy	2.7	1.3	0.9	-0.2	1.7
Spain	3.6	2.3	1.0	-0.6	1.7
Portugal	2.9	2.2	1.4	0.6	1.9
Greece	1.8	1.8	1.4	1.1	1.7
United Kingdom	3.2	-2.2	-0.6	1.8	2.9
EC average	2.8	1.4	1.1	-0.4	1.8
United States	3.3	-1.2	2.1	2.6	3.1
Japan	4.3	4.0	1.3	1.0	3.3

Source: OECD, Economic Outlook, no. 53 (June 1993); and no. 55 (June 1994).
Note: The first column shows average annual percentage rates of change between 1982 and 1990.

What is clear from table 5.7 is that both the United States and Japan have had higher increases in GDP growth than those economies in the European Community since the 1980s (at current and constant prices), while the Community has been a slow growth area.

Declining Government Capital Formation

Almost all the EC countries experienced higher levels of gross capital formation and capital outlays (percent of total government outlays, at current and constant prices) of general government in the mid-1970s than in the mid-1980s. (Portugal is the only exception.)

The rates of gross capital formation and capital outlays of government vary from one member state to another. Portugal (12.9 percent), Germany (12.6 percent), and Italy (11.3 percent) experienced the highest rates in the mid-1970s, while France (10.5 percent) experienced the lowest. The other countries in the EC experienced rates of over 10 percent in the mid-1970s. However, the picture changes in the mid-1980s and the mid-1990s. Portugal (19.7 percent), Spain (14.1 percent), and Italy (10.8 percent) experienced the highest rates in the mid-1980s, while Denmark (5.3 percent) and Belgium (5.6 percent) experienced the lowest. The other EC countries experienced rates varying from 6 percent to 10 percent in the mid-1980s.

In the mid-1990s, France (10.3 percent) and Italy (9.3 percent) experienced the highest rates and Denmark (4.2 percent) the lowest. In the EC area, on average, the rates of gross capital formation and capital outlays of government decreased from 11.4 percent in the mid-1970s to 9.8 percent in the mid-1980s, and fell further to 8.4 percent in the mid-1990s. The tendency by most OECD governments to accept the principle of a more limited role of the state has had the effect of arresting the growth of government expenditure (and, therefore, the growth of gross capital formation and capital outlays of general government), as a ratio of GDP during the last two decades.

The United States and Japan are also chosen as reference points. Both of them experienced higher rates of gross capital formation and capital outlays of general government (percent of total government outlays) in the mid-1970s than in the mid-1980s, but their rates increased by 1990. Also, Japan and Italy experienced the highest rates of state investment (percent of GDP) in the 1990s.

Clearly, a disturbing picture of the Community's comparative record emerges when Japan is taken into consideration. The rates of gross capital formation and capital outlays of the Japanese government are high—much higher than those of the EC/EU and the United States. In fact, this observation is in accordance with the view that the Japanese government relies heavily on government investments (the state as investor) (see also tables 3.2 and 3.3 in chapter 3).

Direct participation by the state in the allocation of investment spending to industry has been important in both the qualitative and quantitative senses, and the Japanese government has played a very important role in both mobilizing and directing investment funds. All the above figures are shown in table 5.8.

TABLE 5.8
The Share (percent) of Gross Capital Formation and Capital Outlays of Government to Total Government Outlays in the EC, the United States, and Japan (at current prices)[7]

Country	Mid-1970s	Mid-1980s	Mid-1990s
United Kingdom	10.62	6.44	9.83
Germany	12.61	8.49	7.96
France	10.48	8.25	10.30
Denmark	10.78	5.28	4.20
Belgium	n/a	5.63	n/a
Netherlands	10.85	9.56	8.63
Italy	11.25	10.79	9.34
Spain	n/a	14.05	n/a
Portugal	12.95	19.74	n/a
EC average	11.36	9.80	8.37
United States	6.04	4.86	5.10
Japan	21.81	17.24	19.49

Source: OECD, National Accounts (various years) and our estimates.

Industrial Policies in Europe and International Competition

Discussions and controversies about industrial policies and growing interest in various issues and problems related to them are certainly not new. On the theoretical side, one may contrast two main conceptions of industrial development. The traditional view of international differences in growth rates suggests that all countries should converge to the same level of development (Solow 1956).[8] The less advanced countries will catch up with the leading ones and, consequently, enjoy a faster rate of technological progress.

At the center of this catch-up argument is the belief that industrial latecomers are expected to innovate faster than the advanced countries located in the technological frontier area. The alternative view, favored by Myrdal (1957), Kaldor (1966), and recently, by the industrial strategy theorists, contends that countries follow their own national growth paths and build their own technological capabilities, usually with divergent growth paths and little tendency for convergence in income or productivity levels.

Therefore, economic growth and development take place in a context of cumulative causation (many factors influence the cumulative mechanisms). On the other hand, recent endogenous growth models (Romer 1986; Lucas 1988) have focused on the possibilities of divergent growth paths between different countries. The national accumulation of skills and technology is the endogenous outcome of investment expenditure in human capital formation and knowledge-intensive industries.

During the last five decades, and on the side of policy making, government interventions have usually been of a microeconomic nature and industrial policies are usually considered as minor complements of national macroeconomic policies. Governments have often worried about the effect of international competition on the prosperity of domestic firms, have tried either to shield industries from foreign competition or to help them in world competition, and have been seen to support (more or less) the industrial sectors, to correct their micro-imperfections and to offer protection to them. Market failure has usually been the reason for subsidies and other forms of financial support to industries.

Although forms and commitments vary significantly from one country to another, government industrial policies are seen to be limited to the promotion of R&D and to the selective promotion of activities designed to:

- promote new industries and high technology;
- help old ones to restructure;
- keep declining sectors alive in order to save jobs and avoid social and political tensions (Price 1981: 18).[9]

There is now a recognition by governments that their actions will have a major influence on the development and performance of industry, because they can promote structural transformation and the necessary accelerators of competency and growth in the context of industrial policy for improved industrial competitiveness. The policy orientation of the EC governments and their support to industry are described in tables 5.9 and 5.10.

TABLE 5.9
Government Support to Industry in the EC, Average 1986-1998

Country	R&D	SME	EXP	HOB	SFSP	RAI	Total
Belgium	0.37	1.05	0.54	0.95	0.51	0.88	4.3
Germany	0.46	0.22	0.05	0.21	0.19	1.59	2.7
France	0.32	0.19	0.92	0.27	1.68	0.28	3.7
Denmark	0.75	0.02	0.32	0.26	0.39	0.11	1.9
Ireland	0.28	0.36	2.24	0.00	0.84	2.38	6.1
Luxembourg	0.14	0.50	0.07	0.36	0.00	1.37	2.5
Netherlands	0.72	1.09	0.05	0.61	0.20	0.47	3.2
Italy	0.32	0.58	0.42	0.67	1.04	3.21	6.2
Spain	0.27	0.06	0.05	0.23	4.20	0.11	4.9
Portugal	0.09	0.12	0.09	3.05	1.61	0.21	5.2
Greece	0.92	0.59	4.95	0.00	3.11	6.10	15.7
UK	0.25	0.22	0.23	0.18	0.87	0.83	2.6
EC 1986-98	0.38	0.32	0.37	0.36	1.04	1.37	3.8

Source: CEC, European Economy no. 48 (Brussels, 1991); CEC (1999c); and, OECD, Economic Surveys: Sweden 1991/1992 (Paris, 1992).
Note: R&D: research and technological development; SME: small and medium-sized enterprises; EXP: export promotion; HOB: other horizontal objectives; SFSP: sectorial and firm specific; and RAI: regional aid.

TABLE 5.10

State Aid to Industry, Average 1980-1998

	Lx	It	Irl	Fr	Ge	Be	UK	Nl	Dk	Gr	EC
% of GE	19	15	12	11	10	10	5	4	3	-	10
% of GDP	6.0	5.7	5.3	2.7	2.5	4.1	1.8	1.5	1.3	2.5	3.0
% of MVA	7.3	17	13	4.9	3.0	6.4	3.8	4.1	2.6	13	6.3

Source: Commission of the European Community (1999c).
Note: MVA stands for manufacturing value added and GE for government expenditure.

Table 5.9 indicates that different governments have different orientations and set different industrial policy priorities. Government support to small and medium-sized industries is a very important priority for Belgium and the Netherlands. Greece and Ireland place more emphasis on export promotion and regional aid, which also expresses their particular economic weakness in these two areas. Spain places emphasis on sectorial and firm specific support much more than all the other EC countries and Italy on regional aid.

Although privately funded R&D has usually been larger than state spending on R&D in most OECD countries (Eurostat 1998), most governments often encourage investment spending in high-risk ventures by sponsoring research activities; by offering special support and provision for investment in R&D; or by directly and indirectly subsidizing innovations.

If all expenditure on R&D is considered together, the Community devotes just over 2 percent of its GDP to it which is below that of the United States and Japan (roughly 2.8 percent). The gap is even greater if these figures are related to population. The research situation in the EC/EU countries is also marked by tremendous diversity and the resources which are allocated to research vary considerably from country to country. Moreover, research potential is unevenly distributed with considerable regional differences within the EC area. It is estimated that the technology gap between the most and the least advanced regions is in the order of one to one hundred, seven times greater than the highest differences amongst individual member states (Eurostat 1992; 1998).

European manufacturing industry remains a major force in the world economy, and even though its share of the European economy as a whole has dropped, it still contributes more than one-third (34.4 percent) of gross value-added—more than in the United States, but less than in Japan. Since 1974, the value-added in manufacturing industry (as a percent of GDP) has slowed down and, since 1983, industrial production recorded sustained growth peaking at 4 percent per year in general by the end of the decade. But the rate of growth in industrial production in the EC was slower during the 1980s and 1990s than in the United States and Japan (OECD 1992; 2000).

Japan was in a better position than the EC or the United States during the same period. In short, industry in the Community had lost ground against the United States and particularly, against the Japanese industry. Over the last two decades, the annual growth in the productivity of the EC/EU industry was slightly higher than in the United States (3.4 percent as against 3.2 percent) but appreciably lower than in Japan (5.5 percent). With industrial output growing more or less in line with productivity, there has been no immediate pressure for a massive shake-out similar to that experienced in the United States and the leading European economies in the 1980s.

Lastly, the EC/EU Commission contends that the maintenance of an international ability to compete requires the advanced EU economies to become internationally competitive and to specialize in higher technology industrial sectors, given that there is increasing competition, especially from newly industrializing countries in low technology products. It considers that Japan and the United States are,

> continually pushing ahead with specialization in the high-tech industries, and that . . . the relatively low level of productivity achieved by European countries in the high-tech industries goes a long way towards explai-ning weak performance in international trade in a number of sectors. . . . Furthermore, completion of the internal market is likely to give a fresh boost to these new advanced technology industries and, through a cumulative process, revive European competitiveness. (EC 1988: 25, 115, 129)

However, scientists (such as Hughes 1992; 1993) support the view that a shift into high-tech sectors is neither necessary nor sufficient for improved performance, as there is no apparent relationship between technological specialization and trade performance. For example, Japan, Germany, and Italy, with the best overall trade performance in the 1980s, had their best performance in high, medium and low technology products respectively; while the United Kingdom and the United States, with a relatively poor overall performance, had their best performance in high technology sectors (Hughes 1992: 175). Moreover, Hughes argues that

> both EC economies and the United States had problems with respect to R&D and to skill with respect to Japan. [Thus] competitiveness is determined by a variety of factors in ways that vary across countries. (Hughes 1993: 156)
> The determinants of overall patterns of competitiveness are clearly more complex than a simple interpretation of [neoclassical] theories of trade would imply, and depend on [many] other factors than innovation. (Hughes 1992: 181)

CONCLUSION

This chapter has sought to exhibit some of the existing problems in the EC area, based on the inefficiencies of the market system; to explain the issues surrounding these problems; and, finally, to look at the role of the government. The key point is that imperfections and inflexibilities always emerge in market economies.

Regional disparities in unemployment rates or per capita incomes persist for long periods of time and have harmful economic, political, and social effects. Therefore, left to themselves, market forces will not solve economic and social problems and will not generate full employment either.

The neoclassical and New Right schools have failed to offer successful development solutions; thus, they have little to say about the success of their economic and social policy recommendations. There is no reason to believe that the invisible hand of the market will promote balanced regional growth and development, since it is evident that the process of cumulative causation is largely responsible for the creation of winners and losers, whether firms or regions.

Moreover, these views make assumptions which are unrealistic and produce conclusions that are startling in their implications. This is the main reason that these views and these policies cannot offer solutions to economic and social problems.

Active government policies can strengthen the links between aggregate demand management and substantial regional development. The appropriate role of a modern state would appear to be one of aiding the meeting of social needs, future requirements and long-term development objectives. The Developmental State, which is organized and concerned with promoting endogenous competency and industrial competitiveness, can offer solutions. However, these important notions should be part of a more meaningful and developmental role for the government sector in its specific policies.

NOTES

1. What Myrdal (1957) had in mind was a type of multiplier-accelerator mechanism producing increasing returns in the favored region.

2. According to his view, and applying the Verdoorn Law, the higher the rates of growth of productivity, the higher the rates of growth of output, and differences in the rates of productivity growth will tend to exceed the associated differences in the rates of growth of employment.

3. The center and the periphery concept can be applied at a number of levels, of which the regional and national will be the two discussed here.

4. See also: CEC, *Third Periodic Report from the Commission on the Social and Economic Situation and Development of the Community* (1987); CEC, *Fourth Periodic Report on the Social and Economic Situation and Development of the Regions of the Community* (1991); J. Delors, *Regional Implications of Economic and Monetary Integration* (1989); Eurostat, *Population and Social Conditions* 1990-1997 (1999); and *Europe in Figures* (1992).

5. The most common criteria for redistribution are: equality (the lower the income of the lagging region, the greater the fiscal transfer it will receive), needs, tax capacity, and level of development.

6. Using only fiscal transfers seems to be a partial and unsuccessful economic and political response to regional disparities and to the weakness of market systems, since economic development and self-sustained growth are not simply a function of the amount of resources transferred. Active policies and a Developmental State are also necessary if substantial regional development is to be achieved.

7. The share of capital formation and capital outlays of general government to total government outlays can be obtained either at current or at constant prices, because:

$$\sigma_{ct} = [(KF/deflator)/(GE/deflator)] \times 100 = (KF/GE) \times 100 = \sigma_{cur}$$

8. The neoclassical approach assumes that all countries have access to the same technology and the rate of change of technology.

9. The New Right (neoliberal) schools argue that by keeping resources locked up in declining sectors, industrial policy reduces national income below what it would have been in its absence and society bears an additional burden.

Chapter 6

Developmental State and EC/EU

INTRODUCTION

This chapter concentrates on national, regional, and industrial policies pursued by some of the EC governments. Almost every country in the EC/EU area faces regional and industrial problems, although inequalities and disparities vary considerably between them due to a wide range of causes.

In the face of such significant disparities, most European countries have adopted regional and industrial policies. In the late 1980s, over $10 billion per year, which remains below 1 percent of the Community GDP, was spent in the EC countries on grants and soft loans to firms alone and, in addition, there were a wide range of other financial incentives including depreciation allowances, tax concessions, and employment subsidies (CEC 1989).

At the European level, there is a marked tendency for various regional and industrial difficulties to increase towards the periphery (south) of Europe and such problems, and the policy response toward them, have been of considerable significance. Some elements, both internal and external, may have had some negative influence on the prospects for additional growth and development. In addition, the political and social characteristics are of great importance as the way in which these elements can be combined into an effective national policy package naturally varies with a country's circumstances.

On the other hand, different views about how market economies operate have led to quite different policy considerations. The visible hand of the state, rather than the invisible hand of the free market system, can overcome natural disadvantages, inequalities, and disparities. Hence, a high quality of government intervention and, especially, developmentalist policies are needed.

EXPERIENCES IN THE EC AREA AND THE
DEVELOPMENTAL STATE VIEW

In many industrial countries, in the postwar period, and especially in the golden ages of capitalism, it was felt that a primary duty of governments was to maintain conditions appropriate to steady economic growth, full, or almost full, employment, industrial development and balance in the economy. The need for the government to play an important role in development is far from new and has been apparent, both in theory and in practice, at least since the writings of List and the German industrialization effort in the latter half of the nineteenth century.

The room for government interventions in the economy has been greatly enlarged in most developed economies since the Second World War, both in the long-term (by favoring investment expenditure, improving human capital, etc.) and in the short-term. After World War II, with a large number of states facing the important task of creating basic economic and social infrastructure, ranging from roads, schools and hospitals to machinery and capital equipment, there has been a spate of interest in development theory that was expected to guide the attempts of governments to foster development.

Dore (1986b) classifies, in a rough way, state interventions in the economy as follows:

- Regulation of individual transactions in order to make markets work more efficiently;
- Regulation of the structure of production and trade in order to prevent monopoly and oligopoly;
- Intervention to promote economic growth, of which two sub-categories: (a) state actions taken wholly with regard to the domestic economy (domestic developmentalism), and (b) state actions taken explicitly to promote the industrial competitiveness of the nation in the global economy (competitive developmentalism); and,
- Pork barrel intervention–the use of state power to promote particular sectional interests, either for personal or electoral advantage.

During the postwar period, various regional and industrial policies were often considered as minor complements of standard national macroeconomic policies. Regional policies that were designed to influence the geographical distribution of economic activity and encourage growth in depressed areas are in accordance with what has been observed in the last five decades.

Forms and commitments of state intervention vary from one country to another. Some countries have adopted more comprehensive policies while others have reduced specific policies to correcting microimperfections. The distinction between the market-failure Anglo-Saxon tradition versus the comprehensive-developmentalist tradition reproduces the above distinction on regional, industrial, and full employment economic policies. Clearly, different countries pose different experiences. There are numerous examples of development in the post-war era, and some are briefly discussed here.

British Regional and Industrial Policies

Reducing regional disparities in unemployment and achieving a better balance (or a greater dispersion) in the geographical distribution of industry have un-doubtedly been the main objectives underlying regional policy in Britain in the 1950s, 1960s, and 1970s. Concern has been expressed about Britain's postwar growth performance compared to other industrialized countries (regional policy was thus seen as helping to achieve a faster rate of national growth) and about the problems of excessive growth in the greater London area. A large proportion of public spending on regional and industrial aid has been directed at encourag-ing capital investment by industries in assisted areas, on the assumption that jobs would follow investments, such as loans, subsidies, tax incentives, and grants (Armstrong and Taylor 1985: 174-78).

In the early 1960s, the purpose of growth zones or growth areas policy was to concentrate special public investment in those parts of the regions that had the most favorable prospect for self-sustaining growth and were best located to gen-erate activity over a large area through direct or indirect incentives. But in 1966, the growth zones were replaced by broad development areas within which no special provision was made for growth zones.

Unemployment patterns in the United Kingdom have been dominated by problems of old industries; consequently, regional policies have concentrated on stimulating new industrial activities. In fact, there has been some restructuring of sun-set industries (e.g., textiles) and much of this occurred during the 1950s and 1960s. Selective state intervention has also attempted to improve industrial performance (e.g., the nationalization of steel and shipbuilding industries).

At the end of the 1960s, the regional policy framework comprised four ma-jor elements:

1. employment subsidies—the Regional Employment Premium (REP);
2. controls on location decisions—Industrial Development Certificates (IDCs);
3. automatic subsidies for investment in assisted areas (differential investment grants); and,
4. discretionary financial assistance (soft loans and grants).

This regional policy was directed at raising economic activity in three types of assisted areas: intermediate areas, development areas, and special development areas. The first two categories were distinguished primarily by levels of unem-ployment while the third one was distinguished by levels of unemployment plus anticipated unemployment arising from heavy dependence on the declining in-dustries of coal and shipbuilding (*Industrial Development Act* 1966).

During the later 1960s, governments pursued policies of much more direct intervention in the restructuring of British manufacturing industry, at a time when international competition was increasing and major industries, like steel-making, and mechanical and electrical engineering, were experiencing new difficulties. At this time the effectiveness of regional development policy in creating jobs in depressed areas was undermined by falling employment in many key industries, by an increasing south/north gap in terms of employment and by the operation of other economic policies (Armstrong and Taylor 1985; Wood 1987; Bowers 1991).

At the beginning of the 1970s, the automatic element of regional policy was the Regional Development Grant (RDG), and the discretionary element was the Regional Selective Assistance (RSA) that helped companies to maintain their profitability, to maintain existing employment and/or to create new employment (*Industry Act* 1972, *Industry Act* 1975 and *Local Employment Act* 1972).[1] The government's intention was "to continue and develop the financial and other incentives now available for the location of new industry and the expansion of existing industry in the assisted areas" (House of Commons, *Parliamentary Debates* Vol. 872: cols. 347-48, session 1974).

In the 1970s, and especially after the oil crisis of 1973, many industries reduced their labor force, and rising unemployment, with all its severe regional consequences, became politically unacceptable. The Labor government's nationalization program not only transferred ownership into the public sector but also changed the industrial structure. But since 1979, the privatization program has transferred many of these firms back to the private sector, in spite of a considerable loss of jobs, especially in heavily depressed areas, and the government has viewed ownership as a more important determinant of economic performance than competition. Furthermore, regional policy has been further downgraded.

Indeed, there has been inadequate emphasis on government investments on the accelerators of industrial growth and competitiveness. In the other areas of policy identified as the supply side, British governments did relatively little and spent only little on regional infrastructure and other modern factors of development (see table 6.1 below and tables 6.2-6.7 in the appendix).

TABLE 6.1
Government Expenditure on Regional Policy (£m, current and constant prices)

Year	Payments to Firms	Percent of Total	Infrastructure	Percent of Total	Total GE
1972-73	233.3	80.1	58.3	19.9	291.6
1975-76	622.6 (397.9)	89.9	70.1 (44.7)	10.1	692.7 (442.6)
1978-79	520.7 (210.3)	91.1	51.2 (20.5)	8.9	571.9 (230.8)
1979-80	399.2 (141.3)	87.9	55.4 (19.5)	12.1	454.6 (160.8)

Source: CSO, Abstract of Regional Statistics (1974); and, Regional Trends (1981).
Notes: 1. The term "Payments to Firms" means the sum of REP, automatic payments and discretionary payments. Total GE means the total public expenditure on regional policy.
2. The figures in parentheses express government spending on regional policy at constant (1972/73) prices.

Most industrial policies in the United Kingdom have been based on the concern for the promotion of competition and on the assumption that the government's task is to promote price competition (Best 1990: 46). Situations of market failure suggest state intervention of a regulatory kind and limit this intervention to correct market imperfections. Indeed, the regulatory role relates to government interventions, mainly in industrial affairs, through regulation. Especially during the 1980s and 1990s, the main thrust of British industrial policy has been for the government sector to adopt a regulatory, rather than developmental, role with particular emphasis on competition policy.

Following Dore's classification, British industrial policies can be placed under the term "regulation"; but there have also been elements of policies which could be placed under the term "developmentalism." These elements have particularly arisen from Labor governments, for example, a number of economic policies pursued during the 1960s and 1970s, and can be seen as involving a more developmental role for the state.

However, the timid nature and brief life of those policies (e.g., the National Plan of 1965-66 and the industrial strategy of 1975-79), which are seen as interventionist responses to pressing problems, along with the hostile academic response they received, indicate the dominance of the market failure analysis (Sawyer 1992a: 57). For example, training and training schemes have often been dictated by the pressure of unemployment and lack of qualified manpower (i.e., reactive policy). As a result, no strategic planning took place because of changes in government and/or shifts in policy making.

Moreover, the Developmental State view suggests much more government spending on infrastructure and accelerators rather than on various payments to industries and firms. The accelerators of growth and development should be considered as a complete package of development tools. Indeed, improvements in production result from a sophisticated combination of skills, R&D, new technologies, and innovation. In addition, investment spending in human resource development can overcome many of the characteristics of the labor force that act as impediments to greater productivity (i.e., the potential benefits of investment in human capital).

In brief, the dominance of the market failure tradition is obvious in most British regional and industrial policies, even though there have been elements of developmental policies that have arisen particularly from Labor governments. However, these policies have not achieved significant regional restructuring, desirable industrial performance and competitiveness.

German Regional and Industrial Policies

An important feature of the German government has been its federal constitution (eleven provinces), which reflects the relatively weak sense of central identity in the country as a whole (Littlechild 1982: 155). It has been described as the most decentralized system in Europe.

Fundamental to German economic policies has been the belief that a steady reliance on a market economy—free competition, rather than state intervention, at an international, national or regional level—linked to improvements in social services, should be the guiding force behind economic development (i.e., social market economy).

Indeed, the private industrial sector appears to have revived with relatively little state intervention. Since the 1960s, large firms have come to dominate key industrial sectors such as oil and gas, automobiles, shipbuilding, electric power, and chemical and electrical engineering (Statistisches Bundesamt 1971) (see tables 6.8-6.10 in the appendix).

The government actively encouraged mergers between German companies throughout the 1960s on the grounds that only large industrial units could hope to compete with American-based multinational enterprises. But since 1973, the key element in German industrial policy has been the antitrust legislation which seeks to encourage competition.

During the entire lifespan of German regional and industrial policies "there has been a strong sense of responsibility at all levels of government, and there have often been 'implicit' regional considerations in the pattern of government expenditure and commitment to a uniform standard of living in all parts of the country" (Blacksell 1987: 250).

From time to time, state involvement is seen directly in regional aid policy; in subsidizing coal production; in promoting certain high-tech sectors; and, in occasionally providing adjustment assistance, for example, in 1974 in the case of Volkswagen. In the case of company failures, the state would not provide assistance, although the private banking system may do so (i.e., competition policy which has evolved alongside some developmental elements).

From the mid-1970s and onward, one of the serious weaknesses of German regional policy has been national coordination. In 1975, further attempts were made to coordinate regional policies with those of the federal government (Mellor 1978). In the 1980s, the provinces started to place more emphasis on their own development plans whereas, at the same time, the federal government began to question the effectiveness of regional financial incentives as a means of stimulating local development, given the very rigid division of responsibilities between the different levels of government.

Furthermore, the composition of German industry has altered considerably over the past four decades. In 1984, for example, the chemical industry was the most important national industry in terms of turnover, followed by vehicle manufacturing, food production/processing, heavy engineering, electrical engineering, and oil refining (Statistisches Bundesamt 1985). Iron and steel remain among the cornerstones of the economy.

In the 1980s, all the major sectors of manufacturing industry went through a process of reorganization and rationalization, which may have produced only some short-term efficiency improvements in some areas, and one of the main results has been a reduction in the need for manpower. Although some other sectors, notably services, are expanding, they are not growing fast enough to compensate and unemployment has been a serious problem (Riquet 1976a, b; Blacksell 1987: 245-46).

In contrast, the Developmental State analysis suggests the widespread and intensive use of government policy to purposefully guide the market economy. There is public/private cooperation in which the state independently develops national goals. German economic policies have focused largely on the market mechanism. The Developmental State analysis supports the view that the state can play a positive enabling role in the economy and, thus, there is a degree of complementarity between the market system and an active government (i.e. the manipulation of the market).

The potential partnership between government and private firms implies that the state adopts a principal role and is, thereby, able to create opportunities that would not otherwise exist. German state policies are seen to be "market-conforming" rather than "market-augmenting," to use Amsden's phrases.

A serious problem for German government policy-making has been the insufficient and inefficient coordination between the federal government and local governments as well as the adoption of short-term perspectives in decision-making.[2] This fact effectively precludes discussions of the range of government policies which may prove useful in the encouragement of industrial strategies.

The Developmental State view places great emphasis on strategic planning. This planning, which is different from intervention, involves "conscious attempts by the government of a country—usually with the participation of other collective bodies—to coordinate public policies more rationally in order to reach more fully and rapidly the desirable ends for future development which are determined by the political process as it evolves" (Myrdal 1960: 15).

Further, sufficient empirical evidence has emerged to show that, probably, the main factor in determining the distribution of new high technology industrial activities among nations is the location of investment expenditure in knowledge, R&D, and technological innovation rather than economic incentives (Giese and Nipper 1984; Amsden 1989; DeLong and Summers 1991; Archibugi 1993; Amable 1992; Amable and Petit 1996; Munnell 1992; Dowrick 1993; Boyer and Caroli 1995).

However, cuts in public spending on education, technological improvement, research, etcetera, during the last two decades or so (in the name of fiscal prudence) can harm the long-term growth prospects of the German economy. Besides, concepts such as state investment planning, comprehensive government policies, long-term economic and, especially, industrial strategies, etcetera, have not been taken into account sufficiently by German policymakers.

In sum, Germany could be considered to be following standard economic policies and reducing the functions of the government to those of regulation and restriction. German economic policies seem to be losing momentum and effectiveness (e.g., economic and social problems, regional inequalities, "Eurosclerosis"). However, the Developmental State—New Competition line of argument recommends a comprehensive and supportive role for the state that is different from standard policy making.

French Regional and Industrial Policies

In France, a series of national plans, as well as other measures, were often used to foster economic development. The French plans were significant, not because they really plan the French economy but because they create close links between industry and the public sector. Besides, French governments have been extensively involved in many sectors like telecommunications, electronics, gas, coal, oil refining, transport, steel, motor cars, chemicals, computers, nuclear energy, and insurance, and have often adopted growth pole developmentalist policies in order to counterbalance the dominance of Paris.

The growth pole policies were strengthened in varying degrees during the 1960s and 1970s, partly in response to policies for moving selected industrial plants and relocating manufacturing and tertiary jobs. But all the growth poles remained strongly subordinate to Paris and only few attracted really significant decision-making functions (Clout 1987: 179). A limited number of key factories had been moved from Paris to the provinces (see table 6.11 in the appendix).

During the 1960s, grants were made widely available and aid was extended to areas of underemployment in the countryside as well as to old manufacturing areas, while the relocation of employment in offices, higher education and research activities had to be included in schemes for regional development if these were to keep in line with major trends in French economic life.

In the 1970s, financial aid for tertiary development was extended to all areas that qualified for industrial grants, to the growth poles and many other provincial cities. The state entered into new agreements with banking and insurance firms for further relocation schemes and incentives, and continued to talk about the desirability of transferring some of its administrative and research activities, and the management of the countryside.

However, many large private firms and international corporations either stayed in Paris or moved relatively close to it, while the national economy shifted from the secondary to the tertiary sector (Clout 1987: 181). Traditional sectors, such as clothing, shoes and textiles collapsed; new industries, such as steel, coal, oil refining, and car industry went into decline; jobs were lost; and, firms were particularly badly placed, poorly managed, spatially fragmented, overstaffed, financially uncompetitive and inefficient.

During the 1960-80 period, the route that was initially followed in France was the use of government investment plans. Such a national plan presented a consistent economic framework against which individual businesses could make their investment and other decisions. There was also an element of expectations becoming self-fulfilling: the expectation of fast growth became translated into a high level of investment which then enabled the growth to occur.

In general, French governments pursued economic policies of support for national champions in certain strategic, high-tech large industries. Assistance was provided for such industries on a highly selective basis, and ranged from the provision of subsidies, the use of government investment programs, protection from foreign competition, etcetera.

During the 1980s, French governments placed special emphasis on decentralization that would strengthen the rights, powers and responsibilities of local authorities and regions. Substantial industrial sections came under state control, but policymakers tried to make these industries more efficient by improving management, closing surplus capacity, and dismissing labor.

These policies also tried to cover urban and rural planning, job creation and relocation, the improvement of services, etcetera. The main grant came from the central government and was available for both manufacturing and service firms, although the spatial grading of assistance varied for the two sectors (Brunet and Sallois 1986).

Despite the operation of specific policies, Paris experienced a remarkable population growth and service employment, and most high level industrial operations remained in or near Paris (Clout 1987: 192). Faced with a growing employment crisis in the early 1980s, extra sources of public finance were also available from the government in order to improve industrial sites in special development areas and accelerate schemes for training young people and retraining a surplus labor force for employment in modern industries or the tertiary sector.

Therefore, in the French case, the government directed an inward-oriented economic growth and development policy ("domestic developmentalism" to use Dore's phrase). Indeed, government actions were taken wholly with regard to the domestic economy. However, the growing openness of national economies to international competition and the "national ability to compete on international grounds" (as the New Competition view suggests) were not taken seriously into consideration.

Another point of argument is the role and contribution of indicative plans for economic development and growth in France. These plans, although they played an important role in French economic and industrial development, do not seem to have guided the market successfully. In contrast, the Developmental State analysis supports the view that economic policies should be designed to shape the market system and influence private economic decisions in ways that the government considers to be desirable and developmental.

French governments have also placed much emphasis on various incentives and financial schemes, instead of government investments on the accelerators of growth and competency, which should be considered of primary importance for the improvement of the competitiveness of the French economy. In fact, there has been an inadequate and partial consideration of the modern factors of development and competitiveness by French governments that has arisen because of particular pressing economic and social problems, for example, training dictated by the pressure of unemployment.

The accelerators of growth and competitiveness should be considered as a thorough and necessary package of useful tools for the promotion of outward-oriented economic development, since these accelerators seem to be the main factors in determining the distribution among economies of new high technology industries. Besides, faced with growing unemployment, and the social and political pressure that this implies, strategic planning has neither been thorough nor adequate enough.

Finally, resources in the less developed locations and relatively depressed regions in France have been underutilized and the growth of resources, such as industrial infrastructure, capital equipment, etcetera, has been relatively slow. Higher level activities have gravitated to Paris (the power of attraction of the center). State investments in regions and rural areas should be designed to:

1. support and develop indigenous resources, firms and industries;
2. add to the sum total of investment capital, training, current research, technical progress, innovation and services available; and,
3. add to the opportunities for significant regional/local growth and regeneration, and social welfare.

In brief, the national champions policy implemented by French governments has reached its limit, and has neither achieved a better distribution of industry nor reduced regional disparities. However, in order for firms to grow, they must improve their "ability to compete on international grounds," thereby operating successfully outside the national territory.

Italian Regional and Industrial Policies

Regional planning and supportive state intervention within the dominantly free enterprise environment of the Western world was the main belief of regional and industrial policies in Italy after the World War II (King 1987: 129). The process of encouraging new factories to settle and expand in the South, and the influx of new industrial activities, was accompanied by a simultaneous decrease of industrial, as well as agricultural, employment and investments in other branches of industry, and continuing high levels of out-migration.

A large proportion of southern growth is the result of help from northern Italy or abroad; thus, the south's model of industrial and regional development has been dependent on the north and multinational capital (King 1987: 149; see also King 1977: 87-102). Not only has there been a highly unbalanced spatial concentration of the southern industrial development efforts, but also new employment has been highly concentrated sectorally, with 73 percent of the jobs created by 1980 accounted for by the chemical, metallurgical, and mechanical branches, mostly in large capital-intensive units.

Furthermore, there has been only a limited development of smaller and more labor-intensive enterprises in traditional industrial branches like food production/processing, wood products, and textiles (Giannola 1982: 67-92) (see also tables 6.12-6.13 in the appendix). More than half of the investment expenditure in southern industry has been accounted for by state firms since 1957 (ISTAT, various years).

During the 1970s, a redistribution of political power took place in Italy, reflecting the participation of left-wing elements in regional governments. As a result, the regions started having power in the following main areas: economic development, administrative organization, planning matters and social services (King 1987: 160).

Moreover, relations between the regions and central government have been antagonistic, with consequences for the financial independence of the regions as well as the autonomy of regional policy making. In fact, the financial and bureaucratic structures of central administration have been reproduced at the regional level (Freddi 1980: 383-98).

However, the deep crisis in its national economic planning has provided no development framework of priorities for action in the regions. Behind all else lies the objective of using development policy, which appeared to be a response to political pressure, as a means of recruiting political support for the ruling party, the Christian Democrats (Wade 1979; Allum 1980).

Italy (and especially its north-central part or "NC Italy") offers a different experience. In general, Italian industrial policy has been used as a buffer against international crises and to compensate for structural features of the domestic industrial and financial system. NC Italy, as distinct from the industrial north and the agricultural south of Italy, is based on groups of small firms (Best 1990: 87; 118). They are entrepreneurial firms that pursue a strategy of continuous innovation and flexible production methods.

Furthermore, there is a large number of cooperative institutions, mainly quasi-public development agencies, within NC Italy that serve as functional equivalents to managerial hierarchy and contribute to the development of the industrial district as a collective entrepreneur. However, although NC Italy is led by internationally competitive, independent small firms, there has been a variety of forms of cooperation between firms, and between firms and government, which appear to have been economically successful.

Interfirm cooperation and an administrative governmental structure, which actually does not base decision-making authorities on ownership, are very important. Cooperation in the provision of services with substantial economies of scale has helped small firms to maintain their independence in production.

NC Italy, as well as Japan and NICs, offers an approach to the promotion of small and medium-size firms; both depend upon a combination of cooperation and competition, and this combination seeks to develop sector strategies and to promote R&D and innovation, which will encourage enterprises to learn to cooperate (specialization by activity).

In the case of Italy, the state has adopted some elements of a developmental role. The Italian policies can be placed under the term "developmentalism" (as identified by Dore 1986b). But the antagonistic relations between central administration and local governments, especially during the 1970s, have caused a deep crisis in, and lack of, national strategic planning. Consequently, the state can neither develop national goals nor provide the developmental framework for action to firms and, especially, to regions.

In contrast, the Developmental State argument suggests that both central administration and local governments have a significant and strategic role to

play, as they can enhance the operation of the market system and create opportunities which would not otherwise have existed.

There are strong forces of cumulative causation at work, both at the level of
the firm and at the level of the region. In fact, the operation of centripetal market
forces generates uneven development between the north and the south of Italy.
A Developmental State is concerned with offsetting regional disparities and the
lack of human and material resources, and can add to the opportunities for local
growth. Investments are enhanced by high levels of capacity utilization and are
preferable to financial incentives, since public investments in human resource
development and R&D can improve, renew, and increase the productive capacity and competitiveness of an economy.

Lastly, the convergence of economic and political functions in the Italian
state and the crisis in its political system have had disastrous effects in the economic sphere. The Italian government has used the state's power to promote
particular interests for both personal and electoral advantage (pork barrel policies). Compared to an autonomous, strong Developmental State, the Italian state
systematically underprovides economically desirable policy actions, and systematically overprovides politically motivated and economically harmful interventions.

In sum, pork barrel intervention in Italy has been subjected to a number of
conflicting forces with deleterious effects on the country's comprehensive economic policies (i.e., multiple consequences on regional/local growth and regeneration, industrial performance, and competitiveness).

Greek Regional and Industrial Policies

Greek regional and industrial policies have adopted largely empirical and local
attitudes to national development. Regional development has emphasized the
improvement of transport and communication networks, power and water supplies, educational and banking facilities, workers' housing, and where appropriate, the installation of industrial zones.

In addition, development towns or growth centers have been favored for the
provision of health, social, and cultural facilities for the surrounding population.
The main idea behind each of these proposals has been to build up provincial
equipment and infrastructures in order to discourage out-migration to greater
Athens or abroad (see table 6.14 in the appendix).

Until 1980, Greece had pursued an active regional development policy for
over fifteen years, but none of the regional planning studies were implemented
as a legal framework for state policy making. Official regional policy was utilized to steer private investments into regional incentive schemes through grants,
low interest rates, and tax concessions and this may be interpreted as part of the
general objective of decentralizing activities from the capital.

Thus, both the character and implementation of regional policy remained
inadequate and unsuccessful. But regional planning policy still faced the dilemma of having to decide between the contrasting targets of social equity and eco-

nomic efficiency. Policies tended to gravitate one way or the other depending on particular needs and political pressures (Carter 1987: 429).

In the 1980s, the Greek government was committed to encouraging both endogenous development and industrial investment in the economy. The main aims were to accelerate decentralization, promote regional economic and social development, and encourage greater coordination in government administration. This emphasis was reflected in laws, passed during 1982-83, in which assistance was allocated according to a multicriteria procedure.

These laws not only embraced regional but also technological and other important factors for financing technical centers, and industrial and agricultural cooperatives. Considerable investment spending was given to projects that made use of new technology and which were geared to applied research and increased production (Carter 1987: 430).

Government grants ranged from 10 to 50 percent of a project's cost, depending on its location as well as a combination of predetermined commercial and socioeconomic criteria. For the purpose of investment policy, the country was divided into four zones (no grants were available in zone A; zones B, C, and D—the undeveloped frontier area—received grants ranging from 10 to 25 percent, 15 to 40 percent, and 20 to 50 percent of project investment costs respectively).

Moreover, the government set in motion a large decentralization program with reforms requiring considerable consultation between interested social segments and/or parties, in order to encourage greater regional/local autonomy with respect to administration and economic affairs, and central government representatives no longer had a casting vote in municipal affairs. Thus, only in the 1980s can Greece be considered as being in favor of developmentalist (comprehensive) regional and industrial policies.[3]

In the Greek case, the policies pursued have been a varying mixture of the four types of policies identified by Dore (1986b). Greek governments have used state power in order to promote particular interests for personal and electoral advantage. In fact, pork barrel policy nurtures the proliferation of special interest groups, whose various rent seeking activities seriously impede state capacity for effective intervention.

In complete contrast, Developmental State strategies and policies are neither responsive nor reducible to various political pressures, private interests, and rent seeking. In fact, the Developmental State has relative autonomy from dominant classes, interest groups, private interests, and political pressures so that it can direct an outward-oriented developmentalist strategy.

Until 1981, economic policy making focused on the market system and the rhetoric of business that invoked perfect competition as bringing benefits for the economy, particularly consumers. These policies suggest state intervention of a regulatory kind. The Developmental State approach, in contrast, suggests a developmental role for the state and complementarity between market and plan.

Greek economic policies do not seem to have addressed adequately and successfully problems like the adoption of short-term perspectives in decision-making, a lack of interfirm cooperation, technical inefficiencies, and failures to develop and promote new products and processes. The idea of interfirm cooperation and coordination seeks to develop sector strategies and to promote R&D and innovation, which encourage firms to learn to cooperate.

Greek governments have tended to place little emphasis on government investments on the accelerators of industrial competency and too much emphasis on financial incentives. Human capital formation is inadequate as there is a serious lack of R&D, innovation, on-the-job, and institutional training and retraining, etcetera. Particular emphasis needs to be placed on investment spending on the accelerators of development and growth, rather than on incentives and financial schemes, which will substantially improve production capability and competitiveness.

Resources in the less developed locations and relatively depressed regions in Greece are underutilized and the growth of resources, especially, capital equipment, machinery and new technology, has been slow. Various higher level activities have been seen to gravitate to Athens. Strategic planning combined with investment injections in regions and rural areas should be designed to provide all the essential requirements for a thorough supply-side strategy, which is seen to be necessary to solve the deeper structural problems of the Greek economy.

In short, pork barrel intervention has had harmful effects on Greek economic policies. Traditional policy making has neither been able to achieve substantial regional/local growth and industrial regeneration nor a significant improvement in competitiveness.

A CONTEMPORARY EVALUATION

During the last two decades, the real economic problem facing the EC/EU area has been slow growth and insufficient productive activity–due to a lack of effective demand and inadequate levels of investment spending–which lower demand further, constrain potential supply, and can destroy the desire to engage in productive activity. A review of the European economy shows that all is not well. At root, this is a failure of the orthodox development theory and policy making.

The cumulative causation principle can explain successfully the unequal or uneven regional incidence of development within the EC/EU area, and relates to the tendency for higher level economic activities and occupations to gravitate to the center, toward the success and the winners, whether firms, regions, or nations. Market forces usually produce cumulative movements away from spatial equilibrium; within the market system there are vicious and virtuous circles of cumulative causation.

Furthermore, regional problems are basically problems of spatial economic imbalance. This is, in part, a reflection of the general unattractiveness of agricultural problem regions to industrial investments and services, due to a lack of modern factors of growth and endogenous competency, an underdeveloped infrastructure, etc. Resources in the depressed areas in the EC have been underutilized and the growth of resources has been slow.

Since the 1950s, most regional and industrial policies in the EC area have been based on mainstream market failure analysis, and most state interventions have usually taken the form of ad hoc responses to pressing problems. In contrast, thorough strategic actions and longer-run structural reforms instead of short-run measures constitute fundamental characteristics of the Developmental State–New Competition analysis.

The policies pursued by European governments have not achieved a better balance in the geographical distribution of industry, nor have they reduced regional disparities. The forces of cumulative causation operate at the level of the firm and at the aggregate level of a region or nation breeding both success and failure. Yet, EC/EU governments have often put great faith in the ability of private firms to stimulate industrial growth and regeneration; however, this has not been translated into significant regional/local development, desirable industrial performance and competitiveness.

Of course, a fundamental question centers around the compatibility of the Developmental State model with political liberalization and democratic forms of governance. Another critical issue concerns the lessons to be drawn from the East Asian experience, which can subsequently be generalized to, and applied in EC/EU member countries. The available evidence clearly demonstrates that the Asian countries' success story is the product of specific historical circumstances. Consequently, there may exist significant constraints on its transferability to, or replicability in, different or alternative national contexts (Onis 1991: 120-21).

It would generally be wrong to consider that the Developmental State model could, or indeed should, be transplanted to EC/EU countries that have quite different history and culture. What is important to learn from these Far Eastern experiences is the approach to the development problems—that is, the strategic approach. The development challenge, therefore, for the EU decision and policymakers is to devise forms of industrial policy that are consistent with the norms of democratic accountability and perhaps with more limited concentration of state and private power than has been the case in the East Asian context (Onis 1991: 123).

CONCLUSION

This chapter has presented a survey of the regional and industrial policies of a number of EC countries. It is clear that these governments' ability to pursue supply-side policies has faced specific limitations (for example, on the use of government subsidies), and this implies that both demand management policies and supply-side policies are clearly necessary and needed.

Furthermore, the development of a regional and an industrial policy in the European Community has been subject to a number of conflicting forces. It was argued above that there are different traditions among the member countries, though the Treaty of Rome and the *Single European Act* tend to support more the Anglo-Saxon antitrust approach. In complete contrast, the New Competition and the Developmental State perspectives clearly suggest a more interventionist and supportive role from an industrial policy.

It also needs to be mentioned that a description of the policy objectives of a single state at a given moment of time would be difficult enough; instead, long-term development plans are needed. Although the European Community/Union is essentially an economic community, its political dimension must also be taken into account as, in many cases, the underlying political aims are opposed to the explicit economic goals.

Lastly, social, political and cultural factors and linkages, as well as the capacity of local, regional and other economic and social organizations and institutions to handle their responsibilities should be taken into consideration. In the long run, political will should not be an obstacle for each individual EC/EU country nor for the European Union as a whole.

NOTES

1. See: Office of the Minister for Science, *Report of the Committee on the Management and Control of Research and Development* [Zuckerman Report], London: HMSO (1961) and CSO, *Research and Development Expenditure,* London: HMSO (1973); Department of Trade and Industry, *The Machine Tool Industry. Report of the Machine Tool Expert Committee* (p. 76), London: HMSO (1971); Department of Industry, *Survey of the United Kingdom Aerospace Industry,* London: HMSO (1975); Shipbuilding Industry Board, *Shipbuilding Industry Board 1967-1971,* London (1971), and Department of Trade and Industry, *British Shipbuilding 1972,* London: HMSO (1973); and Department of Trade and Industry, *Industrial and Regional Development* (Cmnd. 4942), London: HMSO (1972); Treasury, *An Approach to Industrial Strategy* (Cmnd. 6315), London: HMSO (1975); Department of Industry, *Industry Act 1972: Annual Report for the Year Ending March 31* (especially paragraph 26 and Appendix A: "Criteria for Assistance to Industry"), London: HMSO (1976).

2. Of course, regional policy in Germany needs to seriously consider the special problems caused by the incorporation of East Germany in the German economy, which are special challenges for the Developmental State.

3. Recently, since the mid-1990s, the Greek government pursues Developmental State type policies: large-scale investments on infrastructure and the modern factors of development and competitiveness, technically proficient planning, and comprehensive regional and industrial strategies.

APPENDIX

TABLE 6.2
GDP per Head (factor cost: current prices)

Region	1966	1970	1980	1990	1993
United Kingdom	100.0	100.0	100.0	100.0	100.0
North	84.0	84.8	92.2	88.1	89.4
Yorkrshire/	96.4	94.2	92.9	90.8	91.2
Humberside					
East Midlands	98.4	96.4	97.0	95.9	95.8
East Anglia	95.6	96.0	96.1	101.3	101.7
South East	114.4	115.6	116.5	118.5	116.0
South West	93.2	93.5	92.7	94.6	96.6
West Midlands	108.1	104.3	93.0	92.8	93.1
North West	96.1	94.5	96.1	90.5	90.8
England	103.4	102.9	102.3	102.2	101.7
Wales	85.7	86.1	84.0	84.6	84.7
Scotland	88.9	91.1	94.2	92.6	98.4
Northern Ireland	62.5	68.7	77.9	75.4	81.9

Source: CSO, Abstract of Regional Statistics (1974); Regional Trends (1981, 1990, and 1996).

TABLE 6.3
UK Unemployment Rates (percent)

Region	1966	1970	1979	1990	1994
United Kingdom	1.5	2.6	5.8	6.8	9.5
North	2.5	4.7	8.6	10.3	11.7
Yorkshire/	1.1	2.9	5.7	7.4	9.8
Humberside					
East Midlands	1.0	2.2	4.7	6.6	8.3
East Anglia	1.4	2.1	4.5	4.8	7.4
South East	0.9	1.6	3.7	5.2	9.6
South West	1.7	2.8	5.7	5.0	7.5
West Midlands	0.8	2.0	5.5	6.7	9.9
North West	1.4	2.7	7.1	7.9	10.2
England	1.2	2.3	5.2	6.3	9.5
Wales	2.8	3.9	8.0	8.1	9.4
Scotland	2.7	4.2	8.0	9.3	9.9
Northern Ireland	5.9	6.9	11.3	11.6	11.5

Source: CSO, Abstract of Regional Statistics (1974); Regional Trends (1981, 1990, and 1996).

TABLE 6.4
UK: Shares of Investment in the Manufacturing Industry (percent)

Year	North England	Scotland and Wales
1971	39.6	17.9
1975	37.9	19.5
1979	34.3	16.1
1982	28.9	16.6

Source: CSO, Abstract of Regional Statistics (1974); Regional Trends (1981 and 1984).

TABLE 6.5
UK: Shares of Investment in Housing and Community
Development (percent)

Year	North England	Scotland and Wales
1971	25.2	17.5
1975	21.2	17.8
1979	24.6	18.4
1982	22.6	26.4

Source: CSO, Abstract of Regional Statistics (1974); Regional Trends (1981 and 1984).

TABLE 6.6
UK: Shares of Investment in Human Capital (percent)

Year	North England	Scotland and Wales
1971	26.1	15.4
1975	26.6	16.7
1979	28.4	16.8
1982	29.9	17.9

Source: CSO, Abstract of Regional Statistics (1974); Regional Trends (1981 and 1984).

TABLE 6.7
UK: Shares of Investment in Economic Services (percent)

Year	North England	Scotland and Wales
1971	28.5	19.7
1975	22.9	22.6
1979	19.1	32.5
1982	20.0	24.5

Source: CSO, Abstract of Regional Statistics (1974); Regional Trends (1981 and 1984).

TABLE 6.8
West Germany: Manufacturing Industry (Leading Sectors, 1984)

	Turnover (Million)	Employees (000)	Firms
Chemical Industry	170368	568	1156
Vehicles	163053	793	1798
Food Processing	153255	453	3862
Heavy Engineering	141821	927	4545
Electrical Engineering	136742	932	2299
Oil Refining	110437	36	50
Iron & Steel	51679	234	101
Textiles	34529	236	1419
Plastics	32133	191	1659

Source: Statistisches Bundesamt Statistisches Jahrbuch 1985 fur die Bundersrpublik Deutschland, W. Kohlhammer, Stuttgart and Mainz (1985).

TABLE 6.9
West Germany: Employment in the Major Economic Sectors by Land (percent)

	Population	Agriculture & Forestry	Manufac-ture	Transport & Com/ation	Other Services
Schleswig-Holstein	4.2	5.2	3.1	5.2	5.2
Hamburg	2.6	—	1.7	4.4	3.4
Niedersachsen	11.8	15.4	10.3	11.8	11.5
Bremen	1.1	—	0.7	0.1	1.2
Nordrhein-Westfalen	27.4	13.3	27.3	25.9	24.7
Hessen	9.1	6.0	8.5	10.0	10.1
Rheinland-Pfalz	5.9	6.3	5.8	5.6	5.9
Baden-Wurttemberg	15.1	17.2	18.9	13.6	14.4
Bayern	17.9	35.3	19.8	17.3	17.9
Saarland	1.7	—	1.6	1.5	1.5
West Berlin	3.0	0.4	2.2	3.3	4.2

Source: Statistisches Bundesamt Statistisches Jahrbuch 1985 fur die Bundersrepublik Deutschland, W. Kohlhammer, Stuttgart and Mainz (1985).

TABLE 6.10
West Germany: Unemployment by Land, 1974 and 1984 (percent)

	1974	1984
Schleswig-Holstein	3.2	10.7
Hamburg	1.7	11.2
Niedersachsen	3.2	11.9
Bremen	2.6	13.8
Nordrhein-Westfalen	2.9	10.7
Hessen	2.4	7.4
Rheinland-Pfalz	2.8	8.3
Baden-Wurttemberg	1.4	5.6
Bayern	2.7	7.8
Saarland	3.9	12.7
West Berlin	2.0	10.2
Federal average	2.6	9.1

Source: Statistisches Bundesamt Statistisches Jahrbuch 1985 fur die Bundersrepublik Deutschland, W. Kohlhammer, Stuttgart and Mainz (1985).

TABLE 6.11
France: Employment in Manufacturing, 1954-1975 (by Region)

	Percentage in Manufacturing Employment (1975)	Percentage Change in Manufacturing 1954-75
Alsace	36.4	+21.1
Aquitaine	22.4	+7.6
Auvergne	30.2	+21.7
Bourgogne	32.7	+45.2
Bretagne	18.5	+39.3
Centre	32.9	+65.6
Champagne	30.9	+5.4
Franche-Comte	38.3	+16.3
Languedoc	15.3	-10.1
Limousin	20.5	+1.9
Lorraine	38.4	+1.9
Midi-Pyrenees	22.8	+20.4
Nord	38.3	-19.0
Normandie (Basse)	26.9	+91.1
Normandie (Haute)	36.6	+49.2
Pays de la Loire	28.9	+99.8
Picardie	39.2	+27.5
Poitou-Charentes	20.5	+17.6
Provence	19.0	+16.0
Rhone-Alpes	35.4	+10.9
Region Parisienne	28.7	-0.5

Source: R. Brunet and J Sallois, *France: Les Dynamiques du Territoire* (Montpellier: GIP RECLUS, 1986).

TABLE 6.12
Italy: Sectoral Distribution of the Working Population, 1951-1981 (percent)

		1951	1961	1971	1981
Italy:	Agriculture	42.2	29.3	17.6	11.2
	Industry	32.0	40.7	44.7	39.8
	Service Sector	25.8	30.0	37.9	49.0
North-West:	Agriculture	24.0	14.9	7.8	5.4
	Industry	48.1	54.5	56.1	48.6
	Service Sector	27.9	30.6	36.1	46.0
North-East:	Agriculture	44.5	28.0	16.2	8.4
	Industry	30.1	40.4	44.8	42.3
	Service Sector	25.4	31.6	39.0	49.3
Center:	Agriculture	42.5	26.9	13.5	7.8
	Industry	28.0	36.8	40.0	37.3
	Service sector	29.5	36.3	46.5	59.9
South:	Agriculture	55.3	43.3	29.7	20.4
	Industry	22.7	30.9	34.9	30.6
	Service Sector	22.0	25.8	35.4	49.0

Sources: SVIMEZ, *Un Quarto di Secolo Nelle Statistiche Nord-Sud 1951-76* (Milan
and Rome: Giuffre, 1978); *12o Censimento Generale della Popolazione 1981* (Rome:
ISTAT Dati Provvisori, 1983); and *6o Censimento Generale dell' Industria e del
Commercio 1981* (Rome: ISTAT Dati Provvisori, 1983).

TABLE 6.13
Italy: Industrial Workers (Manufacturing Only), 1951-1981 (percent)

	1951	1961	1971	1981
Italy	100.0	100.0	100.0	100.0
North-West	52.9	51.4	48.1	43.2
North-East	17.5	19.9	21.9	23.9
Center	13.8	15.0	16.5	18.2
South	15.8	13.7	13.5	14.7

Sources: SVIMEZ, *Un Quarto di Secolo Nelle Statistiche Nord-Sud 1951-76* (Milan and
Rome: Giuffre, 1978); *12o Censimento Generale della Popolazione 1981* (Rome: ISTAT
Dati Provvisori, 1983); and *6o Censimento Generale dell' Industria e del Commercio
1981* (Rome: ISTAT Dati Provvisori, 1983).

TABLE 6.14
Aspects of Employment in Greece, 1982 (percent by Region)

	Registered for Employment	Found Employment	Unemployed
Greater Athens	29.6	38.8	29.7
Central Greece & Euboea	5.5	7.6	4.7
Peloponnisos	5.2	6.8	4.1
Ionian Islands	3.5	1.8	4.8
Epirus	2.9	1.1	3.0
Thessalia	6.3	4.7	5.7
Macedonia	32.2	30.1	34.5
Thrace	4.6	2.4	3.8
Aegean Islands	4.5	2.7	5.5
Crete	5.7	4.0	4.2

Source: Statistical Yearbook of Greece 1983, Athens (1984).

Chapter 7

Developmental State and the Caribbean

INTRODUCTION

Historically, the islands in the Caribbean have had long political and economic associations with developed western countries as protectorates, departments and colonies. In the most general sense, the model of development throughout the region is one of peripheral capitalism and external dependence. In fact, the Caribbean case of underdevelopment has been conditioned by the development and expansion of the western dominant countries through the mechanisms of the international market.

Political independence established national sovereignty in older and newer Caribbean nations when both groups were integrated into the international system. Consequently, the political process of national independence converted states, societies and nations that had evolved as integral parts of the international system of empire into nation-states. The effect was to legitimize their autonomy based on concepts of self-determination rooted in western culture. In the case of the newer Caribbean nations, national independence coincided with the postwar intensification of the internationalization of capital, labor, production, class relations, and the state and nation-state.

However, the political independence of Caribbean nations has not been accompanied by any significant advances in their national economies: foreign ownership, management and control of production; reliance on high levels of imports; dependence on metropolises' preferences for local services and exports; and a dependent monetary system and absence of developed capital markets are among the outstanding features of Caribbean economies. These Caribbean nations rely on other countries for transfers of income and capital, for banking and financial services, for business and technical skills, and even for ideas about themselves.

The foreign trade sector is one of the spheres in which the dependence of the Caribbean is most apparent. Largely, foreign decisions determine the growth of Caribbean economies while most Caribbean own resources, natural, human and technological, remain basically underdeveloped.

Yet, the globalization of modern technology production is revolutionizing the environment and conditions of international competition, and demands a rethinking of traditional concepts of hegemony, national economic space and production, and the basic attributes of the nation-state, among other issues. Inadequate productive resources and skills, compounded by the size of scale on which Caribbean economies operate and their excessive dependence on western capitalist economies have convinced many that self-propelled development is not a feasible and realistic strategy.

Chapter 7 introduces the Developmental State approach for the Caribbean region. The first section of this chapter provides a brief discussion of the East Asian development experience. The following section identifies and highlights various development-related economic problems in the Caribbean. The last part of the chapter concentrates on an alternative development paradigm as well as on general implications and policy considerations for Caribbean nations which the Developmental State and New Competition views imply and suggest.

THE EAST ASIAN DEVELOPMENT EXPERIENCE

The high-performing Asian economies offer a new and quite different approach to the promotion of industrial development. The remarkable record of high and sustained rates of economic growth of these countries is well known, even though they have experienced difficulties in the last years. These Far Eastern experiences and the interpretations of them have played an important role for theory construction concerning the role of the state as well as development policy recommendations. In view of the above development experience, therefore, it is important to draw the right lessons for the Caribbean region.

Some stress the Asian countries' success in getting the basics right and see the free flow of the market as the principal general force for the economic growth of these countries. As a consequence, resources flowed to their most efficient uses and the limitations of small domestic markets were overcome by exporting manufactured goods at competitive prices. They also assert that the NICs' states have refrained from interfering with price formation, foreign trade, and the economic functioning of private firms. Other interpreters support the view that state intervention was an important factor but only insofar as it offset market failures, provided a stable macroeconomic environment and a reliable legal framework, and incentives for export-oriented industrial development. Thus, according to the "market-supremacy" views:

- Let markets work unless it is demonstrably better to step in. It is usually a mistake for the state to carry out physical production, or to protect the domestic production of a good that can be imported more cheaply and whose local production offers few spillover benefits.
- Put state interventions continually to the discipline of international and domestic markets.
- Make interventions simple, transparent and subject to rules rather than official discretion (Singh 1998: 61).

Moreover, the recent development of the "new institutional" economics has largely focused on constitutional order, normative behavioral codes, and institutional arrangements, and has retained the view of an optimal set of these arrangements on the basis of efficiency considerations. All of the above theoretical issues have been the recent policy gospel for developing and less developed countries, which are recommended to seek their comparative advantage, to get the prices right, and to have free markets as far as possible.

The unorthodox line of argument holds that the states of the NICs have intervened to such an extent that they have governed the markets in critical ways and consciously promoted selective sector development. The prioritized sectors and industries have received both administrative and technical support from the state. In the case of Japan, for example, the role of the state in promoting dynamic industries and bringing about the structural transformation of the Japanese economy has been so crucial that, as Nino (1973: 10) remarked, "whereas the United States is said to be a country of the military industrial complex . . . in this sense, Japan may be called a country of the *government industrial complex*" (emphasis added). In a similar vein, Caves and Uekusa on the operations of the Japanese industrial policy pointed out:

> The Ministry [of International Trade and Industry (MITI)], in addition to its various statutory means of dealing with the economic sector, holds a general implied administrative responsibility and authority that goes well beyond what is customary in the United States and other Western Countries. . . . The industrial bureaus of MITI proliferate sectoral targets and plans; they confer, they tinker, they exhort. This is the economics by admonition to a degree inconceivable in Washington or London. (1976: 149)

The governments of these countries followed thorough industrial strategies and a highly proactive intervention: entry restrictions; investment planning; capacity regulations; production regulations; human capital formation and skills; price control, reporting and inspection; active state technology policy and R&D support (subsidies to R&D, joint R&D projects); financial support (subsidies, tax-reduction or exemption); administrative assistance and guidance (Chang 1994: 115-16).

Moreover, Japan and other East Asian countries (e.g., South Korea and Taiwan) integrated with the world economy in the directions and extent to which it was useful for them to do so (i.e., "managed" or "strategic" integration). Given that a number of factors affect the desirable nature of openness (including the world configuration, the past history of the economy and its state of development, among others), the choice of *strategic* rather than *close* integration with the global economy is fully compatible with the Developmental State theoretical framework (Chakravarty and Singh 1988).[1]

Therefore, the high performing Far Eastern economies do not seem to have followed the market-supremacy approach to development. The experience of these countries is certainly an argument against the hands-off market-friendly approach as enunciated by neoclassical and neoliberal scientists. On the other hand, it does not provide any support for a Soviet-type command planning of production.

In all these cases, subject to certain modifications, the governments followed a set of targeted economic policies, pursued planned aggressive strategies to deliberately change their unsatisfactory economic situation, and used a wide variety of instruments to bring about the structural transformation and endogenous development and growth of these economies.

The government played a proactive role with an active state knowledge-based technology policy that had substantial, long-term, productive effects on the national development of these economies as a whole. Hence, their development experience is certainly an argument against laissez-faire; it is unequivocally an argument for adopting thorough endogenous strategies, for shaping the industrial landscape and purposefully guiding the market system.

THE CARIBBEAN ECONOMIC DEVELOPMENT

General Notions

Small size with insular configurations, passive incorporation into the western system of production and trade, a fairly narrow range of economic activities from which income and wealth are generated, and a peculiar plantation and demographic history impart distinctive features to the functioning of Caribbean economies. These economies can be considered to be structurally dependent, as there is a great divergence between the type of goods supplied and the pattern of domestic demand.

Due to the extreme openness of the Caribbean economies, these countries have a high preponderance of imports vis-à-vis exports. In fact, exporting is concentrated on a few primary products, is dependent on one or two dominant metropolitan markets, and is aggravated by foreign ownership—which, in turn, makes for very little independence in decision making. Yet, many economic decisions regarding trade and aid are made outside of the Caribbean (Jones-Hendrickson 1985: 2).

In general, the international process has been quite episodic providing gains and losses to Caribbean countries over the last three decades. Some countries have moved forward while others have stagnated or retrogressed. Some sectors have registered strong and positive growth while others have declined. Among the population, prosperity coexists with squalor and deprivation.

In a real sense, Caribbean countries are still grappling with the dilemmas of the 1950s, identified clearly in Lewis' view—dualism, unemployment, inequality, low productivity, low rates of domestic savings and productive investments, and weak entrepreneurship. Added to these are the pressing challenges of the new millenium—sweeping technical changes, the astonishing pace of technological innovation, the long and heavy hands of the multilateral institutions, declining concessionary flows, liberalization alongside protectionism, unsympathetic economic blocs, the apparent shift of economic power from the Atlantic to the Pacific, and the threat of environmental retribution (Lalta and Freckleton 1993: 1).

In distinct historical periods—pure plantation (1640-1838), plantation modified (1838-1938) and plantation further modified (1938 to the present)—there were differences in the nature of the plantation system, the staple and the character of the society. Nevertheless, it is argued that an underlying historical uniformity has characterized the Caribbean area. Although there are differences between Caribbean countries, there is also a fundamental similarity in the way their economies function.

Best (1968) and Beckford (1972) attribute this underlying similarity to the legacy of the main institutions bequeathed by plantation organization and the nature of the economic, social, and political organization that it engenders, among others: a bias toward raw materials production, external control over the direction of trade, a monetary system backed by foreign exchange, and allegiance to established trade blocks (Lalta and Freckleton 1993: 13).[2]

In particular, Caribbean countries have tended to have financial systems characterized by branch banks from North American and European institutions rather than indigenous financial intermediaries. Four important implications stand out in this regard. First, the financial flows across the foreign exchanges have increased dramatically in size, making government control of the level of the exchange rate very difficult.

Second, the process of globalization has continued apace; this is reflected not only in the increased financial flows across the foreign exchanges and higher levels of foreign direct investment, but also in the degree of integration between financial markets in different countries and in the organization of production on a transnational basis.[3]

Third, the North American and European institutions prefer funding short-term consumer credit rather than longer-term productive credit. Lastly, the repatriation of profits results in the loss of funds for reinvestment within the Caribbean region in the future.[4]

The Present Context

Recently, there has been much talk of the poor endogenous development and industrial competency of Caribbean nations, although an increasing number of commentators now seem to be becoming increasingly nervous about this, with the trade account of the balance of payments of Caribbean islands in substantial deficit—due to the low levels of exports and high levels of imports—and the slowdown in economic activity causing concern. The central element of these discussions to which people refer (especially in Jamaica) is the continuous increase in the total national debt, and the questions that arise are, what are the sources of this economic performance, and can it be sustained under existing policies?

In the Caribbean, it can be argued that monetary and fiscal policies during the last years attempt to provide an environment conducive to attracting foreign investments while holding down real wages, and supporting the growth of a dual economy. Yet, economic growth has been uneven and relatively weak even though the slowdown in economic activity has not been uniform across all the Caribbean countries. We cannot expect a better performance in the near future under present policies because the real base of economic dynamism has been neglected; indeed that very neglect will undoubtedly hold back the growth of Caribbean economies.

It is clear that, in today's circumstances, neoliberal economic policies cause substantial balance of payments and other economic and social problems. The fundamentals of Caribbean economies are not right, and their much vaunted western-style modernization and laissez-faire antidote are increasingly seen to be an illusion.

In most of the Caribbean economies, the primary sector is struggling to maintain output and, at the same time, in common with worldwide trends, is tending to become less labor intensive. In fact, there has been a significant decline in the proportionate importance of local primary production during the past two decades or so. The declining share of primary production in GDP for most Caribbean islands may reflect the reduced dependence on agriculture. However, most countries in the region are net food importers, and only few Caribbean countries have achieved some success in transforming their economy from a primary production to a service and/or industry-led economy.

The ups and downs in the performance of both the agricultural and agro-industrial sectors during the 1990s were due, in large measure, to the problems experienced in the main export sectors and the general stagnation in the other economic subsectors among and within Caribbean countries. For those local economies reporting favorable, albeit low average growth rates, this may be attributed to improved production techniques in the major export sectors and relatively good performance in domestic food production.[5]

In addition, the manufacturing sector within the Caribbean has had very mixed fortunes during the 1970s, 1980s, and 1990s. Many of the manufacturing units in the region are little more than enclave operations of larger extra-regional firms. As such they tend to transfer only limited skills to the region and are always vulnerable to recession.

Subsidiary manufacturing units are always easier to close down than those closer to the home base of the company concerned, and history has shown that the Caribbean is vulnerable to just this sort of action. Besides, there is a widening gap between these firms (mainly transnational corporations), which typically reside in the Caribbean region and are integrating at a faster pace with the global economy, and other companies in the slower integrating Caribbean countries.

In the past, the agricultural and industrial sectors were seen as not providing sufficient employment opportunities. This is in part a reflection of the general unattractiveness of agricultural problem islands to industrial investment due to factors such as size, scale, a lack of skills, an underdeveloped infrastructure, etc. Additionally, there are few and/or weak development-promoting links between economic sectors (for example, between agriculture and industry). Resources in Caribbean economies have been underutilized and the growth of resources has been very slow. This situation is exacerbated by a range of constraining factors which may be summarized as follows (IICA 1998: 25-27): [6]

Inappropriate Policy Environment
- low overall national capabilities in planning, evaluation and execution of agricultural, industrial and trade policies;
- weak mechanisms to encourage and strengthen linkages between agriculture and manufacturing and tourism sectors;
- lack of a coherent regional development planning system.

Weak Institutional Framework
Various institutional deficiencies are manifest by the poor service, inadequate infrastructure and transportation facilities (and the maintenance of them), and weak structural support to agriculture and manufacturing industry—problems common to Caribbean countries.

Declining Productivity and Competitiveness
- a wide variation and fragility of the natural resource base, socio-economic infrastructure and level of development among Caribbean countries which may affect the efficiency of many firms and industries;
- low levels of human capital and skills, low rate of technological adaptation, underutilization and/or deterioration in capital stock, and underutilization of improved or new technologies resulting in low and highly variable output volumes and poor production and operations quality;
- high reliance on imported inputs (that is evidenced by the increasing trend in agro-chemical, machinery and equipment imports into the Caribbean region) and improper application and utilization of them;
- lack of productivity-enhancing production methods and techniques, limited national research capabilities, low levels of expenditure (both government and private, domestic and foreign) in R&D and inadequate marketing, infrastructure and transportation facilities (including appropriate packaging, grading, storing and transportation, processing facilities, marketing and advertising, maintenance of market shares, diversification of exports, and aggressive penetration of new markets).

Against this background, statistics show that tourism is the only sector of regional GDP that has consistently increased its share of total income during the last two decades. Indeed, allowing for some fluctuations, the tourism industry has been the only major sector that has grown steadily in importance during the 1980s and 1990s in the Caribbean. Additionally, the sector has given Caribbean countries employment to a sizable proportion of their population.

However, tourism has further subjected Caribbean economies to outside dependence, making them highly vulnerable. The result of this dependence makes the Caribbean more susceptible to external shocks and more dependent on foreign exchange. This dependence exacerbates the region's instability in national income levels and employment. Besides, the growth of tourism and other services has had negligible effects on the development of local manufacturing industry. As a consequence, there are few linkages between the sectors of Caribbean economies and a serious lack of diversification in production (Higgins 1994: 5).

TOWARD A NEW DEVELOPMENT PARADIGM

Economic growth requires a higher utilization of present productive capacities. Prospects for future local growth in the Caribbean region have been lowered significantly because of the underutilization and foreign exploitation of existing resources, and the difficulties Caribbean economies have repeatedly faced with their balance of payments. The underutilization of part of their capacity is proof of this considerable growth potential.

Thus, a first requirement of any growth strategy is that aggregate demand is sufficient enough to stimulate production up to the adequate rate of capacity utilization. At the same time, local production growth of Caribbean islands must go hand in hand with special consideration of their external trade. In connection with this, the competitiveness of Caribbean economies must come to the fore.

In order to expand industrial production and employment in the Caribbean, firms must have the financial means to invest in the necessary machinery, capital equipment and all the modern factors of competitiveness, and short run bottlenecks preventing a fuller utilization of capacities have to be taken care of. Hence, a second requirement of an alternative development policy framework is the implementation of short run selective fiscal and monetary policies. Equally important, selective economic policies should also provide the resources and stimuli to carry out the investment spending in both working and fixed capital, infrastructure, and the modern factors necessary to raise output and to improve the production and commercial conditions of firms at national and regional/local levels (Cowling 1990: 24).

Monetary policy ought to provide a stable financial framework for the successful implementation of government policy and ensure that sufficient financial resources are channeled to industries and to intermediary agencies at reasonable interest rates. Therefore, appropriate monetary and exchange rate policies to facilitate private investments as well as higher levels of national savings to finance higher levels of productive spending are absolutely essential.

This will require significant government intervention in the capital markets by means of both direct control measures and interest rate policies. In particular, the government will have to issue direct instructions to the banks, close off the options available for rent seeking and capital flight, and guide prioritized investments by selective credit policies (e.g., policy loans carrying favorable interest rates and promoting longer time horizons).

Active fiscal policy, on the other hand, ought to carry out the investments necessary to improve the supply conditions of firms and to support the other expenditures associated with the selective policy. This may result in a budget deficit; however, a deficit may not entail additional inflationary pressures or a larger trade imbalance if it allows firms' supply conditions to improve.[7] In addition, it should be considered that the increase in output would translate into higher profits and savings (Lopez 1998: 12).[8]

Moreover, bottlenecks at the firm or macro level usually hamper a more efficient resource utilization. These bottlenecks have to be seriously considered, and accordingly, a medium and long-run development strategy should have as a basic requirement a close link with a thorough industrial strategy. Such a planned Developmental State action must select and give priority to investments in new and technically promising activities, to particular branches or sectors.

What has been asserted should not be taken to imply a rejection of the problems that could arise with the proposed Developmental State strategy. But to face them, a sound economic approach ought to complement short-run measures with a thorough, technically proficient plan for the future (which of course includes a long-term industrial or structural change strategy). Such a plan is designed to consolidate and improve existing production while reorienting the economy toward new types of economic activities for both the national and global markets (Bernal 2000: 107).

Greater levels of local production, employment and profits that would be achieved in the short-term owing to the fuller use of available resources, would actually ease or encourage a transition to a more structurally efficient economy. Part of this increased production and income in the Caribbean region would go to higher spending on accelerators and lead to faster development of skills of the labor force. Not only higher profits would allow additional investments but also a greater proportion of income growth will be channeled toward planned investment. Thus, in the future, it would be relatively easier to incorporate more modern technology and increase productivity, while at the same time raising accumulation rates (Lopez 1998: 18-19).

The proposed Developmental State framework would tend to correct the Caribbean recurrent tendency toward external disequilibrium and excessive dependence on foreign economic activity. Additionally, given the recovery of production of Caribbean firms and the improvement of competitiveness, a large part of the additional goods produced will be devoted to exports. Consequently, Caribbean countries would make a greater and better use of their productive resources and capacity, while at the same time easing the constraints on their balance of payments.

This alternative policy framework seems a quite sensible and realistic way to confront the future. Devising the necessary measures to stimulate endogenous growth and industrial regeneration, while giving priority to investment planning necessary to allow the fullest and most efficient utilization of existing resources in the region, seems to be a better option for the growth of Caribbean economies than a frantic search for accelerated western-style modernization and laissez-faire antidote (Lopez 1998: 19).

Lastly, it is of course true that this Developmental State strategy, which assumes a much better state action, would require an efficient and competent administrative machine. But so does any national purpose strategy capable of overcoming barriers and laying down the basis of sustained endogenous growth in any developing economy.

DEVELOPMENT POLICY CONSIDERATIONS

Industrial policy has not been seen to be pivotal in most Caribbean economies and has not, therefore, been developed as an important and necessary part of their governments' approach to development policy making. Liberalization, privatization, and deregulation appear to have been the recent policy gospel for Caribbean countries. The remedy proposed and implemented by neoliberal policymakers has been the extension of market forces into almost every area of production (for example, deregulation of state controlled activities, privatization of public sector assets, and the entry of private enterprise into the provision of public services).

State interventions in the Caribbean have usually been of a regulatory type and the policies which flow from these interventions appear to run counter to the Developmental State approach and to be consonant with the market failure view. Most Caribbean governments have often used their power to promote particular interests, and the general concept of a developmental role for the state is rather alien to their general economic and political culture.

However, there are serious doubts about whether these neoliberal and neoclassical policies have been translated into significant industrial growth, local development, desirable economic performance and competitiveness. While appropriate fiscal, monetary, and exchange rate policies can contribute much toward enhancing the performance of the Caribbean economies, a much sharper focus on industrial strategies needs to be established. Such supply-side strategies are seen to be necessary to resolve the deeper problems of these countries. Some suggestions and policy considerations, in some broad but very important areas, are outlined below.

Appropriate Macroeconomic Policies

An appropriate macroeconomic policy should pay particular attention to:

1. a faster, non-inflationary growth of domestic demand;
2. the efficiency and effectiveness of public sector spending and taxation;
3. sound government finances/investments;
4. competitiveness (the role of imports/exports and the growth of exports);
5. the relationship between the financial sector and the productive sector; and,
6. the social and political environment (and/or sociopolitical elements).

In the Caribbean area, the general instability in employment and national income levels and lack of diversity have led a number of people to seek job security in the public sector. Thus, government institutions and public sector bodies have been absorbing as much labor as possible.[9]

Current public expenditure levels in the region are under continuous upward pressure. It is noticeable that characteristically large percentages of (re)current government spending of Caribbean fiscal budgets has been dedicated to wages and salaries and debt repayments throughout the 1990s, while both the levels and the share of government capital expenditure and social expenditure are low or very low.

On the government revenue side, an important feature of Caribbean states' public finance is the high dependence on trade taxes (mainly import duties) as a percentage of government revenue. Faced by the difficult realities of budgetary stress, a proactive fiscal policy would emphasize a prudent government expenditure management and planning (long-term productive investments in human capital formation, skills, technological capacity, R&D, information and innovation), and would also consider other alternative revenue-raising sources (e.g., Tobin tax).

The consumption patterns of the Household sector of the Caribbean islands, due to their proximity to the large North American markets, are more reflective of a developed rather than a developing economy. Indeed, local demand has been created for products and services in advance of the domestic economies' productive capacity to deliver these items. The result is an endemically exaggerated propensity to import throughout the region coupled with low actual levels of national savings—which, certainly, are inadequate to finance higher levels of investment expenditure (Higgins 1994: 1).[10] In this case, higher levels of output and income ensuing from a higher degree of capacity utilization and/or a better utilization of equipment can be the source of higher levels of savings required to match higher levels of investment, which will bring about further increase in output and income levels.

Furthermore, to the general domination of Caribbean islands by foreign economic activity and foreign interests as well as development problems and limitations associated with the structure of Caribbean economies (few or weak linkages between economic sectors, the "agricultural paradox of the periphery," etc.), must be added the weak capability of their real sector; the inevitable result is low levels of local exports and high levels of imports (i.e., trade deficits, balance-of-payments constraints).

Hence, aggressive export strategies for Caribbean countries must seek to strengthen their national capabilities first, if these economies are to improve their competitiveness (i.e., export growth). What is really required is balanced development consolidating local production and emphasizing diversification of exports.

Complementarity between Market and State

The orthodox Anglo-American analysis focuses on the dichotomy of market and state as mutually exclusive mechanisms of resource allocation. However, this view has proved to be partial and unrealistic; so have the optimistic expectations regarding free markets and minimalist states. In the contemporary world, the experience of many of the NICs shows how private sector coordination and government activities may complement each other. In fact, economic development requires capable, efficient, and responsive activist states.

In the Caribbean region, social, institutional, and political factors keep most Caribbean states weak and prevent them from effectively playing their necessary role in promoting endogenous development. Also, economic achievements may be handicapped by difficult social and political legacies, and other structural impediments. The Caribbean's reliance on foreign economic activity and foreign exchange has created a state of weak national economic capabilities, which deepens the vulnerability of the region as a whole. Consequently, openness and vulnerability impinge on Caribbean economies' ability to be self-sustaining in their growth patterns.

Contrary to the orthodox analysis, a more tenable formulation can, and should, be a synergistic connection between strategic state management and the business sector. This public-private cooperation will allow the Caribbean states to develop realistic national goals and to translate these broad national goals into effective policy action. However, the pursuit of Developmental State policies can be self-defeating in the absence of the political and institutional conditions and reforms (the enduring institutionalization of state capacity, accountability, effectiveness, etc.) required for their effective implementation.

Developmentalism

On the side of policy making in the Caribbean area, government interventions have usually been of a microeconomic type and have taken the form of ad hoc responses to various pressing problems based on short-run, often highly partial, considerations. Governments have been seen to support industries, to correct their microimperfections and to offer—more or less—protection to them (e.g., by using various protectionist barriers or trade restrictions).

Market failure has usually been the reason for loans, subsidies and other forms of financial assistance to industries and firms. However, these traditional incentive policies offer only marginal solutions, and often recommend some temporary assistance without getting at the root of the problems. In contrast, Caribbean states should become more concerned with distilling a vision of future economic direction, and should undertake selective strategic interventions in their economies taking on a central developmental role without necessarily owning most of the productive assets (Cowling 1990: 10). Therefore, the role of the state at the national level "should be limited to the strategic oversight of development which is essential in the case of a limited array of key industries or sectors–many sectors being left to market processes without strategic guidance . . . rather than getting involved with detailed operational decision making in indus-try" (Cowling 1990: 18).

Realistic strategies for Caribbean countries must seek to consolidate and improve existing production as well as create new types of economic activities first, if their economies are to improve their ability to compete internationally (i.e., strategic reorientation, strategic repositioning). Indeed, Caribbean countries must successfully trade if their economies are to grow and be prosperous, and the modern factors of development and competitiveness must be brought to the fore.

Government Investments on the Accelerators

Investments in the Caribbean area have usually been insufficient to bring about the full utilization of existing resources. In addition, most foreign corporations have developed a rentier-like appetite for short run capital gains and, thus, the developmental needs of local economies have taken a secondary place.

The real problems facing the Caribbean economies are slow growth and high and persistent unemployment and underemployment caused by inadequate aggregate demand, which lead to low levels of investment and innovation and constrain potential supply. Therefore, fiscal spending must be directed to long-term productive investments in technological infrastructure and human capital formation, technical change and its implementation. At the same time, private investments on the accelerators of endogenous competency are essential and highly desirable. It is these higher levels of investment that can raise the rates of capital accumulation and the profit rates in the region.

Thorough Industrial Strategies

There is need to recall that it is not necessarily the case that free trade imposes a beneficial discipline in a world of dominant, transnational corporations. Further, the financial institutions usually adopt particularly short-term perspectives with regard to investment spending, and can impose these perspectives on firms and industries (especially the small ones). These central tendencies within modern market economies point to the requirement for national strategic planning in order to achieve efficiency in the allocation and utilization of national economic resources.

Today, development means strategy; hence, a coherent, national strategic planning system should be an essential element of any efficient economic system. In fact, the Caribbean economies need broad industrial strategies, which should involve conscious attempts by Caribbean governments to coordinate public policies more rationally in order to reach more fully and rapidly the desirable ends for future development, competitiveness and efficiency.

Such economic strategies should be imposed, but leaving the market system to do what it is good at doing: looking after the myriad, incremental changes which are required within these broad strategies, and, of course, running those sectors which do not require strategic intervention (Cowling 1990: 17). In fact, proactive state guidance takes the form of industrial modelling, targeting and repositioning: support of propulsive sectors, whose rapid growth would have substantial, long-term effects on the national development and endogenous competency of Caribbean islands, while considering issues of scale and scope.

In some sectors, such as tourism, the Caribbean already has a strong basis on which to build. These sectors require significant investments, rejuvenation, and repositioning, and have to address a number of serious economic, social, and environmental issues simultaneously; but all of these problems are, in principle, solvable. Provided that the immediate problems are solved, the prioritized sectors are clearly capable of considerable further expansion (Clayton 2001: 15).

Therefore, there is potential and market opportunity for the growth of specific local industrial sectors and activities such as food production/processing, organic farming, biological extracts and derivatives, among others,[11] which will set up incentives and open up possibilities for a wide range of new economic activities, for the following reasons:

- there is an increasing demand for a range of food products (domestic demand plus exports to the large North American markets), particularly processed products, not currently produced in the Caribbean. Therefore, they will significantly enhance local food production capabilities and reduce the imported food. There is also an increasing demand for leisure, recreation and holidays from the travelling public;
- they will allow the local capture of a high percentage of value-added, and thus, generate profits and contribute to the process of capital accumulation. They will also encourage the reinvestment of profits within the local economies;
- Caribbean countries can have some significant prospective competitive advantage in these sectors. Higher capability to compete internationally will be responsible for their endogenous growth, thereby establishing an expanding market share and contributing to their balance of payments and foreign exchange earnings;
- the targeted sectors will better utilize domestic resources and offer solutions to the serious problems in the traditional sectors of Caribbean islands;
- they will give a great boost to the structural transformation, reorientation and diversification of Caribbean islands, and will develop and promote stronger intersectoral linkages with multiple short- and, especially, long-

run productive effects resulting from investments on infrastructure and the accelerators;[12]

- the key industries will enhance the local skill/knowledge base, introduce the know-how and innovation, stimulate technological progress, create managerial and entrepreneurial talents, develop a pool of expertise, and increase productivity and, in turn, will impart—through their linkages and complementarities with the other economic sectors and activities—the momentum for "Economic Take-Off";[13]

- the Developmental State approach is a realistic and feasible suggestion for the endogenous competency and overall development of Caribbean economies (which can be successful) and does not require much; rather, it requires employment of existing resources in different ways, a wiser public finance and different state policy choices.

Furthermore, the growth process is expected to lead to a widening of the local markets,[14] which in turn will require and/or bring about a better transportation and communications system. Thus, after resources have been developed and/or put to use, changes in technology will broaden the Caribbean production base, will provide sufficient stimulus to the mobilization of resources of all kinds and/or the inducement to invest, will bring about a net addition to the effective use of resources and, therefore, to the overall growth of the region.

Obviously, increasing and improving capital equipment and infrastructures, improving human resources and R&D status or pursuing a restructuring strategy for the Caribbean will take a long time. The effectiveness of such a thorough policy is a solution in the long term, combines the cooperation of government, business sector, research institutions and funding institutions, and can create dynamic competitive advantages. Such comprehensive knowledge-based strategies would have to be spawned by the University of the West Indies, and place emphasis on infrastructural development, machinery and capital equipment, skills training and upgrading, technical change, technology generation and transfer, technology acquisition and know-how from abroad (where necessary), a higher level of education, research, innovation, continuous development of scientific manpower, better management and marketing methods.

However, the transfer of these planned strategies for Caribbean countries to new environments may be self-defeating in the absence of Developmental State policies required for their effective implementation. Active state policies (e.g., aggregate demand management policies, investments on, and thorough plans for, the accelerators of endogenous competency and competitiveness) are needed to complement these strategies.

Cooperation

An important notion, which mainly emerges from the New Competition view, is that—contrary to the perfect competition view—economies like Japan, NICs, and Italy that are able to generate effective long-term-oriented cooperative arrangements, have created prosperous industries and dynamic sectors.[15] In this sense, the cooperation among local industries in areas that are normally subject to strong competition might be of great importance, and may counterbalance the rules of the foreign dominated markets and shape productive investment strategies.

Proactive Developmental State policies will give priority to those industries and sectors that are viable, warranted, advantageous, and strategically important in a long-term perspective but more or less vulnerable in the short or medium term without significant state intervention. Such industries require nurturing and have to be provided with the resources and commitment to allow them to grow and mature.[16] Thus, Developmental State action has not only to select sectors and enterprises for government attention and support but also to improve their appropriate developmental environment.[17]

Moreover, these kinds of policies must be strategically focused, and must be directed toward mobilizing market forces, building up world-market-standard industries and systematically developing efficient economic locations. Indeed, modern businesses have to improve continuously, emphasize organizational innovations, and develop the capacity to respond quickly to changes in demand in existing and new markets in the world economy.

However, the need to focus attention on the expansion of new products/services and exports for the global market should not diminish attention to be given to other sectors and products. Consolidating existing local production and improving the competitiveness of traditional exports (where feasible) should remain an important objective. Expanding existing services (like tourism) to include new products is also important, as there may be complementarities and linkages between new and old sectors and activities (Bernal 2000: 110-11).

Growth Poles and Clusters

Growth pole strategies in the Caribbean region would seek to promote specific propulsive industries and sectors with economic dynamism or high potential, which would then be capable of spilling their expansionary forces into depressed neighboring areas within the region in order to counterbalance the power and interests of western multinational or transnational firms.

Growth pole strategies and policies would create greater external economies and economies of scale, thereby dealing with issues of scale and scope. The existence of these external economies would create conditions and opportunities conducive to faster growth of existing and incoming industry in the Caribbean, and therefore would make the growth centers more attractive for new industrial development.

Similarly, Caribbean states may emphasize *clusters* as important engines of growth. The effects of these clusters will be to bring together key players in economic development, upgrade technological infrastructure and the quality of skills, accelerate learning and innovation, induce the exchange of important technical and market information, stimulate the formation of new businesses, improve managerial capacity and entrepreneurship, reduce investment risks, and increase profit margins and economic growth rates.[18]

National Purpose

It has been often argued (by Stone, Jones, et al.) that Caribbean governments have been using the state's power to promote particular interests for both personal and electoral advantage, and special-interest-group preferences appear to count more than the preferences of the majority of these countries' individual citizens. In fact, Caribbean states have not credibly precommitted to particular national purpose policies and merely react to demands and actions of private actors, pressure groups and political parties.

Moreover, political institutions have been largely undermined by growing demands of powerful economic interests and distributional conflicts, while corruption and collusion seem to be endemic. This convergence of economic and political functions in Caribbean states has had disastrous effects in their economic sphere (Ahrens 1997: 142).

In contrast, strategic and developmental goals and actions should be neither responsive nor reducible to various political pressures and private economic interests, and Caribbean governments should augment the development impact of interventions and design to influence private economic decisions in line with their view of an appropriate industrial and trade profile for their economies.

Strategic Integration with the World Economy

The Caribbean is not a homogeneous area; spatial disparities within the region are significant. Indeed, there are important differences in output, in income, in unemployment or in levels of development between different countries, between the regions of each country, and between the various regions and islands of the Caribbean as a whole. Further, due to political and economic associations between the Caribbean countries and developed western countries (as well as the Caribbean islands' proximity to North America), inequalities in economic terms generate inequalities in political power between the former and the latter.

Therefore, globalization, international competition, and free trade may favor the rich and the strong economies at the expense of the less developed ones. Additionally, Caribbean economies differ from other economies in structural characteristics, which have important implications for the character of the growth process and the endogenous capacity for adjustment. Should Caribbean governments choose to seek close or strategic integration with the world economy seems to be a very interesting question which may result in a serious policy dilemma.

Institutional Reforms

Analyzing the institutional conditions in today's Caribbean reveals substantial failures in the region; indeed, the region has largely suffered from impeding prevailing institutions as well as a lack of institutional arrangements. Caribbean governance structures lack the ability to prevent arbitrary political action, and rely on clientelism and favoritism.

In addition, policies of the "weak" or "soft" Caribbean states—in Myrdal's sense, what characterises a "weak" state is not the extent of intervention but its quality–are captured by vested interests, dominated by too many rent-seeking activities of lobbying groups, and can hardly implement governance structures that decisively promote economic reforms (Myrdal 1968; Ahrens 1997: 119). Consequently, it is unlikely that significant government intervention would be warranted in the Caribbean given the inadequate capacity and competence of state institutions, and the institutional deficiencies and impediments to economic development in the region.

For this reason, the pursuit of Developmental State strategies requires a careful molding of appropriate institutions, mechanisms, and instruments which are necessary for the formulation and implementation of selective interventions in certain key sectors (such as tourism, food processing, agroindustrial sectors, etc.) of Caribbean islands. By establishing the appropriate institutional network, policies and strategies can be designed and incentives created to channel re-sources and decision makers' commitment into those productive activities that are compatible with sustained economic development and prompt private firms and industries to carry out long-term investments (Ahrens 1997: 118). Thus, Developmental State policies should be accompanied by the needed institutional architecture and reforms, which not only lay the foundation of effective execu-tion and enforcement of growth-oriented policies but also create the suitable environment for endogenous development.[19]

Political Agreements in the Caribbean

A key question for the Caribbean countries is whether economic integration leads to the reduction of income inequalities and other regional disparities. The political drive to unite the Caribbean area has taken insufficient account of the problems posed by regional disparity, and efforts to encourage convergence are in effect attempts to impose the removal of trade distortions.

To hold the whole Caribbean area together, economic gains must be widely distributed; but, in the long run, problems of political will are also important. Designing appropriate actions and policies that will at the same time reduce spa-tial disparities within the region and be politically acceptable will, indeed, be very difficult.[20]

CONCLUSION

This chapter has sought to exhibit various development related problems in the Caribbean, based on external dependence and structural inefficiencies of the market system; to explain the issues surrounding these problems; and, finally, to look at the role of the state. The key point is that economic weaknesses are linked to external vulnerability in the region.

All of these issues need to be addressed urgently by Caribbean governments. Active state policies should aim at creating the necessary preconditions for local sustained growth, and speeding up structural transformation and development.

The state in this context is not the state existing in Caribbean countries, but the state that could be created with the help of political determination, politically induced changes, and comprehensive administrative reforms. Indeed, thorough Developmental State strategies, combined with state-led changes, can improve the longer-run supply potential, endogenous competency, and industrial competitiveness of Caribbean economies and can play an active role in them.

NOTES

1. For further discussion see Singh 1998: 70-71.

2. For further discussion of the sociopolitical and economic characteristics and problems of Caribbean islands see: Demas 1965, 1976, and 1997; Best 1968 and 1971; Beckford 1971 and 1975; Girvan 1971, 1973, and 1975; Thomas 1988; Lalta and Freckleton 1993; Higgins 1994.

3. Some argue that these changes have constrained state action and have reduced the dominance of government in economic affairs. For further discussion see Arestis and Sawyer 1998: 1-3.

4. See Higgins 1994: 7-8.

5. IICA, *Performance and Prospects for Caribbean Agriculture*, Port-of-Spain: IICA (June 1998).

6. IICA 1998.

7. Therefore, the neoliberal objections to a budget deficit are not valid here.

8. Both analysis and development suggestions are based on the views of Kalecki (1971) and Kaldor (1978).

9. For further discussion see Higgins 1994: 1-8.

10. Higgins 1994: 1-8.

11. These productive activities and sectors have a rigorous basis in science and should be seriously considered.

12. What is proposed here, however, is rather more profound: Caribbean nations should look to develop knowledge-based growth-oriented activities across all major sectors in order to restructure and transform their economies.

13. The commodities should have a high value to weight ratio in order to overcome the problem of the high transport costs associated with island production.

14. Moreover, stopover tourists expand the local markets.

15. According to the general equilibrium analysis, long-term relationships appear as rigidities and deviations from the discipline of the free market system.

16. The infant industry argument for intervention is very important and relevant here, as full exposure to competition is likely to precipitate a dramatic reduction in the size of these industries.

17. Once again, special emphasis should be placed on sectors such as food production and processing, a vibrant agro-industry (which is of vital importance to the expansion and diversification of the Caribbean productive activity), tourism industry, etc. In addition, complementarity between agro-industry and services is evident: for example, between tourism and food processing in the small economies of the Caribbean.

18. The "quality" issue has been discussed in previous chapters.

19. Of course, Caribbean countries are characterized by different historical and cultural circumstances and different sociopolitical characteristics. What is important to learn from the East Asian success story is the approach to the problem.

20. Recent calls for globalization, further liberalization and deregulation, minimalist state, and "good" governance seem to entirely miss the point: in today's circumstances, Caribbean societies may not be able to make speedy transitions from poverty without activist states which approximate the model of a developmental state.

Chapter 8

Developmental State and Jamaica

INTRODUCTION

As an economic activity, tourism in the Caribbean is of an importance scarcely matched by any other region in the world. Estimates show that tourism is the only sector of regional GDP that has consistently increased its share of total income during the 1980s and the 1990s. In some countries (e.g., the Bahamas), tourism accounts for around 70 percent of national income, directly and indirectly. In addition, the sector provides employment for a large portion of the Caribbean population, generates tax revenues and foreign exchange, and contributes to Caribbean countries' balance of payments.

However, tourism has further subjected Caribbean economies to outside dependence, making them highly vulnerable. The result of this dependence makes the region more susceptible to external shocks and cycles in the world economy as well as more dependent on foreign exchange, and exacerbates the islands' instability in employment and national income levels (Higgins 1994: 5). Besides, the growth of tourism and other services has had negligible effects on the development of local manufacturing industry. As a consequence, there are only few linkages between the sectors of Caribbean economies and a serious lack of diversification in production.

Moreover, due to the expansion in the service sector and the proximity to the large North American markets, the region exhibits patterns of high consumption or rising expectations. Indeed, demand has been created for products and services in advance of the domestic economies' productive capacity to deliver these items. The result is an endemically exaggerated propensity to import throughout the Caribbean (Higgins 1994: 1). Against this general background, tourism industry is increasingly being seen not just as an economic activity capable of creating income and jobs for the region's inhabitants and earning important foreign exchange, but as one of the most promising sectors for future economic growth.

The line of argument of chapter 8 is as follows. The first main section seeks to summarize the historical development of tourism industry in the Caribbean, to analyze the sector according to its principal characteristics, and to set tourism in the context of economic development. The second part discusses the potential for tourism growth in Jamaica on the grounds of endogenous growth, competency, development-promoting links and competitiveness. The final section of the chapter identifies strategic requirements and offers alternative policy considerations which the Developmental State analysis implies and suggests.

TOURISM IN THE CARIBBEAN AND JAMAICA

Historical Perspective

The Caribbean region presents a wide diversity of historical and cultural backgrounds. Caribbean territories have been under the administration of colonial powers for long time in their history, and economic imperialism laid the foundations of their economic structures, the legacies of which are still visible. In fact, the region today is the result of a combination of colonialism, the way capitalism expanded and took root in the Caribbean and the class structure it generated, and the complex network of relations between external agents and internal elites (Grugel 1995: 3).

Historically, the Caribbean states have had long political and economic associations with Western imperialistic countries as colonies, protectorates, and/or departments. Geographically, they are within close proximity to the large North American markets. Consequently, the role of external actors on the political and economic processes in the Caribbean is a major input in the development process of the region because of its colonial past, the region's geographical location and the economic fragility of the islands that make up the region.

International trade and capital flows are penetrating deeper into the workings of the small, dependent or underdeveloped Caribbean countries affecting their overall economic structure in general, and employment, income distribution, and productivity growth in particular. Therefore, the linkages between labor, resources, technology, production, demand, and needs are of such a character, and are organized in such a way, that these communities have internalized through their social relations of production and the use of their productive forces patterns of consumption and production that lead to the perpetuation of the foreign domination.

In more recent times, the Caribbean has come under the economic, and increasingly the cultural, influence of the United States, a trend that, many believe, is now accelerating as most of the former European influence diminishes. However, with these colonial ties came a diverse range of cultures, values, religions, cuisines, recreational activities, and sporting interests.[1] The sum total is to produce a range of destinations for the leisure visitor as exciting and diverse as any other region in the world.

Amid this beautiful and powerful Caribbean culture, and despite its glamorous image as one of the world's primary destinations for the rich visitors, it is easy to overlook the fact that Caribbean territories are overpopulated, underdeveloped countries in which prosperity coexists with squalor and deprivation, and population growth generally exceeds the rate of employment growth.

The Caribbean's Tourism Performance

The Caribbean islands have founded tourism on the classical essentials of a warm climate, good environment, excellent beaches, and nice scenery—the "sun, sand and sea" combination so often referred to internationally. Tourism in the Caribbean has assumed prominence as a result of consistent stagnation in traditional economic activities. In fact, allowing for some fluctuations, tourism has been the only major sector that has grown steadily in importance during the 1980s and 1990s.

Thus, tourism in the Caribbean is vital to the future development of the region, despite the fact that international tourism has its risks. Given that the Caribbean is on the doorstep of one of the world's major origin markets, the United States, and benefits from this close proximity, the sector is gaining a higher political profile in the context of economic development policies.

By 1990 there were over ten million total tourist arrivals in the region, compared with around six million in 1980. The Caribbean increased its share of world tourism since 1980; it was 2.11 percent in 1980, reached 2.41 percent in 1987, declined slightly to 2.34 percent by 1990, and reached 3.2 percent in the late 1990s (EIU, *Special Report No. R455*, 1993; PIOJ 2000) (see tables 8.1, 8.2 and 8.3 in the appendix).[2]

The United States has always been the largest generating market to the Caribbean, providing well over half the total arrivals in the region. Visitors from Europe grew especially rapidly since the late 1980s. In fact, despite the dominance of the North American market, the main growth impetus for Caribbean tourism has since come from the European market, which has significantly increased its share of arrivals in the region.[3]

Thus, the market for the Caribbean falls into a number of separate and quite distinct categories: the U.S., Canadian, and European markets, each with different tastes and demands; the local market and other newer markets (such as South America and Asia); the summer and winter markets, attracting visitors of different income brackets; and the permutation between these groups. This wide range of international travelers presents the Caribbean islands with a number of conflicting signals on the direction in which tourism should move or be pushed.

Moreover, the cruise ship industry has become one of the most successful sectors of the travel trade, and the Caribbean is the most important region in the world for this industry—an industry that has been growing faster than international tourism in general since the mid-1980s. There is little doubt that cruise ships are an established feature of tourism in the Caribbean area, and forecasts suggest that the growth rate of the industry will continue to outstrip that of the stopover business during the next decade.

Clearly, the North American market dominates the cruise ship industry, accounting for over 80 percent of all cruise passengers during the 1990s (see table 8.4 in the appendix). But the main concern of Caribbean islands as far as cruise tourism is concerned relates to the net economic benefits derived from the cruise ship business compared with those derived from stopover tourism. There are four main areas of concern: the level of spending per cruise ship visitor, the increasing competition offered by on-board shops to shopping facilities onshore, the level of direct state revenues generated by the cruise ship industry, and the impact upon the environment, which is the Caribbean islands' basic tourism resource.

The Caribbean Tourism Organization (CTO) estimates that cruise ship travelers spent well over half a billion U.S. dollars in the 1990s in the region. CTO further points out that stopover visitors account for around 94 percent of total tourism expenditure, and cruise ship passengers for almost 6 percent. No statistics exist in detail on leakage of cruise ship passengers' spending, but many feel that the bulk of the purchases made are of the duty-free type with relatively low local value-added.

Jamaica, in particular, more than doubled its number of stopover arrivals during the last two decades, and maintained its fourth position ranking during the same period. Apart from a poor performance in 1985 and a major setback in 1988, due in part to the effects of hurricane Gilbert and the impact of the stock market crash the previous year causing a sharp decline in U.S. tourist arrivals, the country has a strong tourism growth pattern since the early 1980s (EIU 1993; PIOJ various years; JTB various issues).

Again, the United States remains the single most important origin market for Jamaican tourism industry with arrivals exceeding 60 percent, on average, of the total during the 1980s and 1990s. The European market has been increasing strongly and much of this significant increase has resulted from a flourishing charter business.

Tourism forecasts indicate that world tourism demand will continue growing and the United States will remain the single most important origin market. However, the Caribbean region will have to face strong competition from other tourism destinations, including some well-established ones (such as the Florida coast, the resorts of Mexico, and the Mediterranean) and some new ones as yet not on the international tourism scene.[4]

Furthermore, the region is relatively more expensive than most of its competitors, even though it tends to have a greater price differential between the summer and the winter season than most other tourism destinations.[5] Thus, if the Caribbean is to maintain or even increase its share of the world market, it is essential to ensure that quality standards and value for money are improved. The tourism products now on offer have become more diverse responding to broader demand made by the travelling public (Poon 1993: 268).

The importance of tourism industry as a generator of employment, direct and indirect, in various Caribbean islands is regarded as one of the most important direct economic benefits of this sector. In fact, given the labor-intensive nature of tourism, the sector may offer one of the best hopes of increasing employment. As with most macroeconomic measures of the importance of tourism and other related activities, there are wide variations throughout the Caribbean in the proportionate importance of tourism in employment (Poon 1993: 265-66).

In addition, tourism earnings are vital for the region's balance of payments and the sector is an important earner of hard foreign currency. In fact, tourism receipts rose significantly from almost 18 percent of current account receipts in 1980 to around 37 percent in the 1990s, even though, on average, the leakage of gross foreign exchange earnings might be around 40 percent with wide variations between local economies. Thus, the total accumulated deficit on current account of Caribbean economies would have risen significantly if tourism receipts were excluded (EIU 1993).

However, leakage of tourist receipts can take place at various stages of the spending round within Caribbean economies. First round leakages derive from direct imports, which are needed to sustain both the tourism industry and visitors' needs. This can include consumables such as food and drink; various investment goods required to build and maintain hotels and other accommodation stock such as building material, equipment and spare parts; transport equipment and fuel; and the repatriation of profits. Second and subsequent round leakages also arise, for example, from the import content of investment and consumption of the economy at large.[6]

The Caribbean's tourism product is relatively more expensive. This high cost reflects some of the realities of small island economies, as most territories in the Caribbean area have relatively high import requirements to sustain the tourism industry. Small islands may also suffer from poor economies of scale in the provision of utilities like water and electricity. As tourism is an indispensable source of government revenue for Caribbean states (direct and indirect taxation, import duties, the stimulation of other tax-paying sectors and activities, etc.), these taxes may further increase cost.

Moreover, the Caribbean hotel sector, in terms of the number of establishments, is primarily in the hands of private individuals.[7] Most are long-established, may be old-fashioned and are in need of major investments to upgrade and modernize themselves. This is a major challenge for the region and one that has so far not been effectively tackled.

The cost of building new hotels, and the renewal and refurbishment of old ones, are seriously affected by the imports required–and therefore the costs incurred—as well as, frequently, bureaucratic procedures, which add to the administrative costs faced by hoteliers. As building supplies are rarely available locally, the operating costs and the costs of new developments are high. Once built, frequent renewal or refurbishment is required due to the tropical climate, again necessitating the importation of spare parts and replacement goods with their concomitant high costs. The evidence suggests that initial capital costs can be of less importance than ongoing operating costs. Hence, the costs of new developments and, especially, high operating costs in the Caribbean mean that high revenues may not be translated into high profits (Carey 1989).

Another important reason for the Caribbean accommodation sector's high operating costs is that employment costs are relatively high. Despite high wage rates, training tends to be poor and standards inadequate, resulting in low productivity. Service attitudes and skills are commonly reported by industry managers to be a significant problem in the accommodation sector. Most important, however, is that such standards have not yet been addressed by adequate training programs or facilities. This is an area that is generally recognized by tourism authorities and executive managers as being crucial for future success and attempts are being made to improve training standards and availability, with varying degrees of seriousness and success.

In addition, there is a lack of investment in up-to-date training facilities, a shortage of experienced trainers and an uncoordinated approach to training in the region. As a result, in most countries much of the senior management in hotels is expatriate staff, and the level of junior and middle management tends to be below international quality standards.

An additional deterrent to high productivity is the fact that many hotels in the Caribbean have been slow toward utilizing the new technology, such as, information technology, available to assist in the efficient running and monitoring of their businesses. Infrastructure inadequacies and the cost of utilities can also be a major problem, as these inadequacies provide hotels with an extra burden (hotels often have to make their own arrangements). Coupled with all the above deterrents has to be considered the limited availability and high cost of capital as well as the intensive short-termism of financial institutions (EIU 1993; Poon 1993: 269).

Because of the large number of relatively small hotels and guest houses in the Caribbean region, marketing is a major problem. Small establishments have neither the necessary skills nor the budgets to finance major marketing drives. Marketing budgets and advertising expenses are very high, normally beyond the reach of small hotels and resorts. Thus, they have to rely on the efforts of the national tourist offices and/or boards, links with tour operators and wholesalers, and occasionally attendance.

The larger hotels and resorts, and especially the chains, are in a better position to promote themselves successfully. Most are foreign owned, which very often means that considerable promotion takes place in the investor's home base. Most of the larger establishments have links with European and American tour operators, which place them in their advertising documents. This is a considerable advantage because it provides the large hotel/resort with experienced marketing expertise and ensures guaranteed exposure (EIU 1993).

Furthermore, air transport is key to the region's success as a famous destination, and air access is considered the lifeblood of Caribbean tourism industry. There are frequent scheduled air connections between North America and the region, as well as with Europe. Caribbean islands, nevertheless, are very concerned about two main aspects of air links with its most important markets: the vulnerability of the region to changes in route structure; and the reduction in direct connections, as the major airlines in general, and privatized carriers in particular, are increasingly inclined to take decisions on a strictly commercial basis.

The region's own carriers are small, almost entirely state-owned, often underequipped and at the mercy of the dominant airline blocks of North America and Europe. In particular, American Airlines has become the dominant carrier in the region. For this reason, there is general recognition that the airlines of the region may have to cooperate more and become more aggressively competitive, if the air transport needs of this region are not to pass finally into the hands of powerful external suppliers (Bastian 1984).

Policy toward investment expenditure in, and the development of, tourism in the Caribbean centers on the investment incentives offered and the taxation of tourism. Both may be insufficient to offset some of the perceived disadvantages of the region—bureaucratic inefficiencies; lack of transparency in incentive decisions; high operating costs especially for utilities, tourism facilities and supporting infrastructure; and the difficulties of achieving scale economies in small islands. Thus, investment incentives in general may do little to influence investment decisions. A report by the OAS and the CTO in 1990 concluded that

> Existing incentives for the encouragement of tourism investment in the Caribbean region play a smaller role in attracting new investment than [what] is generally ascribed to them and function differently depending on the stage of development of the tourism sector in the particular country concerned. Overall, the study concluded that incentives play a minor role in the decision by foreign investors to establish operations. (In *The Impact of Tourism Investment Incentives in the Caribbean Region*)

Studies in other countries of investment incentives, often allied to regional policy, have cast similar doubts on the effectiveness of incentive regimes.[8] It has been found that factors such as the general business climate, business strategies, operating costs, political and economic stability, etcetera, have a far greater role in the investment decision. Once a broad decision has been taken on investment location, the incentives available may play a subsidiary role in decision making, but they are rarely the deciding factor.

Recently, much emphasis has been placed on the serious need for tourism awareness programs and the necessity of making the local communities more conscious of the economic advantages of tourism and the opportunities it can offer. Undoubtedly, there are problems when poor local residents encounter the great differences between their own lifestyles and that of the affluent, high-spending foreign tourist. Consumption patterns and expectations—the "North American consumption-driven model"—by local residents can be raised to unsustainable levels by reference to those of the visitors. Further resentment may build up when it is seen that local people have lower-grade jobs in hotels whereas senior management positions are held by expatriate staff.[9]

From the visitor's viewpoint, encountering an attitude of resentment does not make for a positive overall experience. Harassment of tourists by locals and a rise in crime are increasingly becoming problems for Caribbean states to deal with. At its most mild, tourists will tend to stay within the confines of their hotels, under the security by a hotel guard and spending little in the wider community. At worst, incidents may trigger a great deal of publicity and cause a destination considerable disadvertisement.

Nevertheless, a corollary to resentment and envy of foreign tourists by poorer sections of Caribbean communities is the fact that there are serious reservations about tourism becoming a viable engine of economic growth. On the one hand, it is believed that tourism growth would simply result in the substitution of one type of dependence for another—for example, tourism for bananas or sugar. On the other hand, it is believed that tourism is a very volatile industry, making dependence on it very risky.[10]

Yet, there is a fear by the more educated of the disintegration of local culture and mores as other lifestyles are imported and copied by local people, especially the region's youth. Consequently, the Americanization of Caribbean areas, the dilution of local cultures and cuisine or the constant bombardment of small islands by U.S. television channels are being viewed with some caution.

THE POTENTIAL FOR TOURISM GROWTH IN JAMAICA

An Alternative Development Paradigm

An important point that should be made concerns the relationship between the Jamaican government and the community within the context of the kind of problems confronting the society, as well as the goals the government has embraced from the standpoint of endogenous development. Attention will have to be drawn to the part played by tourism in the Jamaican economy. However, it is necessary to juxtapose certain facts relating to the sectorial structure of the Jamaican economy in order to provide what might be called "an integrated development perspective of the system," and to show the relative position of endogenous strategic components.[11]

In formulating policies for economic restructuring and diversification, it is essential, therefore, to recognize the critical elements of the system in terms of deriving a long-term strategy. Failure to do so can easily lead not only to short run, highly partial considerations and short-term measures dictated by pressing problems (e.g., national debt, stagflation) but also to the adoption of ad hoc approach to development, which may be in basic conflict with the goal of a stronger economic fabric. The fact that decisions relating to a particular sector (i.e., tourism industry) tend to have broader implications for the Jamaican national economy as a whole requires a clear examination of the interacting influences between the promising activities from the point of view of endogenous competency, and those that may provide short-term benefits but offer little hope as a secure basis for future national well-being.

A first requirement of the proposed tourism growth strategy is that the expansion of tourism represents a net addition to the effective use of local resources and, therefore, to the overall growth of the system. Tourism growth and, thus, overall economic growth will be led by the growth of demand for the Jamaican tourism product, which would translate into higher profits and savings. In connection with this the competitiveness of the sector must come to the fore.

Furthermore, the renewal of tourism in Jamaica requires investment in tourism plant, facilities and supporting infrastructure, and various short-run bottlenecks preventing a fuller utilization of capacities have to be taken care of. These bottlenecks may include a lack of the necessary resources and skills, difficulties in obtaining finance, and a lack of business confidence.

Hence, a second requirement of such a strategy is the implementation of effective fiscal and monetary policies which would provide the resources and stimuli to carry out the investment in both working and fixed capital, infrastructure, and skills, so as to improve the conditions and organization of tourism product development. Indeed, active fiscal policy ought to carry out the investment spending necessary to improve the service conditions of hotels/resorts and to support the other expenditures associated with the selective policy.

Monetary policy, on the other hand, ought to ensure that the overall development effort is not to be thwarted by endemic short-termism, capital flight, and speculative ventures, which can actually starve the real economy of investment capital. As financial institutions have a critically important role in this development process, it is particularly important that they are well-managed, have a clear set of strategic goals and promote longer time horizons (Clayton 2001: 33). Therefore, the government must take steps to ensure that the financial services sector is properly supervised. Besides, appropriate monetary and exchange rate policies to facilitate productive initiatives, as well as higher levels of national savings to finance higher levels of investment spending, are absolutely essential.

However, bottlenecks at the firm or macro level often hamper a more efficient capacity utilization. These bottlenecks must be seriously considered and, accordingly, a medium- and long-term tourism growth strategy should have as a as a basic requirement a close link with a conscious national purpose strategy. Such a directed action should consolidate and improve existing production lines; select and give priority to investments in new and technically promising activities; and adjust quickly in anticipation of, and in response to, global changes in demand and technological innovation (Lopez 1998: 12-13; Bernal 2000: 107).

What has been asserted should not be taken to imply a rejection of the problems that could arise with this proposed pragmatic attempt. But to face them, an alternative development perspective ought to complement short-run measures with thorough strategic planning. Greater levels of production, employment, and profits that would be achieved in the short-term would actually spur a transition to a more structurally efficient economy. Part of this increased production and income in Jamaica would go to higher spending on the modern factors of endogenous competency and lead to productivity-enhancing technical change. Not only higher profits would allow additional investment expenditure but also a greater proportion of income growth will be channeled toward investment. Thus, in the future, it would be relatively easier to utilize more modern technology and increase productivity, while at the same time increasing capital accumulation (Lopez 1998: 18-19).

In addition, given the recovery of production of local industries and the improvement of competitiveness, a large part of the additional goods produced will be devoted to exports. Consequently, the country would make a greater and better use of its productive resources and capacity, while at the same time easing the constraints on its balance of payments.

Such a sound development management (i.e., monitoring and execution) would stimulate tourism growth and industrial regeneration while raising the quantity and quality of productive investment necessary to allow the fullest and most efficient utilization of existing resources within a reasonable time period. More importantly, such an approach seems to be a better option for the industrial competency and development of the Jamaican economy, and a more sensible way to confront the future, than a frantic search for western-style modernization —a vision that decision- and policy-makers in Jamaica aspire to. The alternative and more realistic development paradigm would require the pursuit of Developmental State strategies and policies. This is what the Jamaican economy needs (Lopez 1998: 19).

Issues of Selection

Initially it is important to divide consideration of the key issues related to the structure of Jamaican industry into three sections: issues influenced by state policy and general policy issues; issues influenced by specific industries or sectors; and market-driven issues.[12] On this account, we limit strategic intervention to those parts of the Jamaican economy where government intervention is going to have its most significant potential impact on the dynamism of the economy as a whole. The criteria are obviously "dynamic and forward-looking" (Cowling 1990: 21).

With this background in mind, there is a potential—determined by the history of the Jamaican economy, its current stage of development and its future prospects—for the growth of tourism industry in Jamaica, which appears viable, warranted, advantageous and indeed strategically important in a long-term perspective, and which will set up incentives and open up possibilities for a wide range of new economic activities, for the following reasons (Cowling 1990: 19):

- there is an increasing demand for holidays, recreational activities, and leisure from the travelling public. Besides, the country is close to one of the world's major markets, the United States;
- it can allow the local capture of a high percentage of value-added, and thus generate profits and contribute to the capital accumulation process;

- Jamaica has some significant competitive advantage in this industry. Greater competitiveness will be responsible for the increase in tourist arrivals, thereby establishing an expanding market share and contributing to the balance of payments and foreign exchange earnings;

- tourism industry growth will be accompanied by a higher degree of domestic resource and capacity utilization. It will build strategic alliances and diagonally integrate with tourism-related and non-related activities;

- it will develop and promote stronger intersectoral linkages, and bring about the structural transformation and diversification of the Jamaican economy;

- the tourism sector, in conjunction with the entire services economy, will improve the quality of the country's human resources, enhance the local skill base, introduce the know-how and innovation (access to best-practice technology), stimulate technical progress, create entrepreneurial and managerial talents, and increase productivity and, in turn, will impart—through its linkages with the agricultural and manufacturing sectors—the momentum for "Economic Take-Off";

- it is a realistic and feasible proposal for the Jamaican endogenous development that would make possible the achievement of national goals.

The proposed tourism industry growth, which must take place within the framework of thorough development planning, takes into account the interrelations among a number of stylized facts: domestic resources, capital, social structure, the level of technology and skills, scale, and transformation. Indeed, economies of scale and learning will bring about multiple effects on, and/or changes in, the structure of the Jamaican production. The objective would be to increase value-added to the sector and strengthen intersectoral linkages, which would then be capable of spilling their expansionary forces into other sectors and activities.

Overcoming the Barriers

One of the most important studies published by the World Bank in recent years has been "The World Development Report (1991): The Challenge of Development." The importance of this publication lies in the fact that it synthesizes and interprets more than forty years of development experience as seen by World Bank economists. The study observes that

> forty-three years ago, an influential government report in an important developing country observed that labor shunned hard, productive jobs and sought easy, merchant-like work. The report showed that workers' productivity had fallen, wages were too high, and enterprises were inefficient and heavily subsidized. The country had virtually priced itself out of international markets and faced a severe competitive threat. . . . This would be the last opportunity, concluded the prime minister in July 1947, to discover whether his country would be able to stand on its own feet. . . . That country was Japan. (World Bank 1991: 13-14)

These are important issues relevant to the Jamaican discussion (e.g., people seek easy, merchant-like work while labor productivity has been declining, many Jamaican enterprises are inefficient and heavily subsidized, the national competitiveness is low).

There is overwhelming evidence, which is generally accepted among the scholars in the field, that the government in Japan pursued aggressive national purpose policies to change its unsatisfactory economic situation. A realistic strategy for Jamaica should aim at adaptation and innovation-led development of certain specific sectors, which will have multiple productive effects, and will achieve sustained economic growth, higher productivity, structural transformation and diversity. This is clearly an issue in the Jamaican context.

Jamaican tourism, in conjunction with the entire services sector, and the agricultural and industrial sectors, can provide the foundation that an alternative development strategy can build on. When "the priorities are right," scarce resources will increasingly be allocated efficiently, productivity and profitability will increase, and the propulsive/dynamic sector will become increasingly attractive to the private sector.

Even if employment and operating costs are high, the average total cost will progressively decrease due to higher levels of stopover arrivals and economies of scale. In addition, investment expenditure in the tourism product (mainly infrastructure, facilities and tourism plant), human capital, skills, talents, managerial competency, and innovation, will result in new and better practices and operations quality, toward creating and sustaining demand in both established and new origin markets. It is the successful responsiveness to the market's desires that will single out repeat visitors and word-of-mouth recommendations.

Obviously, the above alternative strategy links the Jamaican economy to the world economy, and involves promoting further growth through the country's ability to maintain and maximize the earnings from tourism. By focusing on higher levels of stopover visitors, the strategy allows hotels and resorts greater scope and imposes a competitive discipline on domestic businesses that forces them to increase efficiency, productivity, profitability, and quality.

With modern knowledge, improved training, managerial excellence, operations quality, professionalism, and commitment the sector can respond to the new industry best practice that is emerging internationally. Within this context, comprehensive development policy will fuel tourism toward growth, and lead this key sector into a viable, competitive, and profitable future.

The Way Forward: The Strategic Approach

It is clear from the previous discussion that a coherent strategy is necessary for the endogenous development of the Jamaican economy. In doing so, the government adopts a strategic view of prospective industrial development in Jamaica and provides a range of support mechanisms to those sectors (e.g., tourism) deemed to have a key role to play in the future.

First of all, a central core is needed, a Bureau of Industry and Trade—a powerhouse dedicated to raising both the quantity and quality of investment spending toward facilitating the prioritized sectors. This executive team should consist of a small, efficient, entrepreneurial team rather than a vast bureaucracy—we must avoid squandering people and resources over a whole range of bureaucratic activities.

The central core should be recruited partly from within the Jamaican Civil Service, but also from business, professionals, and the academic and scientific world; a new look bureau would need some well-educated, well-trained, and efficient technocratic planners. The bureau should be organized around the requirements of a strategic planning agency with a long-term commitment and the power to intervene decisively and take the necessary policy action (Cowling 1990: 24).[13] With the assistance of consultants, the government forms a consensus on the best policies to pursue.

The next step of tourism policy is to emphasize the upgrading of the accommodation and hotel stock, as high quality standards are essential to the Jamaican tourism if it is to increase its market share. Government finance and guidance has a crucial role to play here, as private sector promotion alone may not be sufficient or effective for the large number of small accommodation establishments in Jamaica. On the other hand, it is essential that new sources of funds from the private sector should support the state efforts. Joint marketing initiatives, with airlines for example, and consistent attempts to encourage the private sector to turn aggressively toward major, like the short-break market from the United States, and new markets are important for bringing new products and services to this fiercely competitive industry.

Improvements in production result from investment spending in plant and equipment, and a combination of skills, innovation, and R&D. Spending from the Jamaican budget must be directed to long-term investments in infrastructure, human capital, and technical change and its implementation. However, private investment on the modern factors of competency and competitiveness is also desirable and absolutely necessary. In fact, investment in advanced training as well as the continuous development of scientific and managerial manpower in Jamaica can overcome many of the characteristics of labor force impediments to greater productivity, and will accelerate the adoption of new and more advanced techniques applied to production.

Generally, decision and policy-makers in Jamaica have formulated no long-term strategies incorporating all these relevant issues. However, the Jamaican economy needs broad industrial strategies on the grounds of long-term, dynamic efficiency. A national economic strategy should be imposed, with the market playing a crucial role. Yet, the transfer of this alternative strategy for Jamaica to highly competitive environments may be self-defeating in the absence of active state policies required for its effective implementation.

A much greater commitment to understanding the extent to which the tourism sector can contribute to the long-term development of Jamaica, and especially how this can be achieved, seems essential. Tourism cannot be considered in isolation: the extent to which the tourist spending leaks out, the degree to which local supply of food, and manufactured products and other services can be stimulated, the country's carrying capacity and public services, the impact of tourism on the community and the environment, all need to be considered in an overall framework.

Above all, such a thorough development strategy requires continuity, consistency and commitment to the process and direction of endogenous development. It also requires a high degree of incentive-compatibility of government policies and development and economic performance, as well as the creation of institutional arrangements that constitute a stable political and economic environment in which consensus-building concerning active developmental strategies works (Ahrens 1997: 119; 126).

Without such commitments, competence, accountability, effectiveness, capacity, and seriousness, this radical policy package will founder on short-term expedients, the inefficiency and ineffectiveness of the civil service, the power of the transnationals or the mindset of the people.[14]

DEVELOPMENTAL STATE POLICY CONSIDERATIONS

Industrial strategy has not been seen to be pivotal in the Jamaican economy; thus, it has never been developed in a systematic or coherent fashion as a centerpiece of the government's approach to economic policy making.[15] State interventions have usually been seen as reactions[16] to pressing problems, and the policies which flow from these interventions appear to be consonant with the market failure approach.[17] In fact, the general concept of an active developmental role for the state is rather alien to the general economic and political culture in Jamaica (Cowling 1990: 6).

Further, interest group politics and patronage in Jamaica explains why policy is often flawed in both formulation and execution. This convergence of economic and political functions in the Jamaican state and the primacy of various political pressures and certain private interests have had disastrous effects in the economic sphere.

During the last two decades or so, neoclassical and neoliberal policies have been the central routes to modern solutions for the Jamaican economy. However, there are serious doubts about whether these economic policies have been translated into significant social and economic development and growth, endogenous competency and competitiveness.

While appropriate macroeconomic management can contribute much toward enhancing the performance of the Jamaican economy, nevertheless such policies only deal with the symptoms of deeper structural problems. For this reason, a much sharper focus on industrial strategies is needed. Such supply-side strategies are seen to be necessary to resolve the country's deeper problems. Some alternative policy recommendations for the development of the Jamaican economy in general, and of tourism industry in particular, are outlined below.

Strategic Partnership between State and Private Sector

At present, the direction in which the Jamaican tourism sector is pointed seems to be somewhat random, depending on the current state of the global market rather than based on a long-term development plan. Hence, we have a basis for recommending a framework of, and establishing a role for, strategic planning in Jamaica.

The second and related reason for requiring national strategic planning is the systematic short-termism of the market system, given that financial institutions usually adopt a short-term perspective with regard to investment and impose their short-term perspective on firms, especially the small ones. Consequently, small or new establishments may be severely constrained in their investment ambitions by the short-term perspective of the financial institutions, since it is these firms and hotels which will find difficulties to fund their own growth. This sort of financial environment is hardly conducive to the rational planning of the long-term future of the industrial base. Short-term decision making is crowding out long-term issues, and leaving businesses weaker in the long term. Thus, within the Jamaican economy, we need to establish an institutional structure to plan for the future (Cowling 1990: 13-14).

For Jamaican tourism to achieve its full potential, it seems imperative that the state should draw up comprehensive strategies for implementation. In fact, the public and private sectors can cooperate in a range of different arrangements, each contributing what it does best and both participating in the financial returns, within the context of a socially defined agenda. The key point is the need for a strong developmental role for the state in order to raise the momentum of industrial change and to ensure that such change fully reflects broader national interests.

This institutionalized public-private partnership will allow the Jamaican State to develop independent national goals, and to translate these broad national goals into effective policy action. However, the consistent pursuit and transfer of specific strategies and policies to new environments would be self-defeating in the absence of appropriate politico-institutional conditions and reforms required for their effective implementation.

Government Investments on the Accelerators

Recent developments in the financial markets have significantly encouraged endemic and excessive short-termism and various speculative ventures. These developments, in conjunction with weak or absent state supervision, can foster a dysfunctional business culture and a casino economy mindset, in which insider trading, more direct forms of corruption and conflicts of interest can increasingly become common (Clayton 2001: 16).

In addition, some assert that the hotel sector's high operating costs is a serious barrier that may discourage productive investments in Jamaica. The only logical alternative, then, is to consider the capacity-creating aspect of government spending, and the Jamaican Government should rely heavily on higher levels of government investment. Indeed, planned investments on knowledge, training, technological innovation, and research will boost the endogenous competency of the Jamaican economy, toward higher rates of economic growth and "high wages high productivity." The key issue here is that investment responsibilities would be closely tailored to the needs of the private sector (once again, private investments in tourism plant, facilities, supporting infrastructure, etc., are highly desirable and essential).

Institutional Reforms

In this chapter, it is argued that industrial and/or sectoral strategies and policies in Jamaica should be concerned with the long-term aim of altering the direction and pace of the country's development. Nevertheless, it is unlikely that significant state intervention would be warranted given the inadequate capacity and competence of government institutions, in terms of intellectual, managerial and fiscal resources; the politico-institutional impediments to the Jamaican economic development.

There are even deeper issues as to the nature of the country's political culture, and the quality of its political leadership and business management. For these important reasons, the pursuit of a highly interventionist strategy as well as a successful and effective policy reform would require the institutional structure and means to formulate, implement, and enforce developmental policies and production-oriented interventions in certain key sectors of the Jamaican economy.

First, a central bureau is absolutely necessary in order to organize the critical interactions between government and industry. This executive new look elite would possess accurate intelligence, inventiveness, commitment, effectiveness as well as active, strategic and sophisticated responseness to a changing economic reality (Evans 1992: 148).

Potentially weak central cores or national governments may be captured by powerful interests, and can hardly implement institutional structures that decisively promote structural changes and economic reforms. In addition, changes in the structure of class relations during the last decades induced erosion of political institutions in Jamaica. In contrast, Developmental States are distinguished by strong politico-institutional structures.[18] Building a strong technostructure and embedding it into a network of cooperative and consultative relations with targeted dynamic industries and other social segments is both feasible and operational in Jamaica.

Secondly, the involvement of business elites and social segments in government policy making through institutionalized channels represents an adequate means to establish a state-business-society interface by which the mutual exchange of information can be encouraged, risk sharing facilitated, bureaucratic autonomy and flexibility enhanced, and a consensual process of policy formulation realized. This combination of social connectedness and bureaucratic autonomy, which Evans (1995) calls embedded autonomy, may represent the institutional basis for effective and accountable state involvement in the Jamaican economy, while being independent of societal pressures (Ahrens 1997: 125).[19]

Thirdly, in order to make state action more effective, both effective procedures and increased participation are of vital importance. Indeed, this new institutional structure must allow for participation at all levels. Besides, loose and transparent links between the strategic planning agency and Ministries and Government Departments involved in the industrial strategy and investment planning (e.g., Education and Training) and sectoral agencies and local authorities/ boards would decentralize much of the work of the central core.

To be successful our planning must be democratic, and our institutional structure must allow for participation at all levels. Indeed, participation by the social partners can improve the organization of production and help restrain the power of interest groups that have access to government decision making (Cowling 1990: 28).

Fourthly, preconditions for the success of these alternative strategies and radical policies in Jamaica should include the government's credible commitment to a production-oriented strategy, which includes agriculture, manufacturing industry and the entire services sector; an improved quality of state action; the replacement of the short-term perspective of the Treasury and the financial institutions with one much more favorable to productive investment and industry; recognition of the importance of state capacity, efficiency, and effectiveness; accountability, autonomy, and manageability of the executive elite; mechanisms of consensual conflict resolution as well as political and social stability through transparent and efficient procedures; the organizational design of, and the incentives within, the government sector and the institutional environment: incentives to pursue collective ends while restraining arbitrary action, favoritism, and corruption (Ahrens 1997: 116).

Lastly, particularly in the course of a fundamental redirection of the existing pattern of development, as in the case of the Jamaican economy, simply matching the proposed radical development policy framework to existing political institutions would be counterproductive. Effective governance is "a dynamic process that requires continuing fine-tuning and adjusting institutions and policy solutions to changing technological, social, political and economic environments" (Ahrens 1997: 119).

To the extent that a chosen path falls short in this respect, this will need changes and adjustments in certain policy areas. However, it is difficult to retain a disposition against change in a world where basic conditions are subject to constant mutation.

Production and Operations Quality

In this technological age, a quality emphasis should encompass the entire organization of the Jamaican production, from producers and suppliers to customers, including facility location and/or expansion; equipment layout; purchasing and installation of proper machinery and equipment; layout strategy (capacity needs, inventory requirements); utility specifications and sanitary arrangements; refrigeration specifications; supporting facilities and utilities; maintenance training; products technology training; quality control programs; and just-in-time decisions and scheduling.

For both Jamaican firms and the Jamaican economy as a whole to compete effectively in the global economy, products and services must meet global quality and price expectations. As the country, as well as the whole Caribbean region, faces many crucial challenges, especially in light of strong international competition, it is essential to ensure that quality standards and value for money are improved. Inferior products will harm the companies' revenues and profitability or market share, and will further deteriorate the Jamaican balance of payments (Heizer and Render 1996: 79-80).

Other Important Issues

The new tourism has already begun taking on a different shape responding to, and internalizing a number of signals, such as social, economic, technological, ecological, cultural, and institutional, which emanate from the international environment. Flexible specialization, as a core element of the "new tourism best practice," is driven by new information technologies as well as new managerial and organizational principles of creativity, scope economies, product differentiation, and niche markets (Poon 1993: 274).

Thus, much more attention has to be placed on these important issues, as the new tourism is a highly complex and volatile sector. Likewise, given that the new tourism depends upon environmental quality, the issue of environmental protection has to be accorded a greater priority by policymakers in order to cope with a product that has already begun to deteriorate. In fact, although the Jamaican environment is the country's basic tourism resource, there seems to be a huge gap between this recognition and putting effective controls in place. Consequently, a much closer link is required between tourism policy and environmental control and preservation.

Furthermore, good air access to the Caribbean territories from all the main generating markets is of outmost importance. As the Caribbean area (and Jamaica in particular) is highly dependent and vulnerable to changes in the structure of air services, the region is facing the prospect of becoming a service taker in its main market regions.

Yet, the growing influence of the major Computer Reservation Systems (CRS) in the United States, Canada, and Europe is a further source of concern to the Caribbean. The only practical solution for the region's carriers could be to form cooperative alliances in the vital areas of marketing and scheduling with some of the major carriers in order to avoid being entirely left out (as cost-effective and efficient marketing and distribution are very important to the success of tourism promotion).[20]

Indeed, the building of strategic alliances and partnerships within and outside of the tourism industry is expected to enhance the competitiveness of the sector (Poon 1993: 273). This action can:

- assist toward establishing a Caribbean-wide air transport policy as well as promoting regional cooperation in air services including marketing agreements;
- improve airport infrastructure;
- monitor CRS developments more closely and ensure that the Caribbean region in general, and Jamaica in particular, is not disadvantaged in this area;
- strengthen the capital and management bases of the airlines;
- monitor and forecast air transport developments in so far as they affect the Caribbean.

With cooperative arrangements and regional approaches to tourism industry, Caribbean islands can share the expenses of building marketing intelligence systems, information technology networks, promotion, and public relations campaigns. It is, indeed, these cooperative arrangements and united effort that can considerably increase the strength of the bargaining power of the entire region (Poon 1993: 276).

CONCLUSION

This chapter has sought to establish the Jamaican case for strategic state action; it has described the form a national development strategy should take; it explained key issues surrounding the potential for tourism growth; and, it outlined the way of creating a network of appropriate institutions. Finally, recommendations were made for an alternative development policy framework.

There is no need for vast bureaucratic machinery and procedure, because the approach is clearly entrepreneurial. Such a strategic approach can utilize and maximize the productive resources available for tourism growth; promote cross-sectoral links and create economies of scale across a range of firms and industries; aggregate demand for the accelerators of development, and services; and, finally, identify inefficiencies and gaps to adequately develop and use new products and processes, enabling both government and private policy making to be better targeted.

However, to begin to be successful will require a high quality of state intervention and a certain degree of commitment by the government to domestic development. While the effective execution of the necessary measures is far from straightforward, there is much that can be done. Jamaican tourism will have a better future, should these issues be tackled soon and successfully.

NOTES

1. See Jones-Hendrickson 1985: 2; Lalta and Freckleton 1993: 1.

2. However, the importance of tourism in the Caribbean is very variable.

3. For North Americans, Caribbean islands represent a relatively short-haul destination. For Europeans, the Caribbean is a long-haul destination and the average length of stay is longer (around ten days compared with around seven for American visitors), and historically it has been seen as relatively expensive (EIU 1993).

4. Florida and Mexico offer similar climatic and scenic attractions within broadly the same parameters of price and distance from home (EIU 1993).

5. There is also a wide variety of choice within the Caribbean.

6. Existing evidence shows that a typical leakage coefficient might be of the order of 40 percent, even though there are wide variations between the different Caribbean countries (EIU 1993).

7. The region's accommodation stock currently comprises a wide variety of properties including large resorts, exclusive hotels, small inns, guesthouses, and the emerging all-inclusive resort, which is becoming a trademark of Caribbean tourism.

8. See Karagiannis 1996; 2000.

9. Many of these issues require sensitive handling by all concerned.

10. In fact, tourism can fall victim to the vagaries of international demand patterns.

11. See also Karagiannis 2000.

12. Obviously, there is a strong relationship between them.

13. In fact,

> Institutions can formalize the commitment to such [development policies] and their structure, procedures and personnel can act to ensure that such commitments cannot easily be reversed, but they are simply ratifying [plans] already established. The history of planning shows how fragile was the commitment [in Jamaica] despite the creation of many new institutions, and [the lack of teeth of these institutions was quite obvious]. With clear goals, and a determination to pursue them, institutions with teeth should be forthcoming. (Cowling 1990: 23)

14. However, this approach allows "considerable autonomy in determining the mode of operation, and adjusting it as experience accumulates." The main objective is "a dynamic economy rather than sticking to a set of rigid rules imposed by a central bureaucracy" (Cowling 1990: 25).

15. The partial nature and brief life of Jamaican plans (according to Davis and Witter 1989: 96: "a kind of tyranny of the short run in the government's decision-making process"), coupled with lack of vision and thoroughness, has always been a serious shortcoming which hampers and frustrates the country's development efforts and policy (for example, the one-year "Emergency Production Plan" of 1977, the recent "Tourism Master Plan," etc.).

16. The period 1974-77 may be seen as an exception.

17. For a complete discussion on the Jamaican economic development (1962-87) see Davis and Witter 1989: 88-100.

18. "Strong" in the sense that the government is able to credibly commit itself to national purpose policy making; serious and capable of signaling its commitment to sustainable economic development (Myrdal 1968).

19. "Embeddedness" does not mean cozy relations between the government and individual private businesses, but a strategic government-business interface that is distin-

guished by transparent consultation, cooperation, and coordination mechanisms (Ahrens 1997: 126).

20. The past history of intra-regional cooperation is not such as to raise hopes very high.

APPENDIX

TABLE 8.1
Stopover Arrivals in the Caribbean's Major Destinations: 1990-1999

Country	1990	1995	1999
Antigua & Barbuda	184,248	191,401	207,862
Aruba	391,443	454,892	569,991
The Bahamas [a]	1,561,600	1,598,015	[b] 1,617,595
Barbados	432,092	442,107	424,809
Bermuda	414,097	387,535	339,159
Cayman Islands	253,158	361,444	394,555
Curacao	207,695	223,788	147,435
Cuba	n/a	519,400	1,212,020
Dominican Republic	1,533,000	n/a	2,665,184
Jamaica	840,777	1,018,946	1,248,397
Martinique	280,644	381,019	453,513
Puerto Rico	511,382	730,250	1,006,699
St. Lucia	141,314	230,805	137,999
St. Maarten/St. Martin	393,962	323,571	444,814
Trinidad & Tobago	158,982	132,845	214,722
U.S. Virgin Islands	691,772	499,913	432,124

Sources: PIOJ, various years; CTO, various issues.
[a] These figures, which are provided by the Ministry of Tourism and the Central Bank of the Bahamas (Nassau), are quite different from those provided by the PIOJ, "Economic and Social Survey Jamaica," Kingston: PIOJ, various years.
[b] 1997 figure. The 1999 figure is not available (Ministry of Tourism; The Central Bank of the Bahamas).

TABLE 8.2
Cruise Ship Arrivals in the Caribbean's Major Destinations: 1990-1999

Country	1990	1995	1999
Antigua & Barbuda	182,621	171,845	325,195
Aruba	122,511	150,776	161,415
The Bahamas [a]	1,853,897	1,543,495	[b] 1,981,481
Barbados	362,611	484,670	313,609
Bermuda	112,551	168,452	194,441
Cayman Islands	361,712	682,885	1,035,522
Curacao	158,552	155,115	n/a
Cuba	n/a	n/a	n/a
Dominican Republic	n/a	n/a	n/a
Jamaica	385,771	605,178	601,370
Martinique	421,259	428,032	n/a
Puerto Rico	599,755	773,267	805,327
St. Lucia	101,948	193,912	240,222

TABLE 8.2 CONTINUED

Country	1990	1995	1999
St. Maarten/St. Martin	n/a	410,235	616,595
Trinidad & Tobago	26,928	n/a	30,464
U.S. Virgin Islands	1,119,569	920,931	991,736

Sources: PIOJ, various years; CTO, various issues.
[a] These figures, which are provided by the Ministry of Tourism and the Central Bank of the Bahamas (Nassau), are quite different from those provided by the PIOJ, "Economic and Social Survey Jamaica," Kingston: PIOJ, various years.
[b] 1997 figure. The 1999 figure is not available (Ministry of Tourism; The Central Bank of the Bahamas).

TABLE 8.3
Tourist Arrivals in the Caribbean by Major Markets: 1985-1999

Country of Origin	1985	1990	1995	1999
United States	433,136	565,504	657,521	870,019
Canada	82,294	113,917	96,327	100,338
United Kingdom	21,951	82,429	101,100	124,930
Other European	9,965	38,620	89,602	83,759
Commonwealth Caribbean	14,237	18,251	21,143	38,023
Latin America	4,659	9,627	21,985	15,635
Japan	915	6,104	23,618	8,411
Other	4,556	6,325	7,650	7,283
Total	571,713	840,777	1,018,946	1,248,398
Percent of total				
United States	75.8	67.3	64.5	69.7
Canada	14.4	13.5	9.5	8.0
United Kingdom	3.8	9.8	9.9	10.0
Other European	1.7	4.6	8.8	6.7
Commonwealth Caribbean	2.5	2.2	2.1	3.0
Latin America	0.8	1.1	2.2	1.3
Japan	0.2	0.7	2.3	0.7
Other	0.8	0.8	0.8	0.6
Total	100.0	100.0	100.0	100.0

Sources: PIOJ, various years; CTO, various issues.

TABLE 8.4
Growth of the Cruise Industry Worldwide: 1980-1999

Country of Passenger Origin	1980	1985	1990	1995	1999
North America [a]	1,431	2,152	3,640	-	-
Germany (former West)	160	150	184	-	-

TABLE 8.4 CONTINUED

Country of Passenger Origin	1980	1985	1990	1995	1999
United Kingdom	115	92	186	-	-
Australia	90	100	79	-	-
Italy	-	55	75	-	-
France	-	55	112	-	-
Rest of Europe/Scandinavia	-	80	110	-	-
Others (including Far East)	-	50	75	-	-
Total	-	2,734	4,461	-	-

Source: EIU, *Special Report No 2104*, Table 2: "The World Cruise Ship Industry in the 1990s" (January 1992).
[a] United States and Canada.

Chapter 9

Alternative Development Policy Considerations for the Twenty-first Century

The purpose of the final chapter is to summarize the major conclusions and policy recommendations discussed in previous chapters, linking development to strategies, political stance, and action. Most of these policy considerations have already been presented at the end of the relevant chapters; however, some of these are quite significant and perhaps need to be reiterated.

High Quality Intervention
State intervention can play an important role in improving the social and economic conditions of a society in certain areas. The state can also actively and adequately contribute to development and this has been apparent, both in theory and in practice, since the writings of List and the German industrialization effort in the latter half of the nineteenth century. About a century of facts proves the historical involvement of the government sector in important development efforts. Apart from the three traditional functions of the government and the fiscal budget (i.e., allocation, stabilization and distribution), particular attention has been focused on its new developmental role. Contrary to the current orthodoxy, development requires better state action and this is most likely achieved from Developmental State policies. What is really important is not the *extent* of intervention but the *quality* of intervention.

Demand Management

Aggregate demand management policies are extremely important in the determination of the level of economic activity. The growth of output depends on the growth of demand which, in turn, provides the opportunities for growth of supply which may or may not be forthcoming. It should be noted that it is difficult and misleading to separate demand and supply effects, since the level of effective demand influences the supply side through capital formation and attachment to the labor force (Sawyer 1995: 20-21).

Hence, it seems that demand management policy is insufficient on its own. Aggregate demand management is clearly necessary for GDP growth, higher levels of employment and good economic performance, but it is not sufficient; supply-side factors (e.g., technical progress, manufacturing, and investment) are also important and needed. One implication is that "there is little independent role for aggregate demand in the determination of the level of economic activity" (Sawyer 1995: 87). The Keynesian model of aggregate demand and aggregate supply is fully capable of providing the following:

- an analysis of the full range of supply considerations (such as technology, etc.);
- a comprehensive theory of inflation;
- an explicit theory of income distribution; and,
- the basis for a theory of economic growth (Weintraub 1958; Davidson 1962; Davidson and Smolensky 1964; Casarosa 1981).

Inequalities, Disparities, and Unevenness

Left to themselves, market forces do not usually generate full capacity utilization and full employment. In addition, the play of forces in the market tends to increase rather than decrease the various inequalities between areas, regions, nations, sexes, social classes, etcetera. Markets are usually seen to perpetuate inequalities and disparities, and modern capitalist economies do not conform to perfect competition.

An OECD report points out that manufacturing expertise "grows by the cumulative effects of learning, scale, etc. and is, contrary to the assumptions of the orthodox theory of comparative advantage, geographically concentrated" (1987: 256). On this view of *cumulative causation*, economic disparities, far from being self-correcting, are rather self-reinforcing.

Thus, although the market tradition sees inequalities and regional imbalance yielding to the natural adjustments of labor and capital in response to price signals, there has been no attempt to understand why these imperfections and inflexibilities emerge in all market economies. The complexities of the real world should not be regarded as a disease. These problems are sketched out by Davidson, who states:

> [Three] decades after Keynesian demand management policies were downgraded by most orthodox economists, the market-oriented system of capitalism . . . has regressed to economic performance levels that have not been prevalent since Keynes' revolution. Over 38 million people are unemployed in OECD na-

tions. Double-digit unemployment rates persist throughout the European Economic Community. The distribution of income within most nations as well as globally has become more unequal while substantial numbers around the world have actually experienced declining living standards since the break up of Bretton Woods. (Davidson 1994: 185-86)

In this period of accelerated globalization, in particular, markets have widened gaps in wealth, income, consumption, power, capabilities, and access, among countries and within them. It seems that the mechanisms of liberalization are as uneven as the outcomes of global growth. This is not just a single unfortunate outcome, but part of a repeated global capitalist record (Thomas 2000: 14).

Evidently, global markets have been skewed against the poorer countries of the world. Statistics illustrate very well some of the processes of unevenness and unequal exchange as well as a number of negative results in the contemporary world:

- Globalization is proceeding apace, but largely for the benefit of the more powerful and dynamic capitalist countries. Uneven growth and development accompany this economic manifestation, and the major global economic performance indicators—output, prices, consumption, investment, and trade—reveal this undesirable state of affairs (Thomas 2000: 12).
- The poorest 20 percent of the world's people saw their share in world income decline from 2.3 to 1.4 percent in the past three decades, while that of the richest 20 percent grew from 70 to 85 percent. The ratio of the shares grew from thirty to one in 1960 to eighty-four to one in 1995. In addition, the assets of the world's 358 billionaires exceeded the combined annual incomes of the 2.5 billion people who comprise the poorest 45 percent of mankind (UNDP, *Human Development Report* 1996: 8).
- The loss to the less developed and developing economies from unequal access to trade, labor and finance is estimated at $500 billion a year, which is 10 times what they receive annually in foreign assistance (UNDP, *Human Development Report* 1997: 87). Furthermore, as a former President and Chairman of the World Bank argues, foreign aid programs constitute a distinct benefit to American business. The three major benefits are: Foreign aid provides a substantial and immediate market for the U.S. goods and services; Foreign aid stimulates the development of new overseas markets for U.S. companies; and Foreign aid orients national economies toward a free enterprise system in which the United States can prosper. In fact, capitalist aid appears to be a calculated business investment. Therefore, it is not the imperialist countries which aid the developing and less developed countries, but the latter which aid the former.
- Private foreign investment is growing spectacularly, but it is concentrated in a few economies and among a few firms, and is facilitated by the growth of cross-border mergers and acquisitions, inter-firm agreements, the worldwide introduction of liberalized FDI regimes, and the recent wave of privatizations, trade and exchange rate liberalization, financial deregulation, labor markets reforms, social welfare reforms, and fiscal and monetary or-

thodoxy (Thomas 2000: 11; Girvan 2000: 68). Eighty-three percent of foreign direct investment goes to rich countries, and three quarters of the remainder goes to developing countries, mostly in East and Southeast Asia and in Latin America. Yet, the countries with the poorest 20 percent of the world's people receive just .2 percent of international commercial lending (*Human Development Report* 1992: 48; 1996: 9).

- Financial capital plays a leading role in globalization (i.e., growth in the volume and speculative character of global financial flows, and the consolidation of huge concentrations of private finance capital–transnational corporations and institutional investors–as the dominant players in world production, trade, and finance). This is reflected not only in the dramatic increase of financial flows across the foreign exchanges and higher levels of foreign direct investment, but also in the degree of integration between financial markets in different countries and regions and in the organization of production on a transnational basis (Arestis and Sawyer 1998: 2). The volume of foreign exchange transactions worldwide reached $1.3 trillion a day in 1995 (with the corresponding figure in the early 1970s being $18 billion a day), equivalent to $312 trillion a year of 240 business days (Tobin 1996: 16). By comparison, at the end of 1995, the annual global trade in goods and services was $5 trillion, the total reserves of central banks around $1.5 trillion, and the annual global turnover in equity markets $21 trillion.

- The share in world trade of the world's poorest countries, with 20 percent of the world's people, has declined from 4 to almost 1 percent during the last four decades. Given the uneven industrial development of trading nations, the structure of modern international trade is such that greatly favors the developed countries at the expense of the less developed and developing countries. Indeed, cumulative terms-of-trade losses by the developing nations have exceeded $300 billion during the last two decades (*Human Development Report* 1996: 9; 1997: 84).

- There is a growing proliferation of various social problems, many of which are transboundary and global in scope. Current global consumption has doubled since the mid-1970s. Consumer markets are integrated worldwide to a point where many fear a global "addiction to consumption" (Thomas 2000: 10-11). Yet, an unprecedented intensification of environmental problems and the rapid pace of environmental degradation threat the sustainability of planet earth.

Thus, the reality seriously challenges the neoliberal view that markets are "free and fair" and lead to optimal outcomes, which is the theoretical underpinning of global and regional trade liberalization.

Developmentalism

The regulatory role is a traditional focus of state intervention in economies like the United States and the United Kingdom, with the state acting as an adjunct to the market, working at the edges of the market system. Market failure has usually been the reason for loans, subsidies, and other forms of financial support to industries. Governments have been seen to support, more or less, the industrial sectors, to correct their microimperfections and to offer, more or less, protection to their respective industries.

These traditional incentive policies may offer only marginal solutions and often recommend some temporary assistance without getting at the root of the problems. In complete contrast, developmentalism is strongly related to, and concerned with, strategic actions for achieving industrial growth, endogenous competency and development, regeneration, and competitiveness while, at the same time, structuring and affecting the direction of private economic activity (i.e., long-term market-shaping activities instead of market-reacting responses).

Obviously an old fashioned protectionism is not recommended, which may not create competitive economic sectors; instead, a mixture of inward- and outward-oriented development strategy is suggested, defined in terms of growth, productivity, and competitiveness, which should constitute the foremost priority of state action.

Hence, the modern state needs to undertake selective strategic intervention, which is going to have the most significant potential impact on the dynamism of the national economy, focus its attention on increasing productivity and profitability, and restrict its intervention to long-term requirements (i.e., targeted policies). On the other hand, the government's fiscal policies must cautiously complement their comprehensive policy making.

Emphasis on the Accelerators

There is a strong relationship between technical change/technological progress and human capital formation (health, education, and labor force skills). Improvements in production result from a combination of technological infrastructure, R&D, learning, skills, invention and innovation. Indeed, human resource development can considerably increase the productivity and earnings of labor and may be preconditions for the introduction of more advanced technology applied to production.

However, if technical advances become immediately available to all firms and industries (i.e., the perfect information assumption of the perfect competition analysis), then there would be no incentive for entrepreneurs to make any effort to improve products and/or processes through, for example, R&D. High quality government policies have much to do with production capability: a high level of education and knowledge, learning-by-doing, upgrading of skills and technical qualifications of the labor force, strategic management, development, and the promotion of research and innovation.

Furthermore, instead of targeting particular firms for subsidization, the state can finance and direct the development of new technologies that can be used by specific dynamic industries in order to improve their efficiency, profitability, and competitiveness. Consequently, the firms can utilize the modern knowledge —such as ideas for raw materials, product designs, manufacturing processes and, ultimately, commercial products—and transform this modern knowledge into new technologies and products. In addition to funding R&D, Developmental State strategies include government support of technical knowledge and new manufacturing techniques, especially to the small firms, which often lag behind in technological development.

Higher Levels of Investments

Special emphasis should be placed on state investments, capital formation, and accumulation of general government. The capacity-creating aspect of public investment is considered very important because the state is seen as an active investor. In fact, the state as a direct player in the organization of investment was very much at the heart of Keynes' thinking and constitutes an explicit long-term policy proposal which can be found in the *General Theory*.

Keynes suggested that two-thirds or three-quarters of total investment would be directly influenced by state authorities and semi-public bodies (Keynes 1980: 322). A collective decision-making body set up to regulate huge funds for more socially desirable investment purposes could be construed as a mechanism of "socializing investment" (i.e., the democratic control of capital formation).

However, Keynes' proposal in favor of government investment has to do with the *composition* of government expenditures and not about whether the share of total government spending out of GDP should rise so as to ultimately monopolize all investment expenditure in the economy (Seccareccia 1994: 379). Kregel (1985) and Smithin (1989) both suggested a separate capital budget for government so as not to confuse investments with the consumption expenditures of the state.

Following the Keynesian tradition, investment not only creates additional income but also increases and improves the productive capacity. In other words, investment adds to the productive potential of the economy. Capital formation enlarges a country's capacity to produce goods and, consequently, capital accumulation (which is central to technological progress) adds to both demand and capacity. Without the undertaking of large investment expenditures by the government sector in basic infrastructure projects, the growth rate of an economy would perhaps be smaller than what had in fact been achieved.

Gross investment spending has to take place in order that technical change (either new products or new processes) can be brought into effect. Technical change/progress is infused into the economic system through the creation of new equipment, which depends on current gross investment spending (Kaldor and Mirrless 1962; Kaldor 1978: 54). Kaldor considers technical progress:

> the main engine of economic growth, determining not only the rate of growth of productivity, but also the rate of obsolescence, the average life-time of equipment, the share of investment in income, the share of profits, and the relationship between investment and potential output, that is, the capital-output ratio on new capital. (Kaldor and Mirrless 1962; Kaldor 1978: 54)
> It is the technical dynamism of the economy . . . which is responsible in a capitalist economy both for making the rate of accumulation of capital and the rate of growth of production relatively small or relatively large. (Kaldor 1978: 37)

Technical change can be expected to influence the volume of investment and opens up new and more profitable opportunities for expansion. Thus, profitability—now and in the future—depends upon technical progress. The rate of technical change can influence both growth and capacity utilization; but the implementation of technical change requires expenditure on investment. Indeed, faster technical change/progress requires more and better new capital equipment to implement the technical change and relies on a higher rate of investment expenditure.

Therefore, there are a number of reasons in favor of government investment; these may include the following:

1. there is a strong and sufficient theoretical background related to government investment;
2. investment expenditure is the only component of aggregate demand which, also, seriously helps the supply side. State investment is more reliable and, therefore, more preferable than the private investment for an investment-led developmentalist strategy;
3. the evidence is quite supportive to the use of government investments. For example, around two thirds of middle-income countries had declining levels of investment throughout the 1980s, and the picture has not changed in the 1990s: World Bank, Table 4: *Gross Domestic Investment* (1988); and,
4. various financial incentives and schemes are seen to be partial, inadequate and unsuccessful measures for a successful regional growth and industrial development. Therefore, there may not be any other (or any better) choice.

Fiscal Policies

Some support the view that various *crowding out* effects are a serious problem. However, a complete crowding-out problem is far from being proved, either on theoretical or empirical grounds. Around half a century ago, Kalecki (1937; 1971) argued that the incidence of taxes will, through their effects on the distribution of income, alter the aggregate demand level (which stands in contrast to various crowding-out effects).

A policy of socializing investment by means of an enlarged rate of public capital formation will, over the long term, enhance private sector economic performance and lead to higher levels of output growth and employment. Instead of being inimical to private sector growth, government investment on social and material infrastructures raises private sector output and productivity.

A complete body of economic literature (mainly within the post-Keynesian and radical analyses) has emerged that is staunchly opposed to the orthodox crowding out hypothesis. It deals with the composition of public spending, and some aspects of this debate have provided valuable insights into the effects of different categories of government spending and of alternative ways of financing such expenditure.

Keynes' advocacy of a large extension of the traditional functions of government to include a substantial "socialization of investment" as a means of securing an approximation to full employment is the classic example of the beneficial extension of government sector activity (Hadjimatheou 1994: 323). An expansionary fiscal policy during recession may have little or no impact on the price level or investment. In this case, the crowding out view should be rejected and, hence, no crowding out problem will occur.

In the same vein, neoliberals argue that the growth of government spending results in high deficits with adverse implications for confidence, economic growth, and employment. Actually, they talk about the concept of budget deficit being defined in terms of a trend rather than a full employment level of activity, and their criticism (i.e., the counter-revolution) is primarily directed at Keynes' notions of the appropriateness of relatively comprehensive state intervention seeking to promote economic development.

The irony is that the consequence of failing to take conscious fiscal action now is likely to perpetuate the level of public sector deficits arising from present economic problems. It is only likely that these deficits will get back to lower levels if we can achieve a higher level of activity. Governments have a range of different instruments for achieving these objectives. Hence, the main stimulus must come from fiscal policy and focused investment.

Obviously, different governments behave in different ways in terms of their policies. The great problem is to secure general agreement that state action can, and should, be taken in order to increase GDP (or GNP) and to reduce public debt and unemployment (as scientific and political prejudice is a large problem).

Industry as the Engine of Further Growth
Industry is recommended as the engine of additional economic growth and development. The expansion of industry represents a net addition to the effective use of productive resources, and can contribute to a higher degree of capacity and resource utilization.

Economic growth is governed by the growth of demand, and the growth of demand for industrial products leads to the growth of output and to important efficiency gains (mechanization, capital accumulation, structural transformation, reallocation of resources, learning, and technical change) which induce further growth of demand, and so on. The growth of industry and, therefore, overall economic growth are led by the growth of demand for industrial products. Thus, industrial strategy should be a very important part of government economic policy making, which means that the government adopts a strategic view of future industrial development in the economy concerned and provides a range of support mechanisms to those sectors deemed to have a key role to play in the future.

In fact, proactive state guidance takes the form of industrial modeling, targeting and repositioning: support of dynamic, propulsive sectors, whose rapid growth would have substantial long-term effects on the national development, and endogenous competency of modern economies.

In the past, there has been a sharp contrast between governments' initial intended economic strategies and the actual policies that governments were forced to follow. Governments should follow a long-term strategy based on a technically proficient national plan and an active industrial policy. Hence, the role of the government on regional and industrial development is very important in attempts for further economic and social development.

The role of industry in the process of regional development and growth is complex. Structural factors must play some role in determining a regions' economic performance. Four major areas of activity may reflect the economic needs of a region and should be the strategic aims for a region's development policy (Martin 1989: 37):

1. the growth of a new local economy based on new-technology industry and innovatory activities, R&D, science parks, and technology transfer centers;
2. the modernization of existing mature industries and firms through the application of new product development and production technologies so as to raise efficiency and competitiveness;
3. the upgrading of skills and technical competency of the labor force through education, training, reskilling, and workplace-experience programs; and,
4. improvement and extension of physical, business, and social infrastructure.

Strategic Planning
If we were to consider seriously the present state of mainstream economics, we would find that there has been little of worth contributed to the concrete tasks of working out a rational strategy for coping with those problems which center on raising the levels of development of the productive forces of modern economies, particularly the developing and less developed economies. Apart from the popular distinction between growth and development, it is surprising how little attention has been paid to developing a consistent strategy aimed at providing a planning frame to deal with the multidimensional problems of both development and underdevelopment (the poverty of orthodox analysis).

Undoubtedly, modern capitalist economies do not operate perfectly, and market forces, left to themselves, tend to keep and perpetuate inequalities and unevenness. The linked notions of cumulative causation (Myrdal 1957) and centripetalism (Cowling 1987; 1990) arise from the operation of the market and other forces. Indeed, the principle of cumulative causation means that the existing economic resources of the weak regions and nations are underutilized and undervalued, while Cowling (1985; 1990) has extended the argument on the effects of cumulative causation into the social and political arena.

Thus, some non-market forces (i.e., the actions of government) are required to offset these tendencies. The policy dilemma here is how to preserve the creative functions of markets along with cautious Developmental State policies (which actually enhance them) while restraining their centripetal tendencies. In fact, the Developmental State is concerned with offsetting these tendencies toward disparities and the underutilization of resources, while carrying out a wide range of economic policies. Hence, there are many types of activity which can be undertaken by such a state.

Based on the above considerations, and taking the main modern economic problems into account, Developmental State policy making emerges as both a necessity and a requirement. A central concern of its productive activity is that of industrial strategy and endogenous competency. Therefore, the following three key notions are of great importance in defining and analyzing the role of the Developmental State:

1. the complementarity of market and plan, which arises from the government setting the developmental framework within which industries operate, and seeking to aid firms to fulfil the strategy;
2. government finance and guidance of higher levels of investment spending on the accelerators of growth, which increase the productive capacity of an economy: investment in machinery, people, and technological change and its implementation; and,
3. strategic planning, where the government acts as a strategic principal in order to direct an investment-led knowledge-based endogenous growth and development.

In its developmental part, the state takes a leading and proactive role and the market works within the long-term parameters set by governments at various levels—local, regional, and national.

Obviously, for purposes of designing endogenous competency strategies, technically proficient strategic planning is absolutely necessary—indeed, it is inevitable—and should be directed toward the creation of new conditions and processes to be effectively and directly determined by the planning authorities. Strategic planning is a pragmatic attempt to increase modern economies' long run capacity by upgrading the socioeconomic infrastructure and raising the skill level in the workforce.

In the development of these strategies, local communities generate not only the capacity to spread the use of modern knowledge and industrial techniques into all elements of the strategic restructuring and/or repositioning so as to spur endogenous industrial activities, but they also create a dynamic basis for a more effective engagement in the world economy through higher levels of competitive exports.

Furthermore, as endogenous technology (i.e., consistent technical progress coupled with human capital formation) is the basis for an organic integration of domestic production and demand structures, investment priorities and the choice of techniques are determined by the strategies of transformation, rejuvenation, and repositioning, as well as by the product choices to which these strategies give rise. The overall purpose is to increase the capacities of modern economies to respond at the level of governments, industries, and the population as a whole. Only under such national strategic planning systems trade can serve a different function, because governments themselves will be reoriented to serve different purposes.

Government strategies designed to invest wisely in infrastructure and the accelerators of industrial competency and competitiveness, and to encourage the establishment of new industries and activities and/or the consolidation, rejuvenation and repositioning of old ones, might have a better prospect of stimulating economic expansion. In this sense, Developmental State action should be concerned with offsetting regional disparities and the lack of modern factors of development.

Indeed, there are concrete linkages between the Developmental State policy on the one hand, and industrial and regional strategies and policies on the other, as Developmental State intervention can drive the process of economic change and successfully contribute to long-term supply-side initiatives aimed at restructuring or promoting the activities of particular firms, sectors and regions (i.e., growth poles strategies, industrial clusters). Hence, the Developmental State should be concerned with offsetting regional disparities and the lack of skills, expertise, R&D, innovation and social services, and can add to the opportunities for regional and local development.

Cooperation

The New Competition analysis identifies the cooperation among small firms in areas normally subject to strong competition (such as, skills, R&D, innovation). Enough evidence exists to show that economies which are able to generate more effective long-term-oriented cooperative arrangements regarding both technological and organizational learning and investments (in human and physical assets) are likely to outperform countries that largely rely on classic free market mechanisms.

Besides, technical inefficiencies and failures to adequately develop and use new products and process often occur, but the nature and causes of the failure seem to be unclear. It is not the traditional market failure which can be corrected by traditional measures (e.g., loans or subsidies) or through regulatory policy. The solution is likely to require cooperation between different firms, and between firms and the state.

Similarly, governments may emphasize "industrial clusters" as important engines of economic growth. The effects of these industrial clusters will be to bring together key players in economic development, upgrade technological infrastructure and skills, accelerate learning and innovation, induce the exchange of important technical and market information, improve managerial capacity and entrepreneurship, stimulate the formation of new businesses, reduce investment risks, and increase profit margins and economic growth rates.

Quality

Quality goods and services are strategically important to firms and countries. Equally important to international businesses is quality management, which has resulted in the development of a number of quality standards. Indeed, in this technological age, quality production is the hallmark of most international operations, as inconsistent quality, inadequate marketing, and irregularities in supply can be severe constraints on exports. If both firms and countries are to compete effectively in the global economy, products and services must meet global market expectations. Inferior products can harm a firm's market share and profitability, and a nation's balance of payments.

Appropriate Politico-Institutional Structures

Developmental State policy-making is concerned with promoting domestic industrial development. However, it is unlikely that significant state intervention would be warranted, given that there are major constraints on developmental policies (e.g., the nature of the civil service, its outlook, etc.). Indeed, public institutions may be limited in their abilities to perform certain tasks (for instance, the ability to react to changing technology, and hence the adoption of the appropriate technology in a changing environment). For these reasons, the pursuit of Developmental State strategies requires the molding of specific institutions, whose task it would be to organize the critical interactions between state and industry.

To implement its industrial policies in manufacturing industry, the Japanese government has relied heavily on the Ministry of International Trade and Industry (MITI); indeed, MITI was a necessary but not sufficient condition for its economic success. Although the Japanese institutional structure cannot be easily transplanted, something akin to MITI will have to be instituted in any country seeking a successful, proactive developmental role for the state (Cowling 1990: 18).

First of all, a central core is absolutely necessary—a Bureau of Industry and Trade (BIT)—composed of a small, entrepreneurial team of well-educated, well-trained, and efficient technocratic planners. This executive new look Bureau should be organized around the requirements of a dedicated and determined Strategic Planning Agency (SPA), with a long-term commitment and the powers to implement the interventionist strategy. With the assistance of consultants from leading corporations, banks, trade unions, and universities, such an institution can form a consensus on the best policies to pursue.

Sectoral Agencies (SA) should also be part of the BIT, close to the firms and industries with whose future they are intimately concerned and responsible for the strategic direction in specific sectors. Hence, the sectoral agency will perform a key role in the industrial regeneration of the region. The process could be started off by the SPA within the BIT identifying sectors in which strategic intervention is warranted and advantageous. Yet, the act of putting the strategic decision-making machinery within the regions would allow officials to tailor and disaggregate development plans to regional/local needs.

Obviously, the proposed type of development planning should be neither centralized nor comprehensive. Loose and transparent links between the core planning agency and government ministries and departments involved in the industrial strategy (treasury, education, training, etc.), and sectoral agencies and regional authorities/boards would decentralize much of the work of the central bureau.

To be successful, state planning must be democratic, and the institutional structure must allow for participation at all levels. Indeed, democratic planning (used here) includes participation as one of its defining features–not simply as a goal but as an aspect of the process itself. Participation by the social partners can improve the organization of production and help restrain the power of small groups which have access to government decision making.

While institutions with a strategic planning role are absolutely necessary, these institutions must be derived from a prior commitment to such fundamental change in policy making, and short-term perspectives should be replaced by ones much more favorable to productive investment, industry, and production. Furthermore, such a network of institutions must provide consistency, continuity, and commitment to the direction and pace of industrial development. Without such commitment, effectiveness, competence, accountability, professionalism, and capacity, Developmental State strategies and policies will founder on short-term expedients, the inefficiency and ineffectiveness of the civil service, the power of the transnationals and other capitalist interests, or the resistance of the people.

Lastly, any economy is underpinned and imbued by social values, codes of behavior, and ethics, which are, in turn, reflected in the structure and functioning of government sector institutions and private sector firms. If modern economies are to develop growth-oriented knowledge-based productive activities, it may be necessary to adopt a number of measures to remodel their key social, economic, and institutional factors that will be required to provide the necessary underpinning.

More importantly, these thorough development strategies assume a much better state action, and would require an efficient and competent administrative machine. But so does any "national purpose" strategy capable of overcoming barriers and laying down the basis of endogenous growth and competency in any economy.

Decentralization and Participation
A dynamic process of endogenous development and growth may require decentralization and participation. Indeed, decentralization can facilitate coordinated planning between various government departments and/or agencies, and make plans more relevant to local needs. The efficiency of central government may also be increased through decentralized forms of government, which may lead to the following (Smith 1985: 47-52):

1. better political and administrative penetration of national government policies into regional and rural areas;
2. the generation of additional productive resources, the encouragement of more efficient use of existing resources, and the opportunity for local authorities to improve and expand the economic and social infrastructure in regional and rural areas;
3. the identification of services requirements and the delivery, planning, or regulation of public services; and,
4. the increased participation (local authorities, unions, etc.) in planning and development.

Indeed, participation by the social partners may improve the organization of production, and can contribute toward a less inequitable distribution of income among its goals, to more efficient economic and social development, etcetera. In addition, a more open style of government can help restrain the power of small groups who have access to government sector decision making.

Finance

Clearly, there is the important question of financing the above investment expenditure. The post-Keynesian analysis has offered the following solutions to this question:

1. an appropriate redistribution of available/existing funds from government consumption to government investment (i.e., more government spending on the accelerators of growth and development and less spending on unnecessary or non-essential types of public expenditure);
2. changes of the structure of taxation;
3. higher levels of savings generated by higher levels of income;
4. the use of government bonds;
5. the use of available pension funds;
6. capital controls and the arrest of speculative ventures, tax evasion, and black economy;
7. the effective use of more available resources (a higher degree of capacity utilization); and,
8. deficit finance, if needed.

Learning the Right Development Lessons

Of course, a key question centers around the compatibility of the Developmental State model with political liberalization and democratic forms of governance. Also, another critical issue concerns the lessons to be drawn from the East Asian success story, which can subsequently be generalized to, and applied in, other countries. The available evidence demonstrates quite clearly that the Asian countries' industrial success is the product of specific historical circumstances. Consequently, there may exist significant constraints on its transferability, or replicability in different or alternative national contexts.

It would generally be wrong to consider that the Developmental State model could, or indeed should, be transplanted to countries which have quite different history and culture. What is important to learn from the Far Eastern experiences is how to approach development problems—the "strategic approach." Hence, the development challenge for decision and policymakers is to devise forms of strategic industrial policy which are consistent with the norms of democratic accountability and, perhaps, with more limited concentration of state and private power than has been the case in the East Asian context.

Furthermore, the recent globalization and the resultant unequal exchange— coupled with the emerging role of regionalization as an unevenly developing, heterogeneous, and multidimensional phenomenon in a globalizing world—has served to accentuate and augment the vicious web of development and less development. Besides, recent multidimensional global changes have arguably cast doubts on the ability of national governments to pursue independent and effective economic policies, and there is an ongoing debate on the relevance of the nation state in this global era given the very real constraints that the global political economy imposes.

However, recent calls for "good" or "democratic" governance—which focus on good administrative, judicial, or electoral practice—seem to entirely miss the point: few societies in the modern world will be able to resolve deeper problems or make speedy transitions from poverty without active state intervention which approximates the model of a developmental state (ideally, but not necessarily, the western democratic type).

Contrary to the current orthodoxy, developmentally driven institutional structures and political purposes can better be achieved from Developmental State policies. In this global era, therefore, the solution may be to bring the nation state back to business.

Bibliography

Ahrens, J. "Prospects of Institutional and Policy Reform in India: Toward a Model of the Developmental State?" *Asian Development Review* 15, no. 1 (1997): 111-46.

Albrechhts, L., et al. "New Perspectives for Regional Policy and Development in the 1990s." In *Regional Policy at the Crossroads*, edited by L. Albrechts, F. Moulaert, P. Roberts, and E. Swyngedouw, 1-9. London: Jessica Kingsley Publishers, 1989.

Albrechts, L., F. Moulaert, P. Roberts, and E. Swyngedouw, eds. *Regional Policy at the Crossroads*. London: Jessica Kingsley Publishers, 1989.

Allen, K., D. Yuill, and J. Bachtler. "Requirements for an Effective Regional Policy." In *Regional Policy at the Crossroads*, edited by L. Albrechts, F. Moulaert, P. Roberts, and E. Swyngedouw, 107-24. London: Jessica Kingsley Publishers, 1989.

Allum, P. "Thirty Years of Southern Policy in Italy." *Political Quarterly* 52, (1980): 314-23.

Amable, B. "Catch-up and Convergence: A Model of Cumulative Growth." *International Review of Applied Economics* 6, no. 1 (1992): 1-25.

Amable, B., and P. Petit. "New Scale and Scope for Industrial Policies in the 1990s." *International Review of Applied Economics* 10, no. 1 (1996): 23-41.

Amsden, A. *Asia's Next Giant*. New York: Oxford University Press, 1989.

Archibugi, D., and M. Pianta. "Patterns of Technological Specialization and Growth of Innovative Activities in Advanced Countries." In *European Competitiveness*, edited by K. S. Hughes, 105-32. Cambridge: Cambridge University Press, 1993.

Arestis, P. *The Post-Keynesian Approach to Economics*. Aldershot, U.K.: Edward Elgar, 1992.

Arestis, P., and M. C. Sawyer, eds. *The Elgar Companion to Radical Political Economy*. Aldershot, U.K.: Edward Elgar, 1994.

Armstrong, H., and J. Taylor. *Regional Economics and Policy*, 2nd edition. Hemel Hempstead, U.K.: Harvester Wheatsheaf, 1993.

Artis, M. J., and D. Cobham, eds. *Labour's Economic Policies: 1974–1979*. Manchester: Manchester University Press, 1991.

Artis, M. J. "Deficit Spending." In *The New Palgrave*, Vol. 1, edited by J. Eatwell et al., 764-65. London: Macmillan, 1987.

Ayres, R. "Development." In *The Elgar Companion to Radical Political Economy*, edited by P. Arestis and M. C. Sawyer, 81-85. Aldershot, U.K.: Edward Elgar, 1994.

Baglioni, G., and C. Crouch, eds. *European Industrial Relations*. London: Sage, 1990.

Baran, P. *The Political Economy of Growth*. New York: Monthly Review Press, 1957.

Baran, P., and P. M. Sweezy. *Monopoly Capital*. London: Pelican, 1973.

Beckford, G. *Persistent Poverty*. Oxford: Oxford University Press, 1971.

———. *Caribbean Economy*. Kingston: ISER, University of the West Indies, 1975.

Bell, C. "Development Economics." In *The New Palgrave*, Vol. 1, edited by J. Eatwell et al., 818-25. London: Macmillan, 1987.

Benn, D., and K. Hall, eds. *Globalization: A Calculus of Inequality*. Kingston: Ian Randle Publishers, 2000.

Bennett, R. J., ed. *Decentralization, Local Governments and Markets*, New York: Oxford University Press, 1990.

Bernal, R. L. "Globalization and Small Developing Countries: The Imperative for Repositioning." In *Globalization: A Calculus of Inequality*, edited by D. Benn and K. Hall, 88-127. Kingston: Ian Randle Publishers, 2000.

Best, M. H. *The New Competition*. Cambridge: Polity Press, 1990.

Blackaby, F. T., ed. *British Economic Policy 1960-74*. Cambridge: Cambridge University Press, 1978.

Blacksell, M. "West Germany." In *Regional Development in Western Europe*, edited by H. D. Clout, 229-56. London: D. Fulton Publishers, 1987.

Blanchard, O. J. "Crowding Out." In *The New Palgrave*, Vol. 1, edited by J. Eatwell et al., 728-30. London: Macmillan, 1987.

Boltho, A., ed. *The European Economy: Growth and Crisis*. Oxford: Oxford University Press, 1982.

Boyer, R., and E. Caroli. "Production Regimes, Education and Training Systems." In *Human Capital and Economic Performance*, edited by C. Buechtemann. New York: Sage, 1995.

Cagan, P. "Monetarism." In *The New Palgrave*, Vol. 3, edited by J. Eatwell et al., 492-96. London: Macmillan, 1987.

Carter, F. W. "Greece." In *Regional Development in Western Europe*, edited by H. D. Clout, 419-34. London: D. Fulton Publishers, 1987.

Cheema, G. S., and D. A. Rondinelli, eds. *Decentralization and Development*. New York: Sage, 1983.

Chiang, A. C. "A Simple Generalization of the Kaldor-Pasinetti Theory of Profit Rate and Income Distribution." *Economica New Series* 40, (1973): 311-13.

Chowdhury, A., and I. Islam. *The Newly Industrializing Economies of East Asia*. London: Routledge, 1993.

Clayton, A. "Developing a Bio-Industry Cluster in Jamaica: A Step Toward Building a Skill-Based Economy." *Social and Economic Studies* 50, no. 2 (June 2001): 1-37.

Clout, H. D. "Regional Development in Western Europe." In *Regional Development in Western Europe*, edited by H. D. Clout, 19-38. London: D. Fulton Publishers, 1987.

———. "France." In *Regional Development in Western Europe*, edited by H. D. Clout, 165-94. London: D. Fulton Publishers, 1987.

———. ed. *Regional Development in Western Europe*, 3rd edition. London: D. Fulton Publishers, 1987.

Cowling, K. "An Industrial Strategy for Britain: The Nature and Role of Planning." *International Review of Applied Economics* 1, no. 1 (1987): 1-22.

———. "The Strategic Approach to Economic and Industrial Policy." In *A New Economic Policy for Britain: Essays on the Development of Industry*, edited by K. Cowling and R. Sugden, 6-34. Manchester: Manchester University Press, 1990.

Cowling, K., and R. Sugden, eds. *A New Economic Policy for Britain: Essays on the Development of Industry*. Manchester: Manchester University Press, 1990.

———. *Current Issues in Industrial Economic Strategy*. Manchester: Manchester University Press, 1992.

Davidson, P. *Post Keynesian Macroeconomic Theory*. Aldershot, U.K.: Edward Elgar, 1994.

———. "The Viability of Keynesian Demand Management in an Open Economy Context." *International Review of Applied Economics* 10, no. 1 (1996): 91-105.

Davidson, P., and J. A. Kregel, eds. *Employment, Growth and Finance*. Aldershot, U.K.: Edward Elgar, 1994.

Davidson, P., and E. Smolensky. *Aggregate Supply and Demand Analysis*. New York: Harper & Row, 1964.

Demas, W. *The Economics of Development in Small Countries*. Montreal: McGill University Press, 1965.

———. *Caribbean Integration and Development*. Kingston: ISER, University of the West Indies, 1976.

De Valk, P., and K. H. Wekwete, eds. *Decentralizing for Participatory Planning*. London: Gower Publishing Company, 1990.

DeLong, J. B., and L. H. Summers. "Equipment Investment and Economic Growth." *Quarterly Journal of Economics* 106, no. 2 (1991): 407-43.

Denicolo, V., and M. Matteuzzi. "Public Debt and the Pasinetti's Paradox." *Cambridge Journal of Economics* 14 (1990): 339-44.

Deprez, J. "Aggregate Supply." In *The Elgar Companion to Radical Political Economy*, edited by P. Arestis and M. C. Sawyer, 10-15. Aldershot, U.K.: Edward Elgar, 1994.

Domar, E. *Essays in the Theory of Economic Growth*. New York: Oxford University Press, 1957.

Dore, R. *Flexible Rigidities, Industrial Policy and Structural Adjustment in the Japanese Economy 1970-80*. London: The Athlone Press, 1986a.

———. "Industrial Policy and How Japanese Do It." *Catalyst* 2, 1986b.

Dyker, D., ed. *The European Economy*. London: Longman, 1992.

———. *The National Economies of Europe*. London: Longman, 1992.

Eccleston, B. *State and Society in Post-War Japan*. Cambridge: Polity Press, 1989.

Eshag, E. "Fiscal and Monetary Policies in Developing Countries." In *The New Palgrave*, Vol. 2, edited by J. Eatwell et al., 363-65. London: Macmillan, 1987.

EUROSTAT. *Europe in Figures*, 3rd edition. Luxembourg, 1992.

Evans, P., D. Rueschemeyer, and T. Skocpol, eds. *Bringing the State Back In*. Cambridge: Cambridge University Press, 1985.

Evans, P. B. "The State as Problem and Solution: Predation, Embedded Autonomy, and Structural Change." In *The Politics of Economic Adjustment*, edited by S. Haggard and R. R. Kaufman. Princeton: Princeton University Press, 1992.

———. *Embedded Autonomy: States and Industrial Transformation*. Princeton: Princeton University Press, 1995.

Fazi, E., and N. Salvadori. "The Existence of a Two-Class Economy in a General Cambridge Model of Growth and Distribution." *Cambridge Journal of Economics* 9 (1981): 155-64.

Fel'dman, G. A. "On the Theory of Growth Rates of National Income." In *Foundations of Soviet Strategy for Economic Growth*, edited by N. Spulber, 174-99. Bloomington: Indiana University Press, 1965.

Feldstein, M. "Government Deficits and Aggregate Demand." *Journal of Monetary Economics* 9 (1982): 1-20.

Fleck, F. H., and C. M. Domenghino. "Cambridge (UK) versus Cambridge (Mass): A Keynesian Solution of Pasinetti's Paradox." *Journal of Post- Keynesian Economics* 10 (1987): 22-36.

Foley, D. "State Expenditure from a Marxist Perspective." *Journal of Public Policy* 9 (1978).

Frenkel, J. A., ed. *International Aspects of Fiscal Policies*. Chicago: Chicago University Press, 1988.

Frenkel, J. A., and A. Razin. *Fiscal Policies and the World Economy*. Cambridge: The MIT Press, 1987.

Georgakopoulos, T., C. C. Paraskevopoulos, and J. Smithin, eds. *Economic Integration between Unequal Partners*. Aldershot, U.K.: Edward Elgar, 1994.

Giannola, A. "The Industrialization, Dualism and Economic Dependence of the Mezzogiorno in the 1980s." *Banco di Roma Review of Economic Conditions in Italy* 36 (1982): 67-92.

Glick, M. A., ed. *Competition, Technology and Money*. Aldershot, U.K.: Edward Elgar, 1994.

Girvan, N. "Globalization and Counter-Globalization: The Caribbean in the Context of the South." In *Globalization: A Calculus of Inequality*, edited by D. Benn and K. Hall, 65-87. Kingston: Ian Randle Publishers, 2000.

Girvan, N., and O. Jefferson, eds. *Readings in the Political Economy of the Caribbean*. Kingston: New World Group, 1971.

Hadjimatheou, G. "Public Expenditure." In *The Elgar Companion to Radical Political Economy*, edited by P. Arestis and M. C. Sawyer, 319-23. Aldershot, U.K.: Edward Elgar, 1994.

Hahn, F. H. "Neoclassical Growth Theory." In *The New Palgrave*, Vol. 3, edited by J. Eatwell et al., 625-34. London: Macmillan, 1987.

Harrod, R. F. *Towards a Dynamic Economics*. London: Macmillan, 1948.

———. "Domar and Dynamic Economics." *Economic Journal* 69 (1959): 451-64.

———. *Economic Dynamics*. London: Macmillan, 1973.

Hayek, F. A. *The Road to Serfdom*. London: Routledge & Kegan Paul, 1944.

Heizer, J., and B. Render. *Production and Operations Management*, 4th edition. N.J.: Prentice Hall, 1996.

Higgins, K. J. *The Bahamian Economy: An Analysis*. Nassau: The Counsellors, 1994.

Higgins, B. *Economic Development*, 2nd edition. London: Constable & Company, 1968.

Higgins, B., and D. J. Savoie, eds. *Regional Economic Development*. London: Unwin Hyman, 1988.

Hillard, J. V. "Aggregate Demand." In *The Elgar Companion to Radical Political Economy*, edited by P. Arestis and M. C. Sawyer, 5-10. Aldershot, U.K.: Edward Elgar, 1994.

Hirschman, A. O. *The Strategy of Economic Development*. New Haven: Yale University Press, 1958.

Hodgson, G. *Economics and Institutions: A Manifesto for a Modern Institutional Economics*. Oxford: Polity Press, 1988.

Holland, S. *Capital versus the Regions*. London: Macmillan, 1976.

Hughes, K. S. "Technology and International Competitiveness." *International Review of Applied Economics* 6, no. 2 (1992): 166-83.

———. "The Role of Technology, Competition and Skill in European Competitiveness." In *European Competitiveness*, edited by Kirsty S. Hughes, 133-57. Cambridge: Cambridge University Press, 1993.

———. ed. *European Competitiveness*. Cambridge: Cambridge University Press, 1993.

Hughes, O. E. *Public Management and Administration*, 2nd edition. London: Macmillan, 1998.

Huque, A. S. "Administering the Dragons: Challenges and Issues." In *Public Administration in the NICs: Challenges and Accomplishments*, edited by A. S. Huque, J. T. M. Lam, and C. Y. Jane. London: Macmillan, 1996.

Huque, A. S., J. T. M. Lam, and C. Y. Jane, eds. *Public Administration in the NICs: Challenges and Accomplishments*. London: Macmillan, 1996.

Ito, T. *The Japanese Economy*. Cambridge: The MIT Press, 1992.

Jaeger, A. M., and R. N. Kanungo, eds. *Management in Developing Countries*, London: Routledge, 1990.

Jessop, R. "Economic Theory of the State." In *The New Palgrave*, Vol. 2, edited by J. Eatwell et al., 75-77. London: Macmillan, 1987.

Jorgensen, J. J. "Organizational Life-Cycle and Effectiveness Criteria in State-Owned Enterprises: The Case of E. Africa." In *Management in Developing Countries*, edited by A. M. Jaeger and R. N. Kanungo, 131-56. London: Routledge, 1990.

Kaldor, N. *Essays on Economic Policy*, Vols. 1 and 2. London: Duckworth, 1964.

———. *Further Essays on Economic Theory*. London: Duckworth, 1978.

———. *Further Essays on Applied Economics*. London: Duckworth, 1978.

Kalecki, M. *Selected Essays on the Dynamics of a Capitalist Economy 1933-1970*. Cambridge: Cambridge University Press, 1971.

———. *Essays on Developing Economies*. Brighton: The Harvester Press, 1976.

Kang, T. W. *Is Korea the Next Japan?* New York: The Free Press, 1989.

Karagiannis, N. *Fiscal Policy and Development: With Special Reference to the EC/EU Countries*. Ph.D. dissertation. Leeds: Leeds University Business School, 1996.

———. "The Development of the Bahamian Economy at the Crossroads." *Social and Economic Studies* 49, no. 4 (December 2000): 37-64.

———. "Creating Industrial Production in the Bahamas." *Regional Development Studies* 7, United Nations (June 2001): 33-53.

Keiser, N. F. *Macroeconomics, Fiscal Policy, and Economic Growth*. New York: John Wiley & Sons, 1964.

Keynes, J. M. *The General Theory of Employment, Interest and Money*. London: Macmillan, 1936.

Kindleberger, C. P. *Economic Development*. New York: McGraw-Hill, 1958.

King, R. "Recent Industrialization in Sardinia: Rebirth or Neocolonialism?" *Erdkunde* 31 (1977): 87-102.

———. "Italy." In *Regional Development in Western Europe*, edited by H. D. Clout, 129-63. London: D. Fulton Publishers, 1987.

Knight, M. D., and P. R. Masson. "Fiscal Policies, Net Saving and Real Exchange Rates: The United States, the Federal Republic of Germany, and Japan." In *International Aspects of Fiscal Policies*, edited by J. A. Frenkel, 21-66. Chicago: Chicago University Press, 1988.

Kochen, M., and K. W. Deutsch. *Decentralization*. Cambridge: Oelgeschlager, Gunn & Hain, 1980.

Kregel, J. A. "Budget Deficits, Stabilization Policy and Liquidity Preference: Keynes' Post-War Proposals." In *Keynes' Relevance Today*, edited by F. Vicarelli. London: Macmillan, 1985.

———. "Effective Demand." In *The Elgar Companion to Radical Political Economy*, edited by P. Arestis and M. C. Sawyer, 114-19. Aldershot, U.K.: Edward Elgar, 1994.

Krugman, P., ed. *Strategic Trade Policy and the New International Economics*. Cambridge: The MIT Press, 1986.

Kurihara, K. K. *National Income and Economic Growth*. London: George Allen & Unwin, 1961.

———. *Macroeconomics and Programming*. London: George Allen & Unwin, 1964.

Kuznets, S. *Economic Growth and Structure.* New York: W. W. Norton & Com-pany, 1965.

Lalta, S., and M. Freckleton, eds. *Caribbean Economic Development: The First Genera-tion.* Kingston: Ian Randle Publishers, 1993.

Laramie, A. J. "Taxation and Kalecki's Distribution Factors." *Journal of Post Keynesian Economics* 4 (1991): 583-94.

Lavoie, M. *Foundations of Post-Keynesian Economic Analysis.* Aldershot, U.K.: Edward Elgar, 1992.

Lawson, T., J. G. Palma, and J. Sender, eds. *Kaldor's Political Economy,* London: Aca-demic Press, 1989.

Le Grand, J., and R. Robinson. *The Economics of Social Problems.* London: Macmillan, 1976.

Lewis, W. A. *The Theory of Economic Growth.* London: George Allen & Unwin, 1955.

Littlechild, M. "Regional Policy in Germany." *Town and Country Planning* 51 (1982): 155-59.

Lutz, F. A., and D. C. Hague, eds. *The Theory of Capital.* London: Macmillan, 1961.

MacKay, R. R. "Automatic Stabilizers, European Union and National Unity." *Cambridge Journal of Economics* 18 (1994): 571-85.

Maclennan, D., and J. B. Parr, eds. *Regional Policy.* Oxford: Martin Robertson, 1979.

Maddison, A. A. *Economic Growth in the West.* London: George Allen & Unwin, 1964.

Mair, D., and A. J. Laramie. "The Macroeconomic Effects of Taxation in a Federal Europe." *International Review of Applied Economics* 10, no. 1 (1996): 7-22.

Mandel, E. *Late Capitalism.* London: Verso, 1978.

———. "Marx, Karl Heinrich (1818-1883)." In *The New Palgrave,* Vol. 3, edited by J. Eatwell et al., 367-83. London: Macmillan, 1987.

Marglin, S. A. *Public Investment Criteria.* London: George Allen & Unwin, 1967.

Martin, R. "The New Economics and Politics of Regional Restructuring: The British Experience." In *Regional Policy at the Crossroads,* edited by L. Albrechts, F. Mou-laert, P. Roberts, and E. Swyngedouw, 27-51. London: Jessica Kingsley Publishers, 1989.

Martinelli, F. "Business Services, Innovation and Regional Policy: Consideration of the Case of Southern Italy." In *Regional Policy at the Crossroads,* edited by L. Al-brechts, F. Moulaert, P. Roberts, and E. Swyngedouw, 10-26. London: Jessica King-sley Publishers, 1989.

Marx, K. *Capital,* Vols. 1-3. London: Lawrence & Wishart, 1970.

Michie, J., and J. G. Smith, eds. *Unemployment in Europe.* London: Academic Press, 1994.

Moore, B., and J. Rhodes. "Regional Distribution of Economic Activity." In *The New Palgrave,* Vol. 4, edited by J. Eatwell et al., 113-17. London: Macmillan, 1987.

Munnell, A. "Policy Watch: Infrastructure Investment and Economic Growth." *Journal of Economic Perspectives* 6, no. 4 (1992): 189-98.

Myrdal, G. *Economic Theory and Underdeveloped Regions.* London: Duckworth, 1957.

———. *Beyond the Welfare State.* London: Duckworth, 1960.

———. *Asian Drama.* New York: Random House, 1968.

Nester, W. R. *Japan's Growing Power over East Asia and the World Economy: Ends and Means.* London: Macmillan, 1990.

———. *Japanese Industrial Targeting.* London: Macmillan, 1991.

Nurkse, R. *Problems of Capital Formation in Underdeveloped Countries.* Oxford: Basil Blackwell, 1953.

OECD. *The OECD Jobs Study: Evidence and Explanations.* Parts 1 and 2. Paris, 1994.

———. *The OECD Jobs Study: Facts, Analysis, Strategies.* Paris, 1994.

———. *Economic Surveys: Sweden 1991/1992.* Paris, 1992.

————. *Employment Outlook*. Paris, July 1991.

————. *Employment Outlook*. Paris, July 1993.

————. *Employment Outlook*. Paris, July 1994.

————. *Historical Statistics: 1960-1990*. Paris, 1992.

————. *Fiscal Policy for a Balanced Economy*. Paris, December 1968.

————. *Fiscal Policy in Seven Countries: 1955-1965*. Paris, March 1969.

Panico, C., and N. Salvadori, eds. *Post Keynesian Theory of Growth and Distribution*. Cambridge: Cambridge University Press & Edward Elgar, 1993.

Pasinetti, L. L. "Rate of Profit and Income Distribution in Relation to the Rate of Economic Growth." *Review of Economic Studies* 29, no. 1 (1962): 267-79.

————. *Growth and Income Distribution: Essays in Economic Theory*. Cambridge: Cambridge University Press, 1974.

————. "Ricardian Debt and Taxation Equivalence in the Kaldor Theory of Profits and Distribution." *Cambridge Journal of Economics* 13 (1989): 26-36.

Pattenati, P. "The Rate of Interest and the Rate of Profits in a Capitalist Society: A Neo-Keynesian Model of Money Distribution and Growth." *Economic Notes* 3, no. 1 (1967): 97-126.

Peacock, A. T., and G. K. Shaw. *The Economic Theory of Fiscal Policy*. 2nd edition. London: George Allen & Unwin, 1976.

Perroux, F. "The Pole of Development's New Place in a General Theory of Economic Activity." In *Regional Economic Development*, edited by B. Higgins and D. J. Savoie, 48-76. London: Unwin Hyman, 1988.

Perry, G. L. "Deficit Financing." In *The New Palgrave*, Vol. 1, edited by J. Eatwell et al., 762-64. London: Macmillan, 1987.

Peston, M. H. "Budgetary Policy." In *The New Palgrave*, Vol. 1, edited by J. Eatwell et al., 283-85. London: Macmillan, 1987.

Piore, M. J., and C. F. Sabel. *The Second Industrial Divide: Possibilities for Prosperity*. New York: Basic Books, 1984.

Pitelis, C. "Market Failure and the Existence of the State: A Restatement and Critique." *International Review of Applied Economics* 5, no. 3 (1991): 325-39.

Price, V. C. *Industrial Policies in the European Community*. New York: St Martin's Press, 1981.

Reading, B. *Japan: The Coming Collapse*. London: Orion, 1993.

Roberts, P. "Local Economic Development: Alternative Forms of Local and Regional Policy for the 1990s." In *Regional Policy at the Crossroads*, edited by L. Albrechts, F. Moulaert, P. Roberts, and E. Swyngedouw, 170-9. London: Jessica Kingsley Publishers, 1989.

Robinson, J. *The Accumulation of Capital*. 3rd edition. London: Macmillan, 1969.

————. *Essays in the Theory of Economic Growth*. London: Macmillan, 1962.

Romer, P. M. "Increasing Returns and Long-Run Growth." *Journal of Political Economy* 94, no. 5 (October 1986): 1002-37.

————. "Endogenous Technological Change." *Journal of Political Economy* 98 (1990): 71-102.

————. "The Origins of Endogenous Growth." *The Journal of Economic Perspectives* 8, no. 1 (Winter 1994): 3-22.

Rosenstein-Rodan, P. "Problems of Industrialization of East and South-East Europe." *Economic Journal* (June-September 1943): 202-11.

Rostow, W. W. *The Process of Economic Growth*. New York: W. W. Norton & Company, 1952.

Sant, M. *Industrial Movement and Regional Development: The British Case*. Oxford: Pergamon Press, 1975.

————. ed. *Regional Policy and Planning for Europe*. Hants, U.K.: Saxon House, 1981.

Sawyer, M. C. *The Challenge of Radical Political Economy*. Hemel Hempstead, U.K.: Harvester Wheatsheaf, 1989.
————. *The Economics of Michal Kalecki*. London: Macmillan, 1985.
————. "Reflections on the Nature and Role of Industrial Policy." *Metroeconomica* 43 (1992a): 51-73.
————. "Unemployment and the Dismal Science." *Discussion Paper Series* G92/15. Leeds: Leeds University Business School, 1992b.
————. "The Intellectual and Institutional Requirements for Full Employment." In *Employment, Growth and Finance*, edited by P. Davidson and J. A. Kregel, 3-17. Aldershot, U.K.: Edward Elgar, 1994.
————. *Unemployment, Imperfect Competition and Macroeconomics: Essays in the Post Keynesian Tradition*. Aldershot, U.K.: Edward Elgar, 1995.
————. ed. *Post-Keynesian Economics*. Aldershot, U.K.: Edward Elgar, 1988.
Sebastiani, M., ed. *Kalecki's Relevance Today*. London: Macmillan, 1989.
Seccareccia, M. "Socialization of Investment." In *The Elgar Companion to Radical Political Economy*, edited by P. Arestis and M. C. Sawyer, 375-79. Aldershot, U.K.: Edward Elgar, 1994.
Singh, A. "Asian Economic Success and Latin American Failure in the 1980s: New Analyses and Future Policy Implications." *International Review of Applied Economics* 7 (1993b): 267-89.
————. "Openness and the Market Friendly Approach to Development: Learning the Right Lessons from Development Experience." *World Development* 22, no. 12 (1994c): 1811-23.
————. "Competitive Markets and Economic Development: A Commentary on World Bank Analyses." *International Papers in Political Economy* 2, no. 1 (1995).
————. "Competitive Markets and Economic Development: A Commentary on World Bank Analyses." In *The Political Economy of Economic Policies*, edited by P. Arestis and M. C. Sawyer, 60-105. London: Macmillan, 1998.
Smith, B. C. *Decentralization*. London: George Allen & Unwin, 1985.
Solow, R. M. "A Contribution to the Theory of Economic Growth." *Quarterly Journal of Economics* (February 1956): 65-94.
————. "Technical Change and the Aggregate Production Function." *Review of Economics and Statistics* 39 (August 1957): 312-20.
————. "Growth Theory." In *Companion to Contemporary Economic Thought*, edited by D. Greenaway, M. Bleaney, and I. Stewart. London: Routledge, 1991.
————. "Perspectives on Growth Theory." *The Journal of Economic Perspectives* 8, no. 1 (Winter 1994): 45-54.
Steedman, I. "The State and the Outcome of the Pasinetti's Process." *Economic Journal* 82 (1972): 1387-95.
Stiglitz, J. E. *The Economic Role of the State*. Oxford: Blackwell, 1989.
Stohr, W. B. "Regional Policy at the Crossroads: An Overview." In *Regional Policy at the Crossroads*, edited by L. Albrechts, F. Moulaert, P. Roberts, and E. Swyngedouw, 191-97. London: Jessica Kingsley Publishers, 1989.
Thirlwall, A. P. *Nicholas Kaldor*. Hemel Hempstead, U.K.: Harvester Wheatsheaf, 1987.
————. *Growth and Development*. 5th edition. London: Macmillam, 1994.
————. ed. *Keynes and Economic Development*. London: Macmillan, 1987.
Thirlwall, A. P., and J. S. L. McCombie. *Economic Growth and the Balance-of-Payments Constraint*. London: Macmillan, 1994.
Thirlwall, A. P., and F. Targetti, eds. *Further Essays on Economic Theory and Policy: Nicholas Kaldor*. London: Duckworth, 1989.
————. eds. *The Essential Kaldor*. London: Duckworth, 1989.

Thomas, C. Y. "Globalization as a Paradigm Shift: Response from the South." In *Globalization: A Calculus of Inequality*, edited by D. Benn and K. Hall, 8-22. Kingston: Ian Randle Publishers, 2000.

Todaro, M. P. *Economic Development*. 7th edition. Harlow, U.K.: Addison Wesley Longman, 2000.

Toye, J. F., ed. *Taxation and Economic Development*. London: Frank Cass, 1978.

United Nations. *Trade and Development Report*. UNCTAD, 1993.

Vanhove, N., and L. H. Klaassen. *Regional Policy: A European Approach*. Hants, U.K.: Saxon House, 1980.

Wade, R. "Fast Growth and Slow Development in Southern Italy." In *Underdeveloped Europe*, edited by D. Seers, B. Schaffer, and M. L. Kiljunen, 197-221. London: D. Fulton Publishers, 1979.

———. "The Italian State and the Underdevelopment of Southern Italy." In *Nation and State in Europe*, edited by R. D. Grillo, 151-71. London: D. Fulton Publishers, 1980.

———. *Governing the Market*. Princeton: Princeton University Press, 1990.

Wood, P. "United Kingdom." In *Regional Development in Western Europe*, edited by H. D. Clout, 257-83. London: D. Fulton Publishers, 1987.

Williamson, O. E. *The Economic Institutions of Capitalism: Firms, Markets, Relational Contracting*. New York: Free Press, 1985.

World Bank. *World Development Report 1991: The Challenge of Development*. New York: Oxford University Press, 1991.

———. *Governance and Development*. Washington, D.C., 1992.

———. *The East Asian Miracle*. New York: Oxford University Press, 1993.

———. *Bureaucrats in Business: The Economics and Politics of Government Ownership*. New York: Oxford University Press, 1995.

———. *World Development Report 1997: The State in a Changing World*. Washington, D.C., 1997.

Index

About the Author

Nikolaos Karagiannis obtained his Ph.D. in economics at the University of Leeds. He is currently teaching economics and development at the University of the West Indies, Mona. He is the author of four books and has published widely in journals and edited books in the areas of economic development, public finance, and political economy. He has engaged in extensive research in the Caribbean region, specifically in the Bahamas and Jamaica. He is particularly interested in Developmental State theory and policy.